CHANGING SCHOOLS

Changing Schools

Pupil perspectives on
transfer to a comprehensive

Lynda Measor and Peter Woods

Open University Press
Milton Keynes · Philadelphia

Open University Press
12 Cofferidge Close
Stony Stratford
Milton Keynes MK11 1BY, England
and 242 Cherry Street
Philadelphia, PA 19106–1906, USA

First published 1984

British Library Cataloguing in Publication Data

Measor, Lynda, —
  Changing schools.
  1. Comprehensive high schools—England
  2. High school students—England—
  Sociology
  I. Title   II. Woods, Peter.
  373.18′1   LA635

ISBN 0-335-10599-8

Library of Congress Cataloguing in Publication No.

LC 84–19092

Text design by C. N.

Typeset by Freeman Graphic, Tonbridge
Printed in Great Britain by M. & A. Thomson Litho Limited
East Kilbride, Glasgow, Scotland.

Contents

Authors' Acknowledgements

We are grateful to a number of people for their comments on parts of previous drafts of the text. We would particularly like to thank Stephen Ball, Douglas Hamblin, Martyn Hammersley, Andy Hargreaves, and the anonymous referees who submitted helpful reports on the original proposal to the Open University Press. Our thanks once more to Mrs Meryl Baker for unfailingly expert secretarial assistance. Above all, we are indebted to the staff and pupils of 'Hayes' and 'Old Town' Schools, and particularly the counselling staff of the latter, for their co-operation, kindness and hospitality.

The research on which this book is based would not have been possible without the financial support of the Open University and the Social Science Research Council (now the Economic and Social Research Council).

Introduction

This is a study of how the pupils of one comprehensive school coped with their transition to that school from their various middle schools at age twelve. Transfer from primary or middle to secondary or upper school is one of the most important and eventful episodes that occurs during a pupil's career.

> It's like starting a new life going to the other school.

> It seems more grown up. You're sort of more important, and I know that happens, because when I see people from [the upper school] in the street, you kind of look away.

> This school just prepares you for [the upper school], that school prepares you for life.

Yet, hitherto, the full richness of pupil experiences during this profound change has not been tapped. Usually, it is the teachers' view of transfer that is examined (as in Galton and Willcocks 1982, and Stillman and Maychell 1982). Over the years, the aspect most considered has been that of selection. This of course reflects the major concerns of the early sociology of education – selection and social mobility. But there has been some consideration of pupils' general problems of adjustment. There are complications, as Hamblin (1978, p. 5) notes:

> Pupils are asked to make the demanding adjustments to secondary school just when many of them are entering the pre-pubertal growth spurt which makes them feel clumsy and very visible . . .

Nisbet and Entwistle (1969), in their study of Aberdeen schoolchildren, found that 57 per cent of the boys and 64 per cent of the girls experienced identifiable problems of adjustment. Other studies have found similar proportions (e.g. Merton 1975, Neal 1975, Spelman 1979, Power and Cotterell 1981). Yet the reasons for these problems have not been examined in any depth.

1

As they reflected major concerns of the day so also did previous studies employ prevailing methods. Nisbet and Entwistle (1966, 1969), the most prominent of these studies, used intelligence, personality and attitude tests and teacher reports, in a five-year longitudinal project, and concentrated in the main on statistical differences between groups of children. Pupil views were garnered through essays on 'My first day at school' (Murdoch 1966) and 'Six weeks later'. These studies were mainly interested in the correlates of academic success. Similarly, Spelman (1979) in a wide survey of schools in Northern Ireland analysed children's reactions over transfer (assessed by attitude scales which yielded seven 'dimensions') in relation to bold characteristics such as large families and manual backgrounds, or reciprocal visits by primary and secondary teachers. For some more qualitative data on children's views, essays were again employed, and content analysed.

The main conclusions reached have been that:

- pupils in schools with carefully thought-out transition programmes have smoother passages than those without.

- considerable anxiety is engendered at first over a number of items (teachers, work, size of school, etc.), but it modifies within a few weeks.

- the working-class child is particularly adversely affected.

- type of school is more significant than transfer arrangements in explaining pupils' attitudes; familiarity with new schools is best predicted by transfer proceedings, alienation by type of school.

Method of study

However, these researches do have their limitations. They are, for the most part, normative studies, cast in terms of what the schools are trying to achieve. There is nothing wrong with this, if that is clearly recognized as the cast. But it does leave a great deal unresearched, and could possibly yield distorted interpretations. Some teachers labour under such distorted views, according to Beck (1972). He argued that their assumptions about pupils' ability, based on a very narrow and technical range of competencies, and their commitment to progressive methods of pastoral care exerted great influence on the accounts they gave of the transition and their view of pupil problems. They omitted to consider the pupils' own 'systems of relevances' (Schutz 1962) and consequently missed the 'authentic cognitive problems' that pupils experienced with transition, and the consequences for the pupil of school policy, practice and organization.

To capture this, we need, now, detailed case study work which embraces the whole breadth and penetrates the depths of pupil experience. As regards breadth, there should be equal coverage of both formal and informal aspects. By formal, we refer to that aspect of pupil experience and career that relates to goals, values and organization specified by teachers in the school acting in their formal capacities. This is the aspect addressed almost exclusively by previous studies on transfer. By informal, we refer to aims and values that exist apart from the formal, best expressed through the peer group or teenage culture. The informal culture derives from the pupil's situation and concerns. It involves the problems of adolescence, puberty and gender; but it also includes pupils' 'unofficial' adaptations to the formal organization. Whereas the formal culture includes both teachers' and pupils' resolution of the problems induced by official aims, the informal culture is the pupils' own resolution, which, on occasions, may run directly counter to the formal (Willis 1977, Ball 1981). This early transitional period, when adaptation to the informal culture is going on, has hardly been touched upon, though there is a growing body of literature on older pupils' informal cultures (e.g. Hargreaves 1967, Lacey 1970, McRobbie and Garber 1976, Hammersley and Woods 1976, Woods 1980, Llewellyn 1980). Yet apart from being of interest in its own right, the informal culture is inextricably woven into the formal area, and has a considerable effect upon it.

As regards the 'depths' of pupil experience, to arrive at an appreciation of childrens' innermost thoughts and feelings and to gain a picture of their subjective experience, we must employ a range of ethnographic techniques over the whole period of transition. As Nisbet and Entwistle (1969, p. 87) astutely observe, after considering pupil responses garnered from essays:

> But we must appreciate that children's experiences may well be more terrifying than they admit to their mothers or in an essay.

Prominent among these techniques are unstructured interview and observation. Pupils are interviewed many times, on different occasions, in different places, and they are observed in the classroom. We shall know, then, that we are not simply capturing a mood of the moment, dependent on a single context. The researcher is based in their school, goes to their lessons, and lives through, with them, the transition. Another of the benefits of this form of 'participant observation' is that it is able not only to capture the nuances of meaning behind standard expressions of anxiety, but also to savour the emotions and degree of subconscious feeling generated by the change.

The researcher lives as close to the role of pupil as he or she can get. This not only affords insights on its own merits, but can be the means of forging very close ties with children. We have found in previous work (Woods 1979) that children will treat the sympathetic 'unattached' adult to many confidences. They have often told us they 'enjoy' talking to us, and this obviously works in a kind of functional counselling way. This, we feel, is of special importance with pupils of 12-plus, for they are at an age of great sensitivity and of some identity confusion.

Armed with this kind of method, therefore, we aimed to explore some of the unanswered questions relating to this crucial experience in the pupil career. What is *their* perspective of this experience? What are the key points of the transition and how did they accomplish it? We felt that detailed, day-to-day observation of the pupils would show the significance of preliminary visits, first encounters, first adaptations, later settling in. We aimed to chart this process to show how the anxious neophyte *became* the secondary school pupil. We sought, also, to link the evaluation of an induction scheme with its mediation through individual pupils and through groups of pupils; in other words, to monitor how the transition was accomplished by the pupils' own criteria, as well as by teacher assessment. We suspected that the accommodation was not all one way, not all a matter of pupils adjusting to school norms; but that teachers, too, accommodated to pupils. What was the nature of the negotiation between teachers and pupils during this initial period? Which forms of negotiation optimized teaching and learning? Which forms, if any, promoted deviance?

Inter-pupil relationships were also of interest. There are indications even to the most casual observer that, for most pupils, the 'informal' culture is of more centrality than the school 'formal' culture. We have some indications of this from previous research, which has pointed to the importance of friendship (Murdoch 1966, Bryan 1980, Meyenn 1980) and status (Hargreaves 1967, Lacey 1970). But, again, there are vast areas unresearched. The peculiarly functional meaning of friendship (Davies 1982) at this age, for example, has not been clearly identified. Nor, of course, have its implications for learning. Here, there is much for us to discover. We have no adequate sociology of learning. From our observations, one major mode of pupil learning is through forms of interaction among the children themselves, mediating the teacher's message through informal groups. We know nothing of this process, except that certain forms of it are likely to be interpreted by teachers as deviant and to provoke censure. Coupled with this is the question of 'who socializes?' Traditionally, we think of the paramount influence of adults on children in this respect. We were interested in the nature and degree of socialization by the peer group and youth culture generally.

Despite a vast literature on adolescence, we know curiously little about pupils' growth at this stage, from their own perspective. It is a time when children are undergoing profound physical and physiological developments. New social identities are assumed, with the gender factor prominent. New horizons appear with the expansion of curricula and division of labour. Yet though there is growth, there is also the experience of loss – loss of status as they move from the top of one ladder to the bottom of another, and loss of the 'family' ethos that characterizes many of our primary schools, as they move into the more functional climate of the secondary. What do the pupils themselves make of all this? What changes in identity are brought about, what are the influences on those changes, and what are the implications for teaching and learning?

In summary, we felt that such a focus could make a useful contribution to educational discussions about:

- the age of transfer
- induction schemes
- inculcation of a 'culture of the school' (or school 'ethos')
- interaction between the formal and informal areas
- pupil learning
- the character of adolescence and its effects on formal school culture.

The schools and their environment

The research was conducted in a 12–18 mixed comprehensive school of about 2000 pupils, and in one of its seven feeder middle schools. The schools were in a town in the Midlands. There was both light and heavy industry in the area, including a car plant and much food processing. The schools were on a post-war estate with a mixture of council and private housing and tower blocks. The town and the area were comparatively prosperous at a time of general recession, and most of the pupils were children of affluent workers, with very few from middle-class homes. Most of the population were 'London overspill', retaining strong links with friends and family in the capital. There were signs in the town, however, of considerable unrest among the young, with gangs, graffiti and, occasionally, violent incidents. Pupils in the study complained of inadequate transport and leisure facilities.

The middle school (8–12), which we shall call 'Hayes', was staffed mainly by women. There was no school uniform and homework was only occasionally given as an 'optional extra'. It was run very much as a junior school, with generalist class teachers and little specialist teaching. Teachers and pupils of both this middle and the upper school felt strongly, in fact, that it was more of a 'junior' than a 'middle' school, with the extra year simply 'tacked on'. Teachers also referred to discipline problems in the extra year, which they saw as the consequence of treating pupils in that year as 'juniors'.

The first year intake into the upper school ('Old Town') was distributed initially across twelve mixed-ability forms, and four houses for pastoral care and sporting activities. During the first term, they were setted for mathematics, during the second, for science, and during the third, for foreign languages. Otherwise they retained mixed-ability groups through to the fifth year. Old Town had a small sixth form (35 in the two years together). School uniform was insisted upon, except for the sixth form, and corporal punishment was used. There was a well-organized pastoral care system run by four senior members of staff (all on Scale 4 posts), two of whom had formal counselling training. The school was popular in the area, with a reputation for successes in exams and good relationships between staff and pupils, and had an annual problem with oversubscribed numbers, as it was first choice (out of three schools) among a majority of parents. There was considerable rivalry among the three comprehensive schools in the area, evident not only in sporting activities and other achievements but in conflicts between gangs of pupils from the schools, which occasionally led to violence.

The research began in the summer of 1979. The research assistant (who did the fieldwork) studied the top year of the middle school, identifying several 'key informants'. She followed these through to the upper school, where she associated primarily with one house. This consisted of three forms, one of which was selected for special study, though for certain subjects and activities members of all three forms came together. She studied pupils' day-to-day experiences and perspectives through the transfer to the upper school, and up to the end of their first year, a period of eighteen months in all. Ethnographic techniques were employed, consisting primarily of unstructured interviews and observation. The pupils were interviewed many times, on different occasions and in different situations, and were observed in lessons in the classroom from day to day.

The research assistant also shared 'out-of-lesson' time with the pupils, conversing with them in the informal areas of corridors and playgrounds, accompanying them on school trips, going with them on the induction visits to the upper school, and attending parents' evenings. Pupils also wrote essays and kept diaries for her at significant points, recording their thoughts and experiences. The research assistant, therefore, lived through the transition with them in the true spirit of 'participant observation'.

In this introduction, we have identified the issue we chose to study, located it within educational thought, indicated the potential gains for teachers and pupils of ethnographic analysis of the matter, and described, briefly, the schools and area of the research. The organization of the book follows the main phases of the transition as we observed them, beginning with the anxieties and expectations of the pupils during their last term at middle school (Chapter 1) and their reactions to the upper school's induction processes (Chapter 2); and moving through the provisional adaptations of the first term, with special emphasis on (a) the initial fronts teachers and pupils presented to each other, and their dissolution (Chapter 3); and (b) the initial formation of friendship groups (Chapter 4). The second term heralded a phase of 'renegotiations', initiated by an attempted coup, when pupils made a distinctive bid to win more control (Chapter 5), and marked by significant developments in the move from childhood to adolescence, and the reorientation of peer relationships in line with newly espoused values (Chapter 6). The third term brought more consolidated adaptations, with indications of more permanence, as pupils 'made space' more realistically for their interests within lessons (Chapter 7), and assumed more thoroughly the characteristics of 'deviant', 'conformist' or 'knife-edger' (Chapter 8). In Chapter 9, we reconsider the theoretical, methodological and educational implications of the study.

I

Last term at middle school

◯ 1 ◯

Identities at risk

During the last term at middle school, a number of indicators signalled the forthcoming transition. The pupils knew it was their last term. Their teachers referred with increasing frequency to the coming transfer, and in due course official contacts with the secondary school were made. This school operated an induction scheme (see chapter 2), which involved, in the first instance, pupils and parents making several visits to the school. They received pamphlets and brochures giving basic information on the school, its organization, dates of terms and the demands of school uniform. Though our first interviews in May had suggested that some had not thought much about the transfer as yet, the induction visits in June provoked a strong reaction. Not surprisingly, there was a high level of anxiety, accompanied by the proliferation of a number of myths, and these are the two main aspects we consider in this chapter.

It was not all apprehension. Pupils varied in the amount and kind of anxiety experienced, and some appeared to feel none at all. At times, a feeling of excitement and optimistic expectation was evident. Where concern was felt, they were frequently able to supply an antidote or comforter of their own. Like the students described by Becker *et al.* (1961), they employed different time perspectives. The transfer was a short-term move in which fears for the moment might predominate, but it had to be seen against the broader backcloth of the pupils's whole career. The general direction of this was towards adult status, which they favoured. They themselves seemed to see the move as a leap on to a higher platform, where they must first struggle to secure a foothold. Somebody might try to kick them off, they might flounder about for help for a while, but none really doubted they would survive.

Even so, anxiety was the paramount characteristic of the anticipation phase. Its main features have been noted in other studies (Murdoch 1966, Merton 1975, Neal 1975, Piggott 1977, Hamblin 1978, Spelman 1979, Bryan 1980). However, we feel that the source of the concern has not yet been properly located. It is our belief that this transition raises basic

8

questions about the pupil's identity. It threatens to strike at some of the foundations of self, so carefully nurtured hitherto, but still insecure because limited, and untried in wider theatres. The prospect of marginality – they were not yet members of the new school, but already phasing out of middle school – put the pupils in a kind of limbo where the referents they used to identify themselves either no longer applied or were as yet unknown factors in the future. The first line of questions was how would they cope with the new demands, new situations, new problems? But behind these was the more important consideration of what they were to become in the process.

Different groups of pupils may have different value systems, but certain matters are common to them all. They evaluate themselves by comparison with others, and by how others judge them. Respect, esteem, acceptance – and in some instances tolerance – are all hard earned. They might now have to be fought for all over again. Have they the strength and skills to win through? Will they become 'proper' people? Complicating this thought is oncoming puberty and profound physical and emotional changes, and the pressure to assume appropriate gender identities. In all of this, friends are of particular importance in two respects. First, they directly help one's own sense of identity, by reflecting, reinforcing and reciprocating valued aspects of self. Secondly, they offer support, help and security in times of need and trouble. But the teachers' relationships with the child are also crucial, for big changes in them are envisaged: they move from a caring, parental role with wide-ranging knowledge of the child to a more functional, subject-based role with more limited personal knowledge.

Pupil anxiety revolved around five major issues: the size and more complex organization of the new school, new forms of discipline and authority, new demands of work, the prospect of being bullied, and the possibility of losing one's friends. We can see both formal areas (the first three items) and informal areas (the last two) represented here, illustrating the fact that pupils have, in effect, to make more than one transition. This compounds their difficulties.

Expressions of being 'frightened', 'worried', 'scared' and 'nervous' about going to the new school were often coupled with comments on its size.

> It will probably be strange at first, getting used to things, how big it is. It looks big, and people always walking around, and everything. It won't be as quiet as this school.

> It is so big – so many places I have to go see, it will take me a whole year to learn all the places, and it will take me longer than that to know all the people there.

Size, complexity, movement and noise bear down on the ignorant and anonymous neophyte. The comfortable, homely environments they have known hitherto, where they have been looked after, will be exchanged for a brash, impersonal, more cosmopolitan and bureaucratic institution where they must find their own solutions. Yet even the first basic tasks they foresee as difficult. Pupils were afraid of losing their way in the maze of corridors and classrooms, and of being late for lessons and 'getting into trouble' with their new teachers. They were worried about asking directions, for in this new anomic state few could be trusted:

> Darrell: I think I will get lost a couple of times. I am sure to. I have heard that if you get lost, and you ask some one, they send you a completely different way.

Others, therefore, might take advantage of their vulnerability. One's self-defences have been removed, and the inner, more fragile, more sensitive kernel exposed to the merciless whims of those who are celebrating their own personal conquest of the transfer. It is not simply a matter of temporary anonymity therefore, but a real threat to the self. However, there are signs of salvation in pupils' own personal resources and past experience:

> Sue: I think it will be big and crowded. I might lose myself, with all the buildings. I will have to get used to it.
>
> R: Do you think you will be able to?
>
> Sue: Yes, because when I came here, I thought it was gigantic, and I got used to it.

The new complex institution would be governed by new rules enforced by a new penal code. In this, corporal punishment loomed large:

> Keith: Old Town is quite a tough school, they are quite strict there. If you do something very wrong, you get a wallop.

Again, one gets a sense of pupils feeling they are moving from a cosy, homely world to a more impersonal, bureaucratic, rule-governed one. Angela said, 'The teachers will be stricter than here, they're soft here'. Darrell saw a certain inevitability in it: 'They'll be a bit more strict, they have to be, they're dealing with fifteen-year-olds, they're like the police really'. Pupils were also moving from a female-dominated to a male-dominated world. 'I've never had a man teacher before, so I don't know what it's like'. They certainly did not expect the homely touches of their middle school teachers to be emulated. At Hayes, the female staff brought in flowered cushions to 'soften' the grey plastic chairs they sat on. They took in small presents at Christmas, and at Easter, selections of tiny Easter eggs, which were placed in small boxes they made in the Spring term. The custom was for one teacher to have one class of children for most of the time, to get to know each one of them very well.

Pupils expected to be treated in a more distant manner by their new teachers. They could see that it would be difficult to evolve close personal relationships where a new organizational pattern required individual subject specialists, as opposed to the integrated curriculum in middle school taught by a single teacher who knew them well: '. . . it's gonna be a lot more difficult to talk to teachers there than here. Like if you don't understand something, Mr Suit, he explains three or four times until you do, but I don't know if it'll be like that over there. They might just tell you to get on with it, or give you detention if you don't'. Another boy said, 'Will they teach me, or will they just expect me to do it?'

However, standard categorizations of teachers came to their aid. Argyle (1969) has argued that we come to terms with new experiences by employing 'schema' – a range of fixed categories which we have built up in consciousness from past experiences. The middle school pupils already employed familiar typifications of teachers such as 'hard' or 'soft', 'willing to have a laugh with you', 'able to explain', and they projected these images on to the upper school teachers. Mark, for example, classified the headmaster as 'a bit of a harder version of Mr Suit' (his form master). There are signs here, therefore, of pupils already beginning to come to terms with the future, or at least making sense of it, by employing existing, tried frameworks.

This was also the case with regard to another anxiety – work. There were signs that anxiety increased with the degree to which children already experienced difficulty with their work, and possibly reflected a picture of themselves they had internalized from teachers and from comparative peer performance in the middle school. Several were worried that the work would be 'too hard for them'. One girl felt that 'sometimes when we learn new things I won't learn it straight away', and she was especially worried about being able to keep up in maths: 'I am worried about maths really, because I am not very good, but my mum and day say "Just try your best"'.

For those who had few problems with work, there was another concern – whether they could re-establish their identities as high achievers and their ranking among their fellows. Phillip, for example, made clear his worry about his performance in relation to others: 'I like being best and I want to come near the top'. He realized the threat from clever children coming from other middle schools but would not mind: 'If I know another kid's brainy, then I won't feel so bad if he beats me than if I think he's thick'. For some pupils, however, who had preferred to 'muck about' at middle school rather than work, the transfer offered an opportunity to establish themselves in the academic hierarchy, and to make a new start.

Again the pupils leant on their past experience and the longer time perspective to provide guidance in the new situation. Stacey said, 'At the end of the third year here, I was worried about the work, but in the fourth year it was all right, just the same really'. Carol referred back to her transfer from first to middle school: 'When I first came to Hayes, I thought, Oh! I don't know my tables and I'll get really far behind, but they learned you your tables, and I think it'll be the same there'. Similarly, Mark had confidence in his own ability, not being 'worried about any work because I do work alright. I'm in the top five for Maths, Mr Suit said, in the school. I can tackle work all right if I try'. He knew, too, that much depended on the teachers, and 'as you get to know them the work will be a bit easier.' Some actually welcomed the thought of subject specialists, because the teachers will 'take more effort in their subject, and they try harder when they haven't got other subjects to think about.' Phillip liked the idea of streaming because 'you don't get stuck in the group that is higher than what you are, and you can't keep up with them, and you get left behind.' It must be said, also, that, for some, work had low priority and consequently few terrors. Sylvia, for example, told us: 'I'm really looking forward to meeting boys, boys are my best subject', and seemed confident in her abilities to make progress in that area.

However, for all pupils, the prospect of homework was singularly depressing. It was not the nature of this work, but the possible amount of it, which could encroach deep into their private time and deprive them of opportunities for free expression and preferred activities. So Darrell said, 'I want time out, and I don't think I will be able to get it, because I'll be studying all the time for homework. They say you get quite a lot of that'. Stacey similarly was 'worried about getting too much homework, and that you will have to do it too quickly and everything.'

The new sports' facilities, and the opportunity to play a wider range of games, was a source of pleasure for some, but not for all. One girl worried about 'Having to run, athletics and everything, I'm no good at it'. Another boy, considerably overweight, admitted: 'I'm worried about games, 'cos of my weight and that'. Some complained about having to take showers after games lessons. Deborah said, 'I'm not really looking forward to the showers, that will be difficult to get used to, that will be a new experience'. Mark said, 'I don't get the idea of having a shower after games. Why do we have to take a shower?'

The other major source of anxiety was older pupils. 'They will take the mickey out of you, the bigger kids', one boy said. Others said, 'I'm a bit worried about being beaten up by bigger pupils', and 'I wonder about the kids there, you know like, if you're in the playground . . . if you get pushed around and that'. Darrell was worried because he had 'heard there's gangs going around, the fifteen year olds.' The girls were more worried about psychological aggression. Deborah, for example, was 'not looking forward to being a first year. I don't fancy being bullied. If you get in their way, they can call you "first years", and "stupid little first years" and call you names.'

Abigail illustrated the gender difference: 'You might bump into them and say "Sorry", and they might think "Well, she did that on purpose", and they will start making fun of you, calling you names. Sometimes if you are a boy, they might have a fight with you. The girls, they just get on each other's nerves, and if they are old enough, they can get gangs on to you – hopefully that won't happen to me'.

Once more it is status, and not simply personal survival, that is at stake. There is a pecking order in the pupils' informal culture, ranked on a seniority principle. New recruits are natural targets for the expression of superior status. It is all the harder for those who had the most senior rank in their previous school. Keith made this clear: 'The kids there, if you are in the playground you get bullied or pushed about, because right now you can't really because you are in the top year. But there, you are in the bottom year, and there might be somebody there who is a bit of a bully, so I don't like the idea of that'.

One important symbol of status is the kind of space that one occupies. For example, senior pupils customarily occupy the seats at the back of the school bus and of the assembly hall, and tend to monopolize the best pupil amenities. In all institutions, people also make their own 'private areas', where they can relax the formal demands of the role and be 'themselves' (Goffman 1961). Moving schools means that these areas have to be fought for all over again, and that the privileged territory held in one is yielded to the least choice pastures in the other. Darrell showed his uncertainty: 'I don't know what they do there, but here, you go into the playground, and like, we've all got different spots, like you play football in one area, and we all have our own area and you don't change; but if someone goes on your area then you tell them to go away, like you protect your own area. But it seemed the same there, at the upper school, 'cos on Monday, they were playing cricket in one place, and on Thursday, they were in the same place. At first I think we will play with the older kids, and then we'll get our own place'.

This is another illustration of how formal and informal areas interact. Formal status governs the distribution of pupil private territory. But that formal status is heavily reinforced by cruder factors of size and strength. Darrell thought they would get 'shoved off because there will be bigger kids there.' For boys, at least, there seemed to be a rigid hierarchy based on principles of size and toughness. They appreciated that, in due course, they themselves would have advantages in that respect. Mark said that the thing they liked about going there was 'that you're sort of more important. I know that happens, because when we're walking down the street and you see Old Town people, you sort of back away . . . because they're big 'uns.' Phillip also acknowledged that they would probably get bullied to some extent, but 'you get used to that, and then you go up, and can push the others around.'

Here, the longer time-perspective comes to the rescue, for the pupils assumed that principles that apply are the same as they were throughout the primary years. Here, status for boys depended on physical toughness, and was signalled by the ability to fight, or having the reputation of such ability. Phillip told us: 'If you get a reputation for getting the cane, it makes people think you are hard, a tough nut, then everybody will come and scrap you, to see if they can beat you. You get a reputation for being a good fighter. . . . People just come up and say, "Can you beat this boy in . . .?" I mean, I have a reputation for being the toughest boy in the school, and people say, "Oh! I don't know about this" . . . he says, "I can't beat him in . . ." but the others keep on saying "Yes you can" and it just carries on until you fight'.

Having such a reputation carried its dangers, however, on transfer. Phillip realized that a 'good fighter' might be a natural target for some of the bigger lads. Pupils who tried to display their toughness might run into trouble. Keith knew 'some kids who have been in this school and have gone up, and, you know, they wear their big boots, and they have been kicked in for wearing the boots. You get some people like that. But I don't think that will happen to me.' Quite literally, they had got too big for their boots, and had been reduced by older pupils to a more appropriate status. This vividly illustrates another important feature of the transition: that is, that the way to adult or adolescent status is not actually open. Pupils have to negotiate their way through. Sometimes older pupils stand in the way. Some of these perceptions, it must be said, were imperfectly realized, and these particular ones did not apply to the girls.

Discretion would appear to be the prime requisite. But the major defence, in all these matters, was 'friends'. For example, they felt that bullying was less likely to happen when 'your mates are there, especially if they're good mates.' 'If there is a group of you, they would have to push through the groups and the group wouldn't like that'. Unsurprisingly, therefore, the pupils' greatest anxiety was whether they would be 'split up' from their friends and placed in different classes. Phillip hoped he would have 'someone I know in the class, 'cos you have to start all over again making new friends, and it can be pretty bad sometimes. You get left out of everything.' It was a big worry among the girls also. Angela hoped quite desperately that she would be in the same class with her friends Stacey and Amina. Deborah realized she would 'have to make a lot of new friends', but felt she found it 'difficult to make new friends.'

Girls and boys differed in their friendship behaviour. Boys had their 'mates', but tended to belong to large groups; girls also had a circle of friends, but also 'best friends', who were especially close. We shall explore these differences further in a later chapter, noting, for the moment, that for all pupils, friendship was functional. That is to say, it served a purpose as well as resting on a sense of mutual regard. At an elementary level, friends provide help, support and reassurance; but they also help in defining the world, in making sense of situations and in establishing one's own identity. Their prime importance among a wide range of schoolchildren has been noted in several studies (Willis 1977, Meyenn 1980, Woods 1979). So important are they, in fact, that in some instances pupils have been observed to have 'contingency friends', in case the best friend or friends is absent (Davies 1982). The prospect of losing friends, therefore – contingency ones included – on transfer is deeply disturbing, for it threatens to knock out the props of one's self-support system.

One illustration of this is the perceived threat to what we term 'co-operation groups'. These illustrate very well how the pupils organize themselves informally to deal with formal demands. We observed them at both middle and upper schools. They were based on friendship ties, and were exclusively single sex. Their function was co-operation and help, the terms of which were clearly specified in a code of rules. Pupils co-operated over materials and work. The co-operative group consisted of those to or from whom you could loan a rubber, ruler, coloured pencils, and so on. One of the most frequent sources of loud protest in the middle school came when a non-member of the group borrowed something without asking. For the co-operation to work, pupils needed to have a very clear picture of who owned what – a rubber that did not smudge, or a certain coloured felt-tip perhaps.

Co-operation over work took the form of either clarifying instructions or finding solutions. 'Do you have to put it in millimetres?' 'How many do we have to do?' Sometimes, points were disputed: 'You're not supposed to do that'. 'She told us to do No. 1'. However, co-operating in finding solutions, especially to difficult work, was regarded as the more significant and sensitive activity. As with the loan of materials, there were firm boundaries around the groups, and sanctions were used against intruders. There were hierarchies within groups, and particular pupils were recognized as being 'worth asking' for help, though they differed between subjects. Also, there were various acceptable pleas for help: 'I'm stuck. . . .' 'Do you know. . . .?' 'Start me off . . .'. Darrell explained, 'I would ask Phillip to show me, not to give me the answer, but show me how to actually do the sum, and maybe I could then work the answer out, just say, 'Give me a hand on this sum'.

Some idea of the importance of these groups to pupils can be gleaned from observations of events when the rules were broken. Gary and Phillip were in different co-operation groups, but one day found themselves seated together in a mixed activity. Gary tried to look over Phillip's shoulder, whereupon Phillip angrily asked, 'Why don't you get your own work done?' and it is the sort of rebuke a teacher would use. Yet Phillip would co-operate with Martin and Darrell in maths, working through problems together quite freely. Andy, by contrast, was partially accepted in this group – help for him was rationed. On one occasion, he pleaded, 'Go on, Phillip, what is it?' about a difficult maths' question. Complete intruders would be given one of a number of stock rebukes, such as 'Cheating again!' One other firm rule was that 'Boys don't ask girls', though the reverse did not seem to apply quite so rigidly.

In this middle school, teachers disapproved of the practice of co-operation. Pupils remarked on teacher views: 'Mr Suit says it doesn't help you in the long run', and 'Well, you can't ask your friends in exams and that'. Some recounted stories of pupils copying from each other, getting caught and being punished. But most found at least some consultation with their fellows indispensable to their learning. As Darrell said, 'Sometimes if you can't get it right, we have to ask someone. If you don't feel like asking the teacher, maybe they are doing something else and are busy, you can ask your mates, and at least have a try. I try not to ask, I try to look it up, but if I don't understand and the teacher is really doing something you can't ask him'.

The change of schools seemed to threaten this informal – but to pupils essential – activity for handling formal requirements. Phillip thought it would be difficult to ask someone you did not know – it might offend some hidden code: 'They wouldn't know you, and you wouldn't know who they were. You wouldn't be able to talk to them, or ask "What did he say?", something like that'. Darrell also felt that 'you would be too shy to just go up and ask someone who is not your mate in case they said "No", whereas 'friends will tell you the answer, or something like that.' But it was not just a question of friendship – we have already suggested that co-operation also involved ability: 'If you make friends with the others, you like to pick out the best ones to see who is good'. Keith said, 'When you are in a new class, you could be asking this kid, and he could not know what he is talking about at all'. And Andy thought that 'if you wanted to ask, or got stuck, you needed to feel you could "rely on them".' Finding out who was good depended, it seemed, on teacher judgements and labels, and was therefore something that would take time to resolve in the new school.

In a very real sense, therefore, the pupils' identities hang in the balance. They do not know how they will measure up to the demands made on them in a situation that they have not experienced before. They do not know where they will stand in relation to fellow pupils, the great majority of whom are strangers, coming as they do from other middle schools; and they cannot be guaranteed the services of their own personal pupil welfare group. It is a major crossroads in the pupil career. The hazards appear great, their vision is limited. No wonder they approach it with apprehension!

However, we have noted that these fears are embedded within a broader span of experience wherein pupils by and large have worked out methods of coping. In this longer time-perspective, pupils see a different picture – a new and more desirable identity, increased skills, enhanced status. As a Schools Council paper rather grandly puts it, 'This is the time for the first real shrugging off of childish things, the first real donning of the adult mantle' (Schools Council 1977, p. 67). There were signs that, in spite of initial fears of status reversal, pupils felt they were entering a more adult world which eventually was to work to their advantage. The move, while it might carry risks of the unknown, was none the less a step nearer the coveted status of adult. Pupils spoke of it as 'moving up' or 'growing up', and saw symbolic value in all sorts of things such as 'wearing uniform', 'the coffee machine', the cafeteria system with 'school dinners'. Boys especially, for reasons we shall examine later, acknowledged a need for what they regarded as a more 'mature' and more 'adult' attitude. Several spoke of their resolve to work hard in order to get 'a good job' and 'get on in life'.

Anxiety, therefore, is often tinged with optimism and a certain hard-headedness which enables some pupils to objectify the circumstance and see it as part of a larger pattern. There is also the obverse of 'loss of identity' – that is, the opportunity to construct a new, richer one, with the appreciation that the social circumstances provide new possibilities and freer rein. There is another resource available to them which is anything but hard-headed, but which is none the less valuable in equipping them to cope with the coming transition. This is the phenomenon of pupil myths, to which we now turn.

Myths

Pupil myths about transfer were revealed initially in observations of pupils conversing among themselves, and then in interviews with both individual pupils and groups. The former accounts inevitably tended to be less complete and less coherent than those given in interview. All the pupils in the final year at middle school knew about these myths, as did all the first year pupils at the upper school, although they had attended seven different feeder schools. Second year pupils also knew about them, as did (we eventually discovered) sixth form pupils and teachers. Parents also reported hearing pupils discuss the myths at home. There was considerable evidence, in fact, that they were repeated in an annual cycle. First year pupils, in July 1979, admitted relaying them to those about to come to the school the following September. These latter pupils, a year later, were in their turn priming the next intake. The myths were told and repeated mainly by boys. The girls knew about them but did not retail them, except for one specific story. We shall discuss the significance of this later.

What constitutes a pupil myth? In the first place, the pupils' own perceptions about the statements they were making provide a clear indication. Pupils typically prefaced their accounts with signalling phrases such as 'There are all these rumours that', or 'There's stories about', or 'I have heard that', which were cues indicating that a particular kind of information was about to be given. For the pupils the information was somehow different from other kinds of comments about, for example, wearing school uniform or doing homework. Secondly, pupils denied their belief in these myths while they continued to repeat them. There was an ambivalence in their attitude, the boys admitting some element of truth in them, while none the less rejecting them.

This well illustrates a key feature of myths. They are of uncertain truth value, but in a curious way they convey more than any straightforward description ever could. As Sykes has argued in his study of myths in the workshop:

> . . . the myth . . . was known to be only partially true insofar as the actual *facts* were concerned. On the other hand, the men believed that the myth represented the truth . . . and expressed their attitudes . . . much more truthfully and accurately than any narrowly factual analysis could have done.
>
> (Sykes 1965, p. 327)

The problem, therefore, is how to divine this truth. Our first approach to understanding pupils myths was to consider prominent views from anthropology that relate to our concerns. From analyses based on cross-cultural comparisons, anthropologists have suggested that myths and change, at both an individual and a wider level, are quite fundamentally connected. Eliade (1959) has argued that myth making is connected with marginality: 'Myths derive from transitions, they are liminal phenomena, something that comes betwixt and between. They are ultimately involved with change and with the way man adapts to and assimilates change' (p. 73). Eliade, however, tells us nothing about *how* man adapts and how he uses myths to aid his assimilation of change.

Much of the analysis on myths has been made within structuralist or functionalist frameworks. Lévi-Strauss is the foremost theorist in the first of these traditions. He started from an existentialist position. 'There is no "I" that is not part of a we'; 'We cannot choose to be alone, it must be "we" or nothing' (Lévi-Strauss 1955, p. 120; see also Leach 1968). He continued, 'there is an almost infinite choice as to what kind of "we" it shall be', and acknowledged that the order which we perceive in the world is something which we impose upon it. 'Man has the choice to order the world in different ways in a quite arbitrary manner' (Leach 1968, p. xviii). He went on to assert that myths are an important tool of communication within culture, in fact they are one of the basic mechanisms by which we make those choices of order clear to ourselves. This complements the views of Malinowski, who described myth as 'a charter for social action, forming the practical rules for the guidance of man' (Malinowski 1926, p. 13).

There is thus substantial agreement about the significance of myths. They carry messages about the normative values of the society, and point out the knots in the social order, the places at which the demands of the social order bite upon the individual. In marginal situations the myth provides an indication of the norms and rules that will apply in the new situation, a prescription for action, and guidance on how to behave in the new community. The guidance tends to include a proscriptive element, for the pain, shame or punishment that follow any deviation from the social charter are likely to be graphically described. Myths, then, provide a kind of anticipatory socialization for those involved in transitions.

On the mechanics of how this communication is achieved, Barthes (1973) has argued that myths operate symbolically and that it is the ambiguities of that symbolic load which sharpen their effectiveness. The messages about the 'new we', the rules and the norms, the charter for social action, are not stated explicitly, but are concealed within symbols, within a hidden code. Hence the need for decoding if we are to understand them correctly. Thus myths, it is argued, have two levels – the surface detail and the deeper meaning. This could be of relevance in our case, since it could explain the pupils' ambiguity of belief towards the myths – the deeper message being accepted, the superficial one questioned.

However, this would be to jump to too hasty a conclusion. The myths must first be sited within the pupils' experience. In structuralist anthropology, there is a tendency to *impose* interpretations along the lines of greatest perceived plausibility and identification of patterned codes which apply generally throughout history and culture. But it is the anthropologist who does the perceiving, though it is the subjects who employ the myths and rituals. On occasions, highly ingenious explanations are offered, which bear no resemblance to anything the subjects may recognize.

Lewis (1980) has argued against this practice, warning that 'It is easy to think about peoples' rites and symbols in terms of our own preoccupations' (p. 15). These may bear little relationship to actor intent. Lewis also questions the structuralist assumption that myths function purely as ways of communicating weighty cultural messages. He stresses their potential emotional and expressive aspects. Pupil myths therefore may be a form of emotional release, and this may be equally, if not more, important for the pupils than the cognitive messages. Myths are not

> ... purely of the intellect, to be analysed in terms of logic and categories, as structures of the mind, abstracted from attitude, motivation and emotion.
>
> (Lewis 1980, p. 114)

Faced with one of the most significant transitions in their school career, pupils have to make profound emotional as well as intellectual adjustments. This explains why myths are both less and more than the truth. Detailed rational explanations of situations may be incomprehensible and/or 'flat'. Myths are artistically shaped, pruned to reveal certain details starkly, to identify people almost stereotypically, and to present action simply, yet dramatically (Lewis 1980, p. 334). This is all in the service of their emotional appeal. Clearly, then, it is not simply a matter of assuming some secret message in the myths that has to be decoded, like some intellectual riddle. We suggest, firstly, following the main anthropological theme, that myths act as a cultural blueprint, a social charter, for future behaviour, which contains both hints on norms and rules to observe, and clues to what kind of identity will be most appropriate in the new circumstances. Given this, it is important to place a myth clearly within the total myth structure of the culture concerned. 'It is only when the full canon of the myths is presented that the meanings can perhaps be fully or clearly elucidated' (Yalman 1968, p. 76). Lévi-Strauss (1955) compared the total corpus of myths to a full score for the orchestra, individual myths being like the scores for individual instruments.

Secondly, we suggest that the cultural message is conveyed more powerfully by myth because it acts both at a conscious and a subconscious level and affects both the intellect and the emotions. The argument is that, in myths, people mean to communicate certain feelings, ideas or relationships that they do not, or cannot, put into words. Lewis writes:

> Involved are sentiments of concern and respect, these are things which cannot be simply seen or described. They are preeminently the sort of thing for which people require symbolic thinking because they are insubstantial and abstract, yet they are felt as real. Symbolic thinking may help a people in a society understand the ideals which the objects and actions stand for.
>
> (Lewis 1980, p. 198)

This symbolic thinking in turn must be related closely to the cultural realities that the pupils actually experience (Douglas 1968).

Let us now consider some of the myths revealed in our study of school transfer. They fall into three broad categories:

1   Situations and activities making new demands of harshness and toughness in the new secondary school world in both formal and informal cultures.

2   Sexual development.

3   New forms of knowledge and work.

It is our contention that these represent all the major concerns of the
pupil during the transition, matching the stated causes of anxiety mentioned
earlier. We must stress again that most of the myths in the first two
categories were told by boys. Girls knew of the myths, but did not consider
that they referred to them.

New demands

Among this category is the 'head flushed down the loo' myth, which we have
heard repeated in many parts of the country, and indeed in Australia, where
it is referred to as 'the royal flush'. Here is one variant of it:

> Darrell: There's rumours that you get . . . they . . . that they flush yer 'ead down
> the toilet on yer birthday.
>
> Interviewer: Do you believe it?
>
> Darrell: I've 'eard me mates talk . . . an' they say . . . I doubt it really . . . well
> . . . it could happen, I suppose. (pause). It could . . . you know what
> gangs are like.

At face value, here is a fairly straightforward expression of anxiety – fear of
being bullied in the new school, where there are a lot of bigger pupils. The
complementary story about being thrown in the shower with all your clothes
on, again on your birthday, carried the same message. But why does the
myth take this particular form? Why the loo or the showers, and why on
your birthday?

Lévi-Strauss (1955) has drawn our attention to the potential usefulness in
interpretation of any element occurring in a myth that is not necessary to
the myth's making sense. Lewis (1980) has termed these elements 'alerting
factors', and gives a range of examples, such as 'An ambiguity of a thing
isolated, or out of place', or 'an action we feel unable to make sense of that
makes us say "this is odd, there is more to this than meets the eye".' (p. 9).
There is such a factor in the head–loo myth, namely the 'birthday'. The
myth would make perfectly good sense without it, when it might be taken as
a simple instance of bullying. The 'birthday' is the extraneous factor, and
we would claim that it holds the key to the real point of the myth, which is to
do with the intersection of the personal and public spheres.

Birthdays are very personal, part of our own intimate identity. The myth
is warning that if this is revealed publicly, the result will be discomfort and
shame. The myth then carries practical rules and fundamental cultural
directives for the adolescent child. The secondary school represents a new,
more impersonal state, where the inner self cannot any longer be safely
revealed. The myth also conveys a sense of harsher realities, where violence
abounds, after the relatively cosy world of primary, or first and middle

school. This seems connected as well to the status inversion involved in the transfer – from the top of one school to the bottom of the other (the graphic parallels in the head–loo myth do not escape us).

Other myths from the complete corpus tended to support this conclusion. These myths captured the sense of fear of potential violence in the status progression, and we suggest carried indications of new masculine identity, and its corresponding need for toughness. Thus there were stories of marauding gangs who could be 'after yer'. Phillip said, 'I've heard that there's these boys, and if you have a fight, they wear punch gloves with spikes, and they hit you and leave punch holes in your face'. Asked if he believed it, Phillip replied, 'Yes, this other kid told me'. The myth then is warning about the possibility of severe penalties for transgressing certain codes of behaviour; it is pointing out that the agents of this violence are older boys in the school. All of this indicates the vulnerability resulting from status inversion.

There may also be another element in the message. The myths single out dangerous places in the school, the toilets and showers, wherever teachers' supervision is least strong, in fact where the control of the informal culture by the formal organization is weakest, and warn against the danger there. The myth therefore epitomizes anxiety and expresses it, at the same time as it allays it, by providing guidance on how to avoid 'trouble'.

This interpretation of the myth is supported by the ethnographic data. The actual incident – head flushing – never seemed to take place, and Keith, in particular, when actually at the upper school boasted about his birthday, the present he received and the party he was to have. So the story did not provide a direct prediction of events. However, there were plenty of incidents of coercion and bullying, of greater or lesser intensity, recorded in our fieldnotes. Phillip, for example, told of an actual event in his first week of secondary school: he and a friend were in the toilets when a fifth form lad entered and scrawled his signature in 'biro' on their scalps. The symbolism of this act, it could be argued, perfectly matches that of the head–loo myth. The underlying message of the myths, therefore, was accurate.

There was a second focus of the myths in this category relating to the formal culture of the school, which seemed also to warn of tougher realities ahead: not in terms of one's peers, but rather in relation to school authorities and teachers. These myths centred specifically around sports' teachers and sports' events. Many boys repeated with some alarm the view that, at the new school, you were frequently expected to go on long distance runs, especially if there was snow on the ground. Mark said, 'and they say you have to run to Brookfield [a village about five miles away from the school]. I don't fancy running to Brookfield and back.' And Bruce: 'Some kids told me, in PE you run to Brookfield and back – it's nearly five miles!' The subject came up in conversation: 'Oh, there you'll be going on five mile runs an' that'.

We might regard this as simply an example of heavier physical demands in conditions that take the pupils to and beyond the limits of endurance.

Yet, even here, elements of the informal culture weave in and out of the myths related to the formal culture of the school. It became clear, in observation of the pupils during the autumn term of their first year at secondary school, that the informal culture, and particularly certain qualities of maleness, are involved. On one occasion, for example, after a long distance run (although not as long as had been predicted) there was a good deal of excited commentary on the event in the following lesson. One boy, Geoffrey, had been unable to keep up and to finish the run. He was marked and taunted for days, and had clearly lost status. This persisted throughout the whole of his first school year.

These two themes – new demands of character and endurance and the pupil's ability to adapt to them – run through all these kinds of myths. As well as expressing anxiety they are providing information, again of a rather exaggerated kind, overblown for more effect, on general situations that *do* arise. They warn of the new powers of physical endurance that will be required, toughness, speed, and a kind of alert watchfulness, both to meet the terms imposed by the teachers and to maintain face among one's peers. Sanctions, naturally, figure prominently in these tales: 'The thing that bothers me most about going there is to run a mile in under eight minutes, and if you do it in over eight minutes, you get sent back to do it again.' Other tales warned of sports' teachers who were monsters of violent surveillance: 'One of them hits you with a corner post if you're not out of the changing room in one minute'.

During observation of the pupils in their first year at the upper school, it was clear that the boys found that this kind of talk had the strongest element of reality in it. They did find the discipline of one particular sports' teacher both severe and irksome. His favourite weapon was a gym shoe. But if somebody 'got the slipper', the first question, as when any boy got the cane, was 'Did he cry?'. The official aim might have been degradation as well as punishment, but it you could put on a brave face, honour and glory might be achieved among your fellows and advantage gained in the informal status network.

There was abundant evidence of informal status hierarchies at the upper school (see also Hargreaves 1967). One boy, who left school with no examination passes and a long record of rebelliousness, clearly stood very high in the boys' status network. He had resisted teacher demands with some flair, even on one occasion completely turning the tables by striking a teacher. Within classes, we witnessed scrambles for position in this status hierarchy, and the retributions that were meted out for failure at cross-country running. On the other hand, Roy, who was the largest pupil in the class and in June won a fight with a third year pupil, was celebrated for meeting the demands for toughness with such aplomb.

Sexual development

A second broad category of myth was concerned with sexual development, and again it should be noted that the age of transfer, 12-plus, comes at a critical phase in the growth and development of the child. The most frequently related myth here concerned a homosexual male teacher. Some boys mentioned this in the writing exercise: 'Some teachers seemed all right, but one of them is supposed to be queer, called Mr Reeder'. The myths usually included a clear warning to stay out of this teacher's way, although they offered no suggestion for action if one were actually taught by this man.

There are a number of interesting issues here. Firstly, among the boys there was considerable confusion about the actual name and precise identity of the teacher alleged to be homosexual. Several names were quoted, in fact. The central issue seemed to be that there certainly was a 'queer' teacher in the secondary school. Secondly, this myth was equally well known to the older boys who were interviewed and who had just finished their first year at secondary school. This also had an assured place in the annual cycle of myths. But, the important point is that boys who had just finished their first year at secondary school gave credence to this tale, which they did not to the others they repeated. The older boys also added an extra element to the tale, a warning against homosexual boys in their own age-grade. This element was not present in the younger boys' tale, nor were there the large number of jokes and insinuations about homosexual tendencies on the part of any particular boy in the middle school. However, in the first year of secondary school, these allegations were often made against one boy, Thomas.

The 1979 intake followed the same process, a year later, and by the summer term of 1980 the first year boys had begun making allegations for example, that Geoffrey (the boy who failed at cross country running) was a 'poufter'. It is also interesting to note that the middle school boys never made allegations of this kind against their own middle school teachers; it was a new element, associated with the upper school. The boys also never made any allegations about 'queer' female teachers – neither did any of the girls.

If we seek to understand this myth, it must stand in the first instance as a clear and strong proscription against homosexuality. The myth is providing information about a new adolescent identity, about the new sexual self, which is explosively emergent at about thirteen. The myth's message then is about the 'normal' life career, about the pattern that is to be followed and the direction that is to be taken. The myth predicts the entry into early adolescent sexual patterns and lays down the demand for the sexual direction that is to be taken. The myth, then, warns the boy to steer clear of this homosexual teacher, to guard his new sexual self against this influence. Another element is thus added to the blueprint on masculine identity. It is interesting that, despite recent changes in legislation and what would appear to be the spread of more tolerant attitudes to homosexuality, the cultural directive at this age is strong and unambiguous.

Observation of the pupils suggested that the amount of interaction between boys and girls increased quite dramatically during the first year in the secondary school. The last two years at middle school seem to involve a withdrawal of children into their own sex groupings and a rejection of cross-gender contacts. The pupils began to emerge from this pattern towards the end of their last year at middle school, but the process was not completed until after the pupils had reached the upper school. This increase in activity, and this changing pattern of activity, would make the need to distance oneself from the homosexual identity all the more important. Other data from the secondary school confirmed this. Within the boys' informal culture, status was in part later to be achieved through taking out either a large number of girls or a small number of very attractive girls and from successful sexual expeditions, news of which were then broadcast throughout the school.

The myths seem to be concerned mostly with the informal culture. They focus on the values and 'codes' of the pupils' world, although they also indicate the points at which the formal and informal cultures intersect. They give a fairly accurate prediction of the realities of peer interaction, and make it clear that the informal culture, with its alternative status hierarchy, can be ignored only at considerable risk. But the myths equally signal the *value* of the informal culture of the school. They are not only giving information about becoming one of 'the lads' but also seem to celebrate the strength and potency of the informal culture, issuing an invitation, which is simultaneously a warning about 'life with the lads'.

New forms of knowledge and work

The third category of myth was concerned with the kind of work the pupils would be required to do, and it was told by girls as well as boys, unlike the others considered so far. Both boys and girls told gory tales of future science lessons, where various animals were dissected. The details of the story vary, as do the emotional reactions. The reactions, however, were divided clearly along gender lines. One boy said simply, 'Yes you cut up rats'; another declared, 'Most of all, I'm looking forward to cutting up rats, or pigs' hearts'. But another boy allowed his imagination to wander on the pupils' day visit to the school, when they were taken around the science laboratories, where older pupils were in fact sitting, reading large textbooks and answering a teacher's questions:

> When we got to the science laboratory, the walls were a bit dirty, we saw a died squid in a bottle. Then we went to a microscope, and look at a bit of eyeball, brain, heart and some other thing. The best bit was two boys about fourteen or fifteen were dissecting a rat. They had pinned its legs, feet and tail down, and cut it open, then they folded the skin back.

This boy took a delight in building up inister details. The walls were dirty, and there is this mysterious 'some other thing' lurking eternally suspended in formaldehyde. All the elements of the childhood world of the grotesque are present, bits of eyeball and brain are laid out for observation. This well illustrates the dramatic skill associated with myth telling. Sykes (1965, pp. 334–5) observed, 'The skill lies in the way the myth is told, the dramatic appeal, the use of words carefully chosen for their emotive effect, the rhetorical cadence, the repetition of key phrases. In brief, the normal devices used by any story-teller to secure the sympathy of his audience and to evoke an emotional response from them'.

By contrast, Stacey, a girl whose main love in life was animals, put it like this:

> One thing I don't want to do is cut up a rat. I don't think that's nice 'cos sometimes they do it alive so that you can see the heartbeat, I don't like rats, but I don't think that's very nice.

Stacey's choice of language is interesting: she repeats the phrase 'I don't think that's nice' twice in this context. The phrase can be taken as expressing a value judgement and a clear normative content. She has a sense that new rules of conduct, new kinds of discriminations are coming into operation in her life, after the move to the new school. Again the myth can be analysed as providing a kind of normative charter.

The myth is in fact based on a kernel of truth. Towards the end of the first year, the science teachers did dissect a white rat, which was, however, safely dead and which had in fact been deep-frozen. The myth again appears to be communicating demands for tough, hard, unemotional attitudes, and warning that the cosy qualities of the middle school must be put aside. The fact that both boys and girls told this myth indicates that the girls equally recognize that the warm familiarity of the middle school with its emotional flexibility and its leniency is disappearing, and that the patterns of secondary schooling are much more rigorous and austere. Thus the myth is also informing and warning the girls of these new demands. However, we must take into account the different responses made across gender lines. The boys seemed to celebrate the rather grizzly ritual that they anticipated. The girls, however, did not; they stood apart and judged it 'not very nice'. This difference was reinforced by some of the boys' comments. Bill, for example, said, 'Yeh, the rat didn't scare me though. But it did the girls, you could hear them all going "Ughh!" when they heard about it'.

There is, then, a difference based broadly on gender in this issue, a rather different normative prescription being laid down for the girls than for the boys. Girls are expected to have different reactions, different emotional responses to things. Girls have to be able to cope with the rigours of secondary schooling, but there are greater spaces allowed for the play of conventional female susceptibilities. An interesting footnote to this came during observation of the lesson in which the notorious rat was dissected. For it was a *boy* not a girl who fainted, and another boy fainted three days later during a film on the birth of a baby. The demands of the adolescent male code may not always be easy to fulfil by the lads who are subjected to it!

Retailing the myths

It remains to consider the setting in which the myths are recounted, and the motivation of those who tell them and maintain the annual cycle of myth recitals. By the end of their first year, boys at the upper school had discovered the surface detail of the myths to be largely untrue. Events did not happen in the manner predicted. This was the case for both the 1978 intake, who were interviewed in July 1979, and for the year 1979 intake, who were interviewed the following year. Yet in that same month (July 1980) they were involved in recounting the same myths to the middle school boys due to enter the school the following September. The cycle was continued.

It becomes important at this point to ask what kind of member construct a myth is. They are employed by the pupils, they have relevance for them, they were undoubtedly generated and embroidered by them, and they are perpetuated by them. But in a sense they exist apart from the pupils. They have become objectivated (Berger and Luckmann 1967), as is clear from the invariant nature of most of them. They belong to the general body of pupils, and not to any one of them personally. They are therefore available for anyone's use. Thus, the objectivated myth with its exaggerated but none the less relevant picture of reality remains in existence. Though the surface detail may have been disproved, the inner message has been proved correct. There have been new physical, psychological and emotional demands to be met, sexual development has made itself felt, new and stronger forms of knowledge and working have appeared. But this would not be sufficient explanation for the continual re-telling of the myths. The key to this, we suggest, lies in the pupils' celebration of their successful negotiation of the transfer. They have survived, literally 'to tell the tale'. It is interesting that it is the largest and 'hardest' boys, who have a clear sense of being able to take care of themselves, who come to discount the myths first, yet who seem to be most prominent in their re-telling. This indicates a clear connection between the two levels of myth – its general impact, and its individual impact. And it sites these particular myths within the whole span of the pupil career. For part of the celebration is to do with codes of masculine hardness and age-grade hierarchies. It is the older, second or third year pupils who are identified by the myths as the threat, as the purveyors of hardness and toughness. This itself constitutes an excellent reason for the first year boys to relay the myths to the incoming recruits, for it gives a substantial buttress to their *own* claims for toughness, and for an automatically elevated place up the ladder of the informal status hierarchy.

A related line of interpretation of the role and place of myth is to be found in Sorel's *Reflections on Violence* (1950); it is concerned with issues of social control and specifically political persuasion. Sorel saw myths as an exceptionally influential tool for the manipulation of consciousness and the winning of political power over people, and he suggested that they should be produced at an official level (see also Sykes 1965). At first sight, this analysis seems to have little point of contact with the traditional anthropological approach. However, it draws attention to *who* tells *what* to *whom*. Frequently, myths are recited by those who have power in a society, and the content of the myth involves the allocation of status and the legitimation of the power of a particular group or individual. Sorel uses the example of a divine intervention, which granted chieftaincy to one particular family. So myths may also act as a kind of political charter, informing about the power relationships of a social group. It is at this level that Sorel's approach to myth can shed insight on the myths told by pupils, for they deal explicitly with the way power is shared out, and the way status is won in the informal culture of the school. The objectivated myth is taken up by boys at the end of their first year and told to the incoming recruits as a tool in this power game, being intended by them to maintain their own status and power in the age-graded structure.

Pupil myths must be considered in their entirety, and analysed against the background of pupil experience. We see them as conveying a social charter and a cultural blueprint for the changes that confront the pupils in their transition to the new school. They prepare the pupil, emotionally as well as socially, for a quite profound shift to the new world of the upper school, which embodies all the tougher and more impersonal realities associated with the adult's as opposed to the children's world, the status hierarchies and peer group subcultures of the informal area, and the mysterious unknown of sexual development.

Being eased in

The staff of the upper school were aware of the importance of this transition in the pupils' careers, and they were aware of at least some of the anxieties that it generated for the pupils. They had devised an induction programme, based on ideas by Douglas Hamblin (1978), in order to deal with the problems. Primarily, the programme aimed to increase the desirability of the passage for the pupils, and to provide accurate first-hand information about the new school, to substitute for some of the rumour and myth. During the induction scheme, teachers emphasized the benefits of higher status at the new school and underlined the opportunities for new and exciting forms of learning. But, this was done within a context of firm control. New opportunities and resources were available, but they could only be used within a disciplined framework. Thus, some of the ground rules that govern teacher–pupil interactions were spelled out. At the same time, there was room for negotiation, and pupils were allowed to feel a degree of elasticity for the play of the informal culture.

The induction scheme had a well-established organization. The seven middle schools included were divided into two groups, each group of children coming for two visits to the school. The first visit lasted for the entire school day, the second for a morning. In addition, there was an open evening for parents of the new intake. These activities all took place in the second half of the summer term prior to transfer. In addition, there were special arrangements for the beginning of the autumn term. On the first day of term, only first year and sixth form pupils were allowed in the school. A range of counselling activities was organized as well.

We monitored the induction scheme through (i) observation of all these activities; (ii) interviews conducted immediately before and after the induction visits in the summer term; (iii) a creative writing exercise, set by the pupils' class teachers, immediately after the visits. How, then, was the scheme put into operation how was it experienced by the pupils, and how effectively were its aims realized?

From the start of the parents' open evening, which was also open to the new pupils, there was a considerable amount of 'impression management' (Goffman 1959) in which 'appearances' was a major theme. All the teachers had changed from their normal, everyday wear to more formal clothes. The school had been specially cleaned, and a work display of pupils' work and teacher aids mounted. The high point of the evening, however, was the modelling of school uniform by first year pupils, which created a great deal of interest among parents and pupils.

Then the headmaster gave an address. he stressed the importance of uniform, but pointed out they had made it as practical, simple and cheap as possible. For example, no special type of outside coat, or shoes, or blazers was demanded. Also, there were certain concessions in some sensitive areas, like the wearing of ties. Boys were allowed to wear roll-necked sweaters, if they wished.

This was well received – clearly the headmaster had grasped the importance of expense and fashion to parents and pupils respectively. In the writing exercise, one child wrote: 'In that school you have to have a uniform, although I know it makes the children look smart, I think it is a bit stupid, making the parents buy a uniform that could cost anything up to fifty pounds. What if a family can't afford the uniform?' On ties, one boy later commented:

> Well I don't like the idea of ties, in fact I hate ties, can't stand ties at all, the uniform that you are given there is alright, because they stretch it a bit, you can wear basically really whatever you like, as long as it is in the right colours, and in the summer you don't have to wear a tie anyway, you are allowed to wear cords sometimes.

But if there were to be concessions in some areas, the headmaster emphasized that in others there was no quarter given. There was strong discipline in the school, and corporal punishment was used in some instances. In consequence, the headmaster claimed, there was no vandalism in the school, no graffiti on the walls, and the school was respected by the pupils. Then he issued an ultimatum: 'I want to make it clear what kind of school this is, we are a bit old-fashioned here. If as a result of what you have heard tonight you want to change your mind and take your child elsewhere, then you should do so. But that is the way we do things here'. He pointed out the rewards of this firm discipline – good academic and sports' results, and numerous enquiries from prospective employers.

Again the head sounded the correct note with these parents, for all those interviewed later were in full agreement with his policy. They drew the comparison with the other secondary schools in the town. One had the reputation of being 'excessively liberal' (there was no school uniform, teachers were called by their Christian names and, it was widely believed, had very little discipline or control). The third school had a reputation for being undisciplined and 'wild'. 'You hear terrible stories about that school' was a very widespread comment. Pupils and parents were both extremely relieved not to be associated with it.

Not many of my mates want to go there . . . they just lay about outside and go to discos, and kids come out. Oy wash yer name . . . want yer 'ead smashed in . . .

Of course, strong discipline and good academic and behavioural achievement might not have appealed to all pupils, and the headmaster was careful to extol the whole range of the school's virtues, which stretched into the extra-curricular area. He especially emphasized the work of the art and craft department and the rural studies project. Goats cropped the playing fields, and there were many other animals. Sports' facilities were extensive, and the school did well in local competitions. Nor did he ignore the pupil culture, and their anxieties within that field. He pointed out that the first day of the autumn term was just for first years. 'They will have the school to themselves'. He hoped that this would enable pupils to find their way around the school and to feel comfortable in it. They would be given a point where they could get information, to avoid getting lost. On bullying, he declared firmly 'You need have no fear. We don't put up with things like bullying. It's a friendly school this. I take a severe view of bullying, when it's reported to me', and he glared out at the audience and paused significantly. He insisted that his staff were tolerant of new pupils' difficulties. 'No teacher is going to get upset if a child gets lost or is late for a lesson in the first week. It will all be dealt with quietly'.

The headmaster in his speech focused unerringly on many of those anxieties that we identified in Chapter 1. He reaffirmed the school's standards of excellence in both work and behaviour, laid down firm disciplinary guidelines, but also conveyed a sense of warmth and caring, and a large measure of common sense. We know from many studies (e.g. Gannaway 1976) that pupils appreciate above all the ability to control and the ability to relate, and they were promised both here. And though he was firm, he was not beyond negotiating in important matters, like ties and blazers. He knew where an acceptable limit lay. He either realized the importance of appearance to the identity (Stone 1962) and the critical nature of this to the young adolescent, or, from experience, that enforcing uniform rules arbitrarily might be counter-productive. To all this he offered the endorsement of the hundreds of potential clients queuing to get into his school. It was a skilful public relations exercise. One pupil wrote, 'I think the head is a good fair man'. Another said 'He's good, and understanding isn't he? He speaks plain and gets his points right and his facts, doesn't he. He's great'.

Later, pupils were allowed to see the lists that had been posted, showing which form each child was in. This told them whether their friends from middle school would be in a class with them, and was probably their major concern. Several of the pupils described the scenes that arose as a result of these discoveries:

Everyone was running around trying to find out which class they were in.

They wanted to know whose class you were in to find it, and when we went home and the next morning, everybody was going 'What are you in?' and I thought that's just my luck, nobody will be in my class, but it so happened that I was lucky and quite a few of them were.

The contrasting reactions of two girls, one of whom was lucky in the arbitrary draw for classmates, is interesting. One girl wrote 'I am in V3 with my friend Jackie out of my own class now'. Another girl, Joanna, was not so fortunate. She clung to her father and was very close to tears: 'I won't be in Vanessa's class'. Her father attempted to comfort her: 'You'll be OK. You'll be fine wherever you are', and he sat with his arm around his daughter for the remainder of the evening.

At first glance, the 'warm, caring' spirit of the school does not appear to be working here. It is more an example of how the rational workings of an impersonal bureaucracy may cause pain to children already undergoing a complex set of changes. This is not a fully accurate picture, though. The secondary school forms divided into four 'houses' for pastoral care. Counselling staff at the school felt it was important to keep siblings in the same house. Over 50 per cent of the children in the 1979 intake had a sibling in the school. This meant certain children had to go into particular forms and hence particular houses. The secondary school asked the middle school for information on friendship groups, and pupils in the middle school put constant pressure on their teachers to transmit this information to the secondary school. Sometimes the information had to be ignored, in order to get house placings right. On other occasions parents or middle school teachers would request that two children who were friends be separated, usually on discipline grounds. In addition, the secondary school practised a policy of mixed ability, and this could lead to an arbitrary placing of children.

In other respects, the tour provided further successful impression management. Visitors saw, for example, selected pupils in glossy white aprons, bringing fairy cakes out of the ovens in the kitchen; and some of the best graphic art that had been done. There were reproductions of Victorian rag dolls in needlework and cheeseboards and plant stands in woodwork. The science department gave its first pyrotechnic exhibition of the 1979 induction scheme. One child (who in the next year consistently came top in science) described it: 'When we went to the Open Evening at Old Town, there was this kid mucking about with a fire extinguisher you know in science, and there was a little flame and a bottle of liquidised gas, he shot the fire extinguisher at it, and it went boom right up in the air. it blew up. It was excellent!' The majority of pupils expressed themselves well satisfied with this first stage of their induction scheme. Michelle rushed up to the researcher the morning after the Open Evening to say how good she thought it was, and to say specifically that the head had answered 'ever so many' of the questions she had had about the new school. Problems remained, of course – most could only be fully resolved by everyday experience at the new school. But parents and pupils clearly thought the induction evening a good start.

A taste of that experience came with the whole day preview of the upper school that the middle school pupils were given. Here, the earlier dual messages about discipline and the fun of learning were followed up by example. At once, on arrival at the lecture theatre, a very clear discipline message was given to pupils by one of the counselling staff, Mr Snow. There was a loud buzz of excitement as pupils made for seats, arguing about who should sit next to whom. Mr Snow allowed them to settle before he demanded quiet. He clapped his hands loudly and paused, waiting for the desired effect. Then he said, 'My name is Mr Snow'. A pupil laughed and made a joke about winter, and he glared and yelled very loudly 'Don't interrupt me, lad!' There was immediate silence. Mr Snow then said, 'All the stories you have heard about Old Town teachers being nasty and sadistic, well now you have a chance to see them come true'. Mr Snow's approach made a dramatic impact upon many of the pupils. 'A big man came along and led us around into a room called the lecture theatre. He began to talk to us. His name was Mr Snow, he had piercing eyes dashing all over the place'. Another boy said, 'We don't like Mr Snow a lot. He looks at you. He don't seem to smile or nothing'. What fewer pupils noticed was that Mr Snow also was fulfilling a 'caring function' in an unobtrusive manner. There were in fact not enough seats for all the pupils, and Mr Snow had asked some of them to share seats temporarily. This involved children from different schools who did not know each other sitting two to a small seat. This senior member of staff then left the hall and personally carried extra seats into the lecture theatre for the extra children, who relaxed perceptibly when he gave them a place of their own.

The strong disciplinary message was conveyed at several points during the day, and on the later visit. It was taken up again by the headmaster, when he addressed them, but it was not without a touch of humour. In his short speech, he embodied the school ethos, aided the pupils' anticipatory socialization by stating his expectations of them, and contextualized the transition into the longer time perspective. 'I'm known high and low as "the boss"', he said, 'and other things as well, but not to my face'. This amused the pupils greatly. He went on to talk about the 'right kind of attitude', being polite, being helpful, being willing to 'try hard' at school work. He also expected them to learn to behave in a mature and responsible way, and acknowledged the importance of this stage in pupil development: 'You come here and you're very childish, well that's all right, you are children, and that's what the adjective means, it's about being a child. But here you have four years to grow up and to gradually put aside childishness, and I want to see that happening'. The head emphasized also the great importance of good relationships with teachers in the school: 'It's a happy school this. It's not, and it shouldn't be, pupil against teacher'. It is significant that the headmaster used humour as a strategy in this introductory speech. It set a pattern for the way he hoped to appear, and showed that he acknowledged its uses as a negotiating tool (Denscombe 1980b). He also showed that he recognized the importance of the facts of the physical stages through which the pupils were passing, and with which they were deeply concerned. In Chapter 1, we showed that pupils felt that going to Old Town was a really important step in growing up, that it represented an institutional proof that they were now more grown up. The head again showed himself aware of their closest personal concerns.

Socialization, reassurance, demystification – these were the order of the day. If the aim was to make the pupils feel 'at home', this was accomplished in other ways as well. The children were very excited during the visit, and although the staff wanted to retain this excitement, it had to be kept in appropriate channels. At other times, high spirits had to be contained. Thus, they were restless during a talk by the deputy head, in which he explained the programme for the day and the organization of the school, and warned them to 'sit quietly'. Some referred to this later: 'Oh no, I thought. I hope we aren't going to have to sit and listen all day'. Another observed, 'I think on Monday it was a bit boring in the lecture theatre sometimes because we had to sit down all the time'. However, this may have been a useful form of containment, and also reassurance, for it carried an element of routine to which they were accustomed.

Just as boredom seemed to serve a useful purpose in this context, so did the 'spaces' between activities, for this provided opportunity for some private interaction and the play of the informal culture. For example, there was a buzz of noise and chatter in between events, tolerated for so long and no longer. Thus the pupils learnt first lessons about the availability of private and public time.

Much of the day was spent in curriculum demonstration, designed to capture pupils within the distinctive flavour of the school ethos. Perhaps the best example of this was the performance by the English faculty, who entered as a large group of fifteen people. The pupils displayed enormous interest in them as they entered, turning around to stare, craning their necks to see, discussing their appearance. The deputy head of the department made a few introductory comments, again using humour in his account of the activities of the department: 'You'll write stories and poems for four years, once you get into my grubby little paws'. This kind of language and teasing was clearly new to the majority of middle school pupils, who were delighted and very amused by it. Then the English teachers did a short play for the pupils, by way of illustrating the work of their department. The play was modern, working-class drama and involved a family, with teenage children having a furious argument. The insults flew thick and fast in the play, which the pupils found uproariously funny. One or two of the teachers used silly voices, imitation accents and ham, overblown gestures. When the play was ended, the deputy head of the department began a discussion with the pupils on the subject of family rows, asking pupils what their families found to argue about. he received the expected collection of answers: the time they came in at night and the time that they went to bed, pocket money, the washing up, and eating spinach. This teacher agreed that the last topic was a problem: 'Isn't it funny how everything that's good for you tastes horrible'. The teaching technique was to use topics relevant to pupils' lives to interest them in an academic subject, and also to put forward an image of self as being in humorous sympathy with their concerns (for a wider discussion of this kind of ethos, see Measor and Woods 1984). The pupils' reactions were very positive: 'We were then shown a little play by some of the teachers that was really quite good'. Another child wrote: 'Other teachers came and they did a play, it was very good. I am looking forward to going [to Old Town] a bit, now'. One boy said, 'Those English teachers, the ones that did the play, that was pretty good. I liked that. It seemed as if they were a good laugh, they had a good sense of humour'.

The formal programme for the day in general appeared to go very well. But we have noted that pupils also undergo a transition within the informal culture. They may have received words of reassurance from the staff, but their biggest test came during the first break when, for the first time, they were left to themselves and ushered out of the school buildings. At this point most of the pupils displayed some degree of anxiety, and clustered together in friendship groups. They were desperate to be with their friends, and there were lots of shouts like 'Hey, Diggers, wait!' and 'Elizabeth, please wait!'

They argued about where to go and which direction to take. Most of them ended up in the playground, where it was very obvious who they were, since they were the only pupils not in school uniform. They kept by and large to the extremities of the playground, in symbolic recognition of their peripheral status in this informal arena. One or two of the boys got involved in an informal game of football, in which *they* came to be used as the football in some cases!

Sisters and brothers came over to talk to the middle school pupils and their friends. Lesley, who is only a year older than her middle school sister, came across and shared sweets and information about directions. Carol came with her, and giggled loudly as she pointed out one of the middle school boys, Gary, a year younger than she is, whom she used to 'go out with'. Some of the middle school boys, friends of Gary's, teased Carol about the black footless tights she was wearing. The bell for the end of break sounded and, as large numbers of pupils attempted to get back into the school, some of the older boys shoved the middle school boys aside very roughly in order to go in first. Pupils later reported getting 'pushed around' during the break. 'We were next to the coffee machine and this bigger boy came through, pushed us all out the way and went into the toilets'.

Here, already, was confirmation of the message conveyed by the myths on bullying and inequalities of size. More on this theme, together with the emphasis on toughness and hardness and the notion of a status hierarchy among the informal culture of the boys was to appear at lunchtime, when the pupils had a longer break and really confronted the older pupils. Many of the pupils behaved in the same way as they had at break, and stood around the edge of the playground in nervous little clusters. However, some of the boys again joined in a game of football, during which there was again considerable pushing and shoving of the smaller lads. One older boy simply lifted up a middle school pupil and replaced him at another spot, out of the way. However, it was noticeable that this did not happen at all to one child, Tom. He was especially tall and large for his age, and was interested in boxing. He had already had, we were informed, a victorious fight with one or two of the older boys. He was exposed to none of the aggression that the smaller boys faced.

The extent to which the pupils already knew each other from living in the same neighbourhood and through the complex kin, sibling and community links rapidly became clear. The lads playing football knew each other, and we were told later that some of them played the same game in the streets at home. The importance of sibling relationships also was demonstrated again. Nicola had a brother in the top form. At lunchtime, he rushed over to her, and picked her right up off her feet, and swung her over his shoulder, and danced around the playground with her. She appeared very flustered and embarrassed. Later, she said to her friends, 'Ooh, he didn't half show me up, my brother'.

We have identified this issue of relationships with older, bigger pupils, and to the informal culture in general, as one of the major anxieties for the middle school pupils. They gave their reactions to the experience later. Most reported some difficulty: 'We played football with the first and second years. But there was too many people playing'. A great many of the pupils mentioned in writings and in interviews the fear of getting bullied. Two of the boys said at first that the day visit had helped make them less anxious: 'I'm less worried, I think they are friendlier than I thought'. Yet within a minute or two of the interview the boy was talking again about his fear of gangs and general bullying. Phillip said that 'talking to the kids in Old Town you know at play times' had helped, and yet within a short time in the interview he admitted 'the pupils just acted as normal and took the mickey out of us.'

After lunch, it 'was time to go back to the lecher theatre' (as it was described in one of the essays), and at once the pupils, and especially the boys, began to exploit the private space presented them as they waited to be let in. But now there was a different quality about their behaviour. They were more boisterous, noisy and aggressive. The middle school pupils from Hayes began to push and fight. One or two went across to the nearby stairs and slid down the bannisters. There were no teachers present. As the level of violence escalated into actual punches getting thrown, the researcher remonstrated fairly sharply with the boys, but in fact had to do so three times before they were prepared to stop. A teacher walked past the group of boys who formed the centre of the mêlée, but they continued fighting and pushing. It needed strong remonstrations from the senior teacher, when he arrived, to quieten them down. The incident gives the lie to views that all pupils employ conformist strategies in initial encounters (Ball 1980), though it should be noted these pupils were a year older than those in Ball's study. It also revealed, for the first time, the relevance of aggression and toughness within their own peer group. The myths had warned specifically about older pupils. The fact that there were none referring to one's own age group in this respect may be because it was a known factor that they had already learnt to live with.

The afternoon of the induction day was given over to curricular demonstrations in the areas of maths and science. Pupils were reassured to hear that in the first term they would do mostly revision work, and they were shielded from the potentially threatening knowledge that they would be streamed in that subject in the second term. 'I'm not really worried now about the work because I think this year, as they said, we will probably be doing a lot of revision to see what they know about us, because they don't know an awful lot, so the first six months, or so, we will probably be going over the same. I'm not saying it's going to be dead easy. We will probably do a couple of different things and slowly build up'.

Ball (1980) and Beynon (1984) have argued that pupils engage in 'sussing out' during initial encounters – that is, behaviour designed to discover the formal rules governing teacher–pupil interaction – and there was a certain amount of that kind of experimentation here. At the beginning of the science teacher's talk, for example, somebody dropped a ruler with a loud clatter. The teacher walked over, picked up the ruler and smashed it down on to the desk with a loud crash. This brought immediate and total silence. Then the teacher said explosively, 'The one thing you will learn, especially in science, is not to fool around, because it's dangerous. You do not fool around like this while I am in the room'. After pausing again to allow this message to sink in, he said, 'When people are talking to you, I want you to sit up straight!' At this point the whole room rustled as all the pupils hurried to obey.

Having got this basic control message across, he began to discuss the work of the department: 'We want you to have some idea of what physics, biology and chemistry are'. There was also a demand for new adult language: 'We hope you will know not to call a 400 cl beaker – a jug'. Then the curricular exhibition began. The biologists appropriated a volunteer, placed him on a static bicycle and fitted a set of temperature electrodes to different parts of his body. The electrodes were connected to a meter, which showed a light that shone brighter as the temperature rose. The blinds were drawn as the boy began to pedal and as soon as the lights began to shine more brightly so he was urged on faster and faster by the others. The children were fascinated, and stood up and moved chairs so as to be able to see better. The biology department then brought in some of the animals they reared and kept. The reaction of twelve-year-olds to white baby rabbits and chicks was a predictable set of 'Oohs' and 'Aahs'. When the two goats were brought in the excitement became even stronger, especially when one of the goats got up on its hind legs and placidly ate the biology teacher's tie! The atmosphere came to resemble a Christmas pantomime, successfully conveying the 'fun' and 'caring' aspects of this particular school ethos.

The 'learning is fun' theme was continued by the chemists and physicists.

They put thick washing-up liquid on a child's hand, and then poured hydrogen into his palm. This was then set alight, making a restrained but impressive explosion in the child's hand. Phillip later opined:

Phillip: Those experiments were great.

R: Which one did you like best?

Phillip: The hydrogen one, or was it helium? When he lit it in Bruce's hand. All that washing liquid condensed into powder when he lit it. All this white powder came off his hands.

Bruce, the boy chosen for the experiment, said with mingled pride and humour in his written account, 'As for that chemistry man, he tried to blow my hand off on Monday'. The science teachers made pupils' hair stand on end by passing electricity through it, and demonstrated the strength of a vacuum. The latter involved a sphere with handles, sealed with a vacuum, which took six pupils to pull apart. They fell over when they succeeded, to great cheers from the rest. The last 'trick' caused a sensation when the teachers passed electricity through a child, who then ignited a bunsen burner with a flick of his finger. Many children mentioned the experiment later. 'Gary put his hand up to spark off a flame with his finger, with the help of a van der Graph machine. He nearly burnt his finger off'. Another child wrote, 'Another man came in and done some experiments which I thought was good, with a van der Graph'. It seemed significant that a child who could not remember when to use 'did' and when to use 'done' (despite the fact that he must have been told how to use them many times) could, however, remember the name of a foreign and complicated piece of machinery. Darrell wrote: 'We all stood up to see what happened – I really liked that science lesson'. The pupils also mentioned the animals with great approval and said they would welcome the opportunity to look after them. Many of the children said that they were very much looking forward to doing science at that new school, though these were almost all boys.

The girls by and large responded far less well, demonstrating already the pull of gender differences in curriculum areas, again as the myths had forecast. Keith was a typically enthusiastic boy:

Keith: Well there is more of a chance to learn there – because in this school they haven't got the proper apparatus and that. Like in science we have been told about these experiments, but we haven't been able to do them, and find out what the result is, because you can say it, but sometimes it doesn't come out. Not only that, but you can make up your own experiments with things, because they have got science labs there and everything.

Mark agreed, disparaging the equipment at the middle school. 'I've got more equipment and chemicals in my chemistry set at home than they do at this school'. But the girls did not feel the same.

Sue: I am worried about their way of doing physics, and I am no good at it, the hard part.

Many of the girls had liked the animals, but recalled the story they had heard that in the secondary school they would be involved in dissecting a rat later in the year. They were horrified at this prospect.

This gender difference in attitude towards curricular areas was even more evident during the pupils next visit, on an afternoon of the same week. Now they were actually to experience some lessons, and were accordingly divided up into 'class' sized groups. Each group had a guided tour around the school and two lessons, the groups being rotated between the teachers concerned. One of these lessons was 'fabrics', and it was made clear that both boys and girls would take this subject during the first year. The teacher explained the work of the department, and demonstrated the skills involved, such as learning to use a sewing machine and dyeing fabrics. She made it clear that the pupils would have a lot of choice about what they made, and asked them to write out suggestions. The room was filled with examples from previous years, and included not only rag dolls and dresses, but also banners of Liverpool Football Club, puppets and bags for fishing tackle. The boys showed some interest in the football banners, and many of them picked up the small, stuffed toys and furry animals.

The girls, however, were clearly excited by the exhibits and equipment and the opportunities offered. Tracey said, with enormous enthusiasm, 'I really like sewing, it's really good'. The boys on the other hand generally displayed a different attitude. Raymond, for example, sat alone, sullen and resentful for the whole of the lesson. When, towards the end of the lesson, the teacher asked for the suggestions that the pupils had written down, all of them came from girls.

The boys clearly objected to doing this subject. The following day, Phillip, a very 'conformist' child under normal circumstances was heard saying very decisively to some other boys, 'I'm not going to do needlework – no way!'. In the written account one boy said, 'The only thing I don't like is needlework'. Simon said in interview, 'Girls are going to work harder at something like needlework, aren't they? Well they are going to like it better than something like cutting up rats. I don't rate needlework as much as other things, like cutting up rats'. Darrell, too, was unhappy. 'I don't like it much, but it's a part you have to do'. Phillip made the strongest objection:

Phillip: Oh boring . . . don't like it . . . that's girls' stuff. I do think it's girls' stuff, needlework. When the blokes going to do it when they are older – when they are not married that's about all, and if they do get married the wife will do it. . . .

. . . They go out and get the money.

The other lesson that pupils experienced on this afternoon was PE. This was interesting, for the myths had referred to dominant games' teachers and strong sanctions for failure at these activities. The school could hardly make its point about establishing control in a more effective manner, but it was done in the usual Old Town way, with attention to the positive aspects of the activity and with humour. The teacher was a large athletic man, and as soon as he entered the gym the children became perfectly quiet. Earlier, waiting in the gym with their own female middle school teacher, the pupils had been noisy, with some of the boys pushing girls around aggressively. One group of boys had repeatedly crept into the store room, and kicked several footballs into the gym. Their silence now may have been, at least in part, the effect of the reputation for strictness and indeed physical violence this teacher enjoyed among the boys, which was not dispelled by his behaviour. He dropped the papers he was carrying on to the floor, and his large bunch of keys, and then kicked the keys hard so that they made a very loud clatter as they slammed into the wall on the other side of the room. The pupils, especially the boys, sat up very straight and were exceptionally attentive and totally quiet. His first words involved a discipline message, and were spoken sternly, without warmth or humour: 'I want you to listen when I explain things, because I only tell you once. Because if there is one thing I hate, its repeating myself. It's very simple'. He then went on to give some information about the range of sports that were available at the school. He relaxed enough to permit the boys to ask questions like 'Will we be able to do basketball?' Whenever he did this, however, he quickly tightened up the discipline frame again with another severe message: 'We are very strict about kit, if you come without your sports' kit, you won't be allowed to do PE. You must have two kinds, indoor and outdoor'. The teacher also told the children that at secondary school the boys would be separated from the girls to do sports.

With control established, it was time for the pupils to experience some of the fun in the activity. They were set playing a game of indoor non-stop cricket, which they obviously very much enjoyed. However, the teacher kept the discipline frame on the game extremely tight. First, he insisted that the bowling used should only be underarm, for the sake of the girls. The boys looked resentful, but made no protest. He also made an insistent demand that the bats should not be flung carelessly away, but had to be placed very gently on the wooden floor before the player ran. He threatened to take five runs away from the total of the team of any child who dropped a bat.

One team did drop two bats very loudly. The teacher stopped the whole game, and with all the pupils in total silence loudly told them they had lost ten runs. One boy, Gary, labelled as one of the tougher troublemakers at his middle school, put down his bat as if it were on eggs. He firmly told the girls behind him to do the same. As the game continued the teacher changed the bowlers and tested his control to the utmost when he selected a particularly unathletic-looking girl to bowl for the boys' team, which was winning. Again, the boys accepted the control and although they exchanged glances there was not even a murmur of disapproval. Gary, who was 'good at games', simply stood very close to her, to catch and rescue anything she dropped. When the teams changed from batting to fielding the teacher watched the noisy scramble to be first to bat, which the larger boys inevitably won. Then he paused until there was silence and said that the two children who were sitting down quietly at the side, patiently waiting their turn, would go first. The game became very competitive, and again the teacher exercised his control by catching balls and dropping them, and getting in the way of players, so as to even up the score. There were no objections.

The pupils all reacted very positively to this lesson, all said they enjoyed it, and that it was 'great'. The discipline message had not been lost upon them, however. They did not actually object to this teacher: 'He is not bad', but they recognized clearly, 'I don't think you can get away with much'. Another pupil, Phillip, said, 'He is pretty strict, but he knew how to be a laugh – he just stood in front of the wicket sometimes, so that you couldn't get everybody out . . . good laugh'. Phillip then elaborated, explaining that he liked teachers who were able to set clear limits, so that he knew where he was. 'As long as you can take it up to a certain extent, and then . . . take it that far and that's all right'. Again, this accords with the reports in the literature on pupils' expectations of teachers (Woods 1979, Furlong 1977, Gannaway 1976). These expectations, in this case, were based on their existing knowledge. These teachers apparently believed in the same kind of principles that the 'best' of their middle school teachers did, and such activity was easily normalized. Such rehearsal, therefore, formed an important bridge between the two schools.

Further plans for the induction scheme at the beginning of the term, such as counselling activities designed around typical pupil problems and involving group discussion, had to be abandoned when staff fell ill. Instead, pupils were regaled with academic testing and a great deal of being 'talked at'. The pupils were unanimous that this was 'awful, too much chat, they just talked at you the first day'. It has to be said as well that the teachers were disappointed at having to do this. The scheme, therefore, stood or fell by the open evening and the two visits. What had been achieved?

The general opinion was one of great appreciation. The days following the visits saw Hayes' pupils talking animatedly to their teachers and to other pupils about the events. One middle school teacher reported: 'The kids came back full of it', and described their experiences, especially of the scientific experiments. This was contrasted with the visit paid by the other pupils to the sister comprehensive. Old Town had given the children over a month's warning of the visit. The sister comprehensive sent out notices only two days before the visit. This had lasted only half a day and had involved a lot of 'getting talked at'. One teacher said, 'They were thoroughly bored'.

By contrast, prospective pupils for Old Town were enthusiastic. One child wrote, 'Before I had been for a visit to Old Town, I felt that I was going to hate everything like the teachers and the homework. Although I still object to the homework, I think I am going to like it very much. On Monday when we went to Old Town it was quite good'. Mark made an even stronger statement of approval: 'I used to be worried about games and getting bullied. I'm not worried about anything now, I'm really looking forward to going over there'. Dawn was interviewed before the induction visit and she had admitted herself frankly 'really scared'. On the way out of the school after the visit she was asked what she thought of the day. 'It was brilliant', she said, 'I'm really glad I'm going to that school'.

Many of the pupils mentioned the equipment and facilities in the comprehensive, and expressed great approval of them. The sports facilities had been noted. 'They have got great big sports halls like down the town in the leisure centre, they have got a great big place where you play basketball, exactly the same as the leisure centre one'. Many of the male pupils expressed a very high level of interest in basketball. it seemed a popular new sport and the new school was valued for its access to the sport. 'Their PE hall is good. I'm looking forward to it, because we have got the opportunity to do basketball'. The girls on more than one occasion expressed annoyance at being excluded from participation in this sport. However, the other sports were also welcomed. One boy was 'looking forward to trying to get into the football team most of all', and cricket too was popular.

Others made less specific comments simply writing 'Their equipment is grate' (sic). Simon told me in interview, 'A couple of us explored the school, you should see it. It is really excellent'. The library was commented upon, 'You walk through our library here, and their library's a big one, as big as the one down in the Town Centre!' The science facilities also made a very positive impression on the kids. 'The science rooms were very well equipped with machinery – and other things'. One child wrote about the science rooms 'having every safety measure.' Another child, however, felt very clearly that equipment was not the only issue: 'I am really looking forward to using all the equipment in science, and just hope I have a good teacher'.

The facilities for doing a wide range of arts and crafts had also been noticed with approval by the pupils. 'Olt tow is a nice school but thick is better than Hayes because it has big art parts'. The pupils looked forward to doing woodwork: 'We do woodwork here, but the tools are not the same as over there, and the wood, we have hardly got any'. Metalwork facilities were also welcomed: 'And after we went to the metal work room, there we saw some of the boys using Furnises.' The equipment and facilities were seen as a recompense for the size of the school: 'The good thing was in a big school there is loads of equipment, especially metal work equipment'.

For many pupils there remained areas of anxiety that were unresolved. One of these actually concerned the size of the school and the possibility of getting lost within it. Andrew, a boy from Hayes, at the time of the visits had repeatedly said on the tour of the school, 'I'm gonna get lost in this school'. Another girl ahead said exactly the same thing to a friend. In the writing and interviews later, the point was repeated: 'Old Town is a very big school. It is at least three times bigger than Rickley'. 'When i first whent to olt tow i thoth it was big, there is a lot of teachers in olt tow'. Some pupils felt that the visit had helped a bit, but still felt rather anxious.

Another problem concerned teachers. The middle school pupils expected a stricter regime at the secondary school than they had experienced at middle school, and many of them had expressed a good deal of fear about very strict teachers who were free to use the cane. The strict discipline that the school had projected had done little to reduce or eliminate this area of anxiety, despite the occasional touch of humour or allowance for negotiation. Mark said, 'Those teachers seemed to go out to scare you. They stand and stare at you and tell you off, then they go on doing it, 'they don't have a joke about it with you'. He compared them unfavourably with his middle school teachers. 'They'll have a laugh, none of them teachers looked like they would have a laugh'. In the writing exercise one boy concluded, 'A few of the teachers look all right, but there again I would not like to get on the wrong side of them'. The myths that the pupils had told about the teachers, especially about the sports teachers, persisted and were still told after the induction visit to the school.

However, it was the anxieties relating to the informal culture of the school that remained most resistant to change by the induction programme. The pupils were still afraid that they would be bullied and perhaps exposed to physical violence. Phillip remained certain: 'I reckon there is quite a bit of bullying, not much vandalism like he said, but quite a bit of bullying'. Many pupils repeated the headmaster's statement, that they should go to him if they were bullied. Michelle, for one, said that she would go. Phillip, however, saw that there was a real problem in this logic, 'Yes . . . if it got out that you had grassed, as it is called, on people who had been bullying then it wouldn't turn out very good for you in the long run; and even the older people who did bully you, they would take it a bit more serious anyway. They don't want to get the cane do they?' It is interesting that myths continued to be told in this area. If the interpretation we have already suggested for pupil myths is correct, and they do refer to areas of uncertainty and anxiety about the informal culture of the new school, then it is hardly surprising that the pupils continued to repeat the myths after the induction visit.

The pupils themselves made two main criticisms of the induction visit, although most of them found it very useful and it probably did resolve many of their anxieties about the formal institution they would be entering. They felt that two major areas of the new school organization had not been dealt with. The first was the matter of punishment. The pupils knew that the two main punishments applied in the school were the cane and detention. There was a real sense of uncertainty about what the nature of a crime had to be before it provoked the response of the cane. There was a lot of fear about the use of the cane, and the very strong discipline message that Old Town had projected made this anxiety stronger. The school itself probably felt this was a useful tactic. Pupils knew very little about detention. 'To give us a rough idea about detention, I know they do that a lot, you do it after school. How long can you stay there for, the maximum. . . . So they couldn't keep you more than . . .'.

The other issue was that of homework. 'But, not like the bit that we have to do home woke'. The pupils felt that the secondary school had not given them enough information about it: 'They didn't tell you much about the homework: actually they didn't tell you anything at all'. Simon agreed with this: 'Not exactly how much homework, but I wished they'd told us when we'd get homework, and sort out roughly how much'. He finished up: 'Do you know when we get it?'

The school's attempt, therefore, to bridge the transition, to remove anxieties, to render the unknown known, to increase the desirability of the passage, and to pre-socialize pupils into the school's own distinctive ethos was, perhaps inevitably, only partially successful. It was particularly strong in conveying a sense of the range of opportunities, the excitement of learning, and of higher status; but less successful in countering anxiety-producing effects arising from bureaucratic features such as size and organization of school, in clarifying forms of discipline and limits of rules, and the effect some new forms of work, such as homework, would have on the pupils. It was especially weak in the area of the informal culture. In fact, the induction scheme only really addressed in substance the transition into the official culture of the school. Perhaps little more could have been achieved in the time available, and under the 'mock' conditions. Perhaps, also, there is little a school *can* do in the area of the informal culture. One might indeed argue that it should not try to do too much, that there are some things pupils need to learn for themselves. What is needed, we suggest, is a supportive framework within which those lessons are learnt, and certainly this school in general provided that extremely well. Perhaps more could have been done, however, in the preservation of friendship groups and the separation of enemies. Some schools also operate sponsorship schemes, whereby older pupils take some responsibility for the new intake during the early days. We discuss these possibilities further in Chapter 9.

In a sense, the school's induction scheme was the teachers' myth about the new order. Activities were dramatically highlighted, main features pronounced. It was all rather larger than life. But it conveyed the essential content, character and emotional feel of the school's particular ethos extremely well. It came over strongly, to researchers as well as to pupils, as a caring community within a disciplined framework, offering reassurance over problem areas, demonstrating the fun and excitement of some forms of learning, and the basic humanity of its staff. Above all, it carried the tone of a successful institution to which people wanted to come.

II

First term at 'High Town': provisional adaptations

◯ 3 ◯

Initial fronts

The initial encounters' phase was marked by teachers and pupils presenting distinctive 'fronts' (Goffman 1959) towards each other. The teachers carried on the themes of the induction scheme, with its emphasis on discipline, caring, and interest and excitement, while pupils, by and large, conformed to the stereotype of the 'good pupil'. After a short while, however, these fronts began to disintegrate. This phase, therefore, contains two sub-phases: (a) a 'honeymoon' period in which teachers and pupils presented their best 'fronts' towards each other, and (b) 'coming out', in which the seamless fronts began to disintegrate and truer identities emerged. We shall examine each in turn.

The 'honeymoon' period

The teachers' front

A considerable proportion of teachers' initial time and energy was given over to the induction of the new pupils into the institutional demands and routines of the school. In fact, the first day at the school was wholly given over to this task and it continued piecemeal after that. Teachers dealt with timetables and maps, with addresses and birthdates, with lunch and with personal possessions, and with absences from school. These duties fell particularly onerously on to form teachers. For other teachers, especially those in craft and science, other demands pressed. Pupils had to learn safety procedures and the regulations about equipment. Rules about homework also had to be given.

How did the pupils react to this wholesale presentation of format? There was some disappointment and indeed resentment at the unilateralism of the proceedings and their own enforced passivity. The teachers' 'front' of 'learning is fun and excitement' had already slipped. Janet commented, 'During the summer holiday, I got excited, no, not excited, I looked a bit more forward to it, but when it came to the day, the first day I was excited, but it was a bit boring, every lesson, chat, chat. . . . That's what you've got to go through really'. Other pupils gave a similar response. The induction scheme had presented a front of high vitality interest that had now gone, to be replaced by a more familiar boredom.

No doubt this was because of the prior need to establish order, which conflicted with the 'excitement' motif. The induction scheme had emphasized discipline, and it remained a prominent teacher concern. A series of procedures were established for first year pupils. They had to queue up outside classrooms before lessons began, and were not allowed to enter until they were silent and orderly. They had to wait for permission to sit down, and were discouraged from any attempt to talk in lessons. A bell signalled the end of a lesson, but pupils had to continue working and wait to be formally dismissed. There was a set of punishments, and teachers made sure that pupils knew about them all.

Some pupils at least saw behind this stringency:

> Keith: Some of them have got their reasons to sort of clamp down a bit, maybe, because of future people . . . no past people, they have probably mucked about too much and so they have thought: Right, I am going to clamp down on this lot and get them learning in a quiet way or they won't get on.

Another element of the institutional front which had been presented at the induction scheme was that of a 'caring community' spirit. Some of this was explicit. For example, there was a well-organized counselling service, and pupils were placed in smaller house groups for pastoral care. Pastoral care was also on offer from form teachers, who had fairly long registration periods to enable them to pick up any problems. Teachers dealt as best they could with pupils' apprehensions about the new school, their new teachers and their own new roles. Pupils responded well to this. Keith, for example, commented, 'Teachers, they understand you'. About his form teacher, he said, 'She cares – like all the other teachers'.

Within lessons, too, there were new procedures and interactions for pupils to learn. Teachers made efforts to induct the pupils gently, and to make a smooth transfer from primary school patterns. They did this by presenting new demands to pupils in ways that were familiar and had a middle school character. One example of this concerned practices for finishing work and getting it checked by teachers. In the first few weeks of the term, teachers allowed pupils to continue their middle school practice of bringing their finished work to them at the front of the classroom. In a way, therefore, teachers presented an 'unreal' front to pupils. On this issue, they made the demands of secondary school look more familiar, more 'middle school' than they really were. This practice was gradually discouraged, so pupils remained in their seats, the teacher coming to them to mark work. This had an additional effect of reducing the amount of mobility that pupils were allowed in the classroom. It was a new demand on the pupils and was introduced gradually.

Similarly, a cautious mixture of old and new was continued in the area of language cues. Teachers need cues to begin and end lessons, and to change rhythm or direction. For example, they need to signal that pupils are to stop listening and start writing. Teachers also mark out significant points in lessons, as when they are about to introduce a new piece of information (Hargreaves *et al.* 1975). Now middle school teachers underlined their cues heavily, 'I really explained it clearly to them, you know the way you do'. In the same way, the secondary teachers in the first few weeks used, probably intuitively, a stronger set of cues than they normally practised. A change of pace, for example, was indicated by a firm 'Right, . . . will you put your pens and pencils down now and listen please'. Then a pause and 'Right . . . pens down now and listen'. The pause, and the repetition, made certain that most pupils had cued in. In another instance, a maths teacher made the cue for a change of direction in a lesson very explicit: 'As I promised you, we are going to change our topic today'. Some new information was about to be introduced. He paused and then said, 'I want you to rule off and put a new heading in your book, and when you have done that, put your pens down and show me that you are ready'. He made certain that he had marshalled everyone's attention in this way, and that everyone knew exactly what they had to do. These patterns did not persist for very long into the school year, but the carry-over from middle school held for pupils a note of reassuring familiarity.

On the whole, the teachers appeared sensitive to pupil problems. They explained instructions and especially new work to pupils very carefully indeed. Mr Davies was typical: 'We're going to do some new work today. Now, what we're going to do today is difficult, that's to say people always find it difficult, but if you don't get it at once, don't worry 'cos we'll go over it enough times till you get it right. Don't worry if you don't get it today'. This same teacher, when giving the pupils their first homework, went over it in very careful detail, to make absolutely certain that everyone understood. In terms of socialization into the new institution, it seemed that teachers attempted to reduce stress by bridging gaps between the old and the new forms, couching what was new in the language and forms of the old, so that what was new seemed familiar.

There were, however, three areas in which teachers were not always aware of the problems pupils faced. As a result, they were not covered in the 'caring community' way, and consequently the 'front' slipped. Firstly, pupils were apprehensive about their new teachers, and, as had been clear during the induction visit, were extremely reluctant to ask anything of a teacher they did not know. For example, in a maths lesson, pupils were only willing to ask the teacher for help if he happened to be standing near them. They were unwilling to raise their hands and ask a question in front of the whole class. The teacher walked around the room a lot in the first few maths lessons and this solved the problem for pupils, for as he walked by they would ask for help. However, there came a point when he sat down at the front of the class for about fifteen minutes. Most of the class simply stopped asking questions, but one continued to seek help. Janet raised her hand, but instead of asking her question in front of the whole class, walked to the front and asked it privately. Informal culture pressures were no doubt operating too, Janet probably fearing that the other, as yet unfamiliar, members of the class knew the answer to her question, and that she might appear stupid to them.

The second problem was a matter of discipline. Towards the end of a maths lesson, in which the pupils worked hard and attentively, their teacher suddenly said sharply to one boy (who was slouching in an ungainly position), 'Are you feeling tired? Sit up straight'. There was a very loud shuffle, as everyone in the class immediately sat up straight. An English teacher also found cause for reprimand. 'A chair has four legs you know, they rest on the floor, that's the thing that stops you falling through into the room below. Use all four legs, will you'. Such discipline messages were repeated in the first few weeks quite often. It was clear from classroom observation at middle school, that the pupils were allowed far more latitude there, adopting more idiosyncratic postures, and draping themselves around chairs in any fashion that suited them. These discipline messages showed up another area in which the upper school had to resocialize the middle school pupils.

The third problem was more difficult to resolve, and concerned the nature of the work task. In middle school, pupils work was largely 'task' oriented. The day was split into several large blocks of time, and maths or English or 'a project' was done within these blocks. If pupils finished quickly they could be allowed to do something else, such as finishing off work from another area. Their learning was much more an individualized programme, and their orientation was toward the accomplishment of tasks. The regime in a secondary school is quite different. At Old Town, the day was divided up neatly into one-hour compartments, its boundaries signalled by a bell. This structured the work of the whole cohort, and it became '*time* oriented' (Sorokin and Merton 1937, Hallowell 1937). Pupils had to adapt from working on a task according to their own timing, to a lesson orientation. When the 'bell went', it meant they had to stop working regardless of the stage of completion of the task. Pupils experienced this as a frustrating difficulty. Sally said, 'I don't think you get long enough with that hour, I think if you had about two hours in every lesson'. Teachers experienced the problem as a discipline one – pupils did not stop work when they were told to.

There were for teachers always pressures on the 'caring community' front, for it stood in opposition to the pressures toward discipline. However, a head-on collision between the two pressures could at this stage be side-stepped, because different personnel took different roles and functions. So classroom teachers could bark rebukes and administer stringent discipline, while form teachers and pastoral staff maintained the caring role. Individual teachers managed the role-split in different ways anyway, as we shall see.

The pupils' front

At first, pupils conformed exactly to the formal demands of the school, and tried to show themselves good pupils. The most noticeable thing about the pupils' first week in secondary school was the absolute quiet that prevailed in their lessons, a silence that was quite unnatural to anyone who was familiar with British secondary schools. There was 'no talking' in the lessons, and pupils got on with their work. In maths, when the teacher turned his back on the class to write on the blackboard, pupils did not use the opportunity to talk. When asked to do some work on their own, pupils quietly got their books out and started working immediately, without chatting or asking each other questions. When another teacher entered the room, and distracted their own teacher's attention, pupils carried on working in total silence.

Pupils demonstrated a great commitment to their work. They were rigidly attentive to any instructions or information given to them by a teacher. They rushed to complete their work, displayed a keen competitiveness, and a great interest in doing well. The appearance and presentation of their work also received careful attention. Pupils wrote out titles in blue ink and underlined them in red. They remembered to put in the date. Diagrams were done in pencil, with the labelling in ink. They even wrote neatly in their rough books. Pupils covered their books, or bought plastic folders to keep them in, and generally took care of them.

One of the characteristics of this phase was referred to by more than one teacher as 'the forest of hands' syndrome. Despite pupils' reluctance to ask for help, they were anxious to show their keenness to answer the teacher's questions. When a teacher asked a question, there were numerous pupils almost desperately keen to answer it. Interest and attentiveness to work were simultaneously signalled. Pupils who got the right answer, and a complimentary remark from a teacher, looked pleased and happy. One boy who got an answer right demanded that the boy next to him congratulate him.

All the pupils completed the homework they were set in the first week at school. One teacher did not set homework in a firm way, but requested pupils to do some extra work if they had time. All had finished it by the next day. Pupils even asked if they could take work home with them to spend extra time on it. Sally wanted to do extra work on her design project in her own time. There was a willingness to conform, even when not to conform would not have shown up during the early days. When the maths teacher went out of the room to fetch materials, pupils did not talk. The class had one English lesson in the library. Andy finished his book five minutes before the end of the lesson, and informed the teacher and asked him what to do next. It would have been easy for Andy to do nothing for the remaining time.

Pupils literally rushed to do what they were asked. In science their teacher, who was the headmaster, pointed out the dangers of leaving bags and coats at the sides of work benches. Someone could trip, and if they were carrying acid or a burning taper, the results could be damaging. Before he had finished his sentence, all of the pupils rushed to remove their possessions and place them carefully under the tables and out of the way.

Pupils demonstrated also their deep anxiety about getting anything at all wrong, in a number of other ways which teachers grouped as 'fussing'. Whenever a teacher gave an instruction, a pupil, or several pupils, demanded clarification of its exact details, and were entirely unwilling to take any initiative on their own. Caroline asked her teacher if she were allowed to cover her maths book, to keep it clean and tidy. In a lesson where the work was based on independent learning through worksheets, numerous pupils asked if they were allowed to turn the page and go on to the next page, before they did so. Pupils wanted to know exactly which book they were expected to do which work in, and which side of the page they were supposed to write on, and what titles had to be underlined, and how much space had to be left between work and the next piece of work. This behaviour was markedly different from that which had characterized pupils at middle school, where they had a confident approach, knowing the location of equipment, and the rules and procedures for presenting and ordering their work; it possibly reflects the demise of their co-operative work links, which could be relied upon to provide extra information on teacher instructions.

The 'front' was symbolized by pupils' appearance. It was very noticeable that all boys had just had their hair cut in 'regulation' style. There was not a 'skinhead' among them. Both boys and girls wore neat new uniforms and clean white shirts, and knotted their ties properly. The appearance of their equipment matched their uniforms, with their names on nearly every item. Aprons, books and bags were clean and without the graffiti of youth culture. They carried neat pencil cases, used simple pens and pencils and erasers. The pupil 'front', like the institutional front, was seamless at this point, every element and aspect of it fitting accurately into the image of circumspect pupilhood.

However, both teachers and pupils recognized the phase to be temporary. They knew it was 'a front'. Sally said, 'I think all the [first year] boys and girls are trying to be as good as they can. When they get older, they will answer the teachers back, but now they are as good as gold, pets'. In the same group interview, her friend Amy agreed, 'They want to get a good name from the teachers', and Rebecca chimed in with 'Reputation!'. Mark looked back on that stage and recognized the process: 'All the people that were in our class when we first got here were totally different . . . everybody was nervous, so they were different, quiet'.

Mr Ship, an English teacher, identified the first year pupils: 'Temporary personae they have for a couple of days'. Some teachers felt that the length of this particular phase had got less over the years. Mr Ship said, 'Five or six years ago, they were all good and quiet until at least half term, you could rely on it'. Mr Jones agreed that things had changed; now he maintained,

'After a week, they're all behaving as if they owned the place'. This may have something to do with the age of transfer. In the days when the 'honeymoon' period had lasted longer at Old Town, pupils transferred at eleven plus. Ball (1980) observed a similar duration for this phase in his 'eleven plus' school.

Whatever the duration, neither school nor pupils can keep up this front for any length of time, and after about a week, things began to change. The main reason for this was that the pupils' nervousness was fading. Phillip reported, 'The first day, you know, I wasn't really looking forward to it, but the first day was better than I expected it to be, and it's gone down, the excitement has, but it's just as good as I thought it would be. Pretty good, Yes'. Jenny agreed, 'I was nervous at first, but I think it's better than I thought it would be'. The successful completion of the first week seemed to reassure many of the pupils, and they found the second week somewhat easier.

'Coming out'

Once this nervous, apprehensive reaction to school had abated, personal concerns became important again. The teachers could not possibly keep up 'the front' either, their own personal differences soon pushing through in places. As the front crumbled, 'real' identities emerged. The main issue was the discipline 'front'. Pupils began to probe for 'living space' for themselves, testing around the edges of the sharply drawn rules, to negotiate the ground rules that actually operated (see also Strauss *et al.* 1964, Delamont 1976, Martin 1976, Woods 1978, Ball 1980, Beynon 1984). Such probing ensured the initial blanket conformity broke down still further as distinctions were discovered. Pupils soon began to discover priorities – important and comparatively unimportant parts of the school day, what they were actually allowed or not allowed to do in lessons, high and low status subject areas of the curriculum, important and less important teachers, and what adjustments to school uniform they could get away with.

Important distinctions among pupil values also began to appear as they reclaimed latent identities, as 'bright' or 'thick', 'good or bad' at a particular subject. Orientations toward school were reaffirmed, as pupils showed themselves conformist or deviant, 'teacher's pet' or 'menace'. Gender identifications were also highly important at this stage of adolescent development, and school was an arena against which they could be highlighted and played out. This phase confirms that pupil adaptations are an active construction on their part, not simply a response to teacher directives. In the rest of this section, we shall document this initial exploratory negotiation.

Appearance

It was the area of appearance, the symbolic manifestation of 'front' that was to change most rapidly; perhaps because first year pupils had older pupils as models. Their appearance made it clear that school uniform could be negotiated; it was more public than what went on in their lessons. The appearance 'front' hardly lasted the first week at school. It was the boys who first began to deviate, particularly those who later in the year were to form an 'oppositional culture' group. Roy and Pete inscribed 'PUNK' on their craft aprons. From such beginnings, deviant strategies grew. By 21 September, Roy was wearing a safety pin in the V-neck of his school jersey, and had a paper clip on the edge of his shirt collar. Pete's group marked the entire surfaces of their personal equipment – aprons, bags and pencil cases – with myriad slogans in rainbow colours. By 26 September, Pete's school books proclaimed uncompromisingly his allegiance to the Sex Pistols, Sid Vicious and Leeds United. Thus the emblems of punk rock began to intrude into the image of circumspection, but only for one group of boys. This group also carried on a consolidated attack against their ties. Keith had his hanging loosely around his neck one day, and he got severely 'told off' in consequence by a senior teacher. 'Why should you go around looking like a rat bag? Dress yourself properly'. Keith's official reaction to this was, 'oh he just tries to scare you. He goes round shouting, just trying to scare people. He don't scare me.' However, Keith did ask his form mistress for help in knotting the offending tie, and asked her anxiously for a mirror to check his appearance. He was making only an exploratory foray into this area of deviance. The rest of the class engaged only partly in this activity. Most boys ceased to wear their ties neatly, and by the fourth week many were wearing them loosely around their necks in their own peculiar styles. Many inscribed the names of football clubs on their own personal equipment, but not on school equipment such as books. Clearly, pupils were beginning to test for the *real* rules that governed appearance and the uniform of the school.

By the third week the girls had joined in the campaign, following the boys' initial explorations. The girls had less stringent uniform demands than the boys. They did not have to wear ties, were allowed to wear jewellery and nail varnish and any kind of shoes they chose. One group of girls intruded the emblems and interests of youth culture on to the formal equipment of the school. They wrote the names of rock groups on pencil cases. Amy said in a craft class to her friends, 'Everyone writes on my pencil case'. Gradually graffiti spread over their aprons, bags and especially their 'rough books', although it took about another month sbefore all spaces were appropriated. This group of girls wrote the names of popular punk groups on their equipment, but the real significance was attached to the writing of the names of boys in the peer group on books and pencil cases. Such elements from the informal culture split the smooth surface of pupil conformity within a very short time of their joining the school.

Spaces

The institutional framework was also tested out during this period. Pupils quickly found the comparatively 'unimportant' interstices of the school day.

For example, the first deviant actions were noted not in a lesson but in registration. Pete answered his name in a silly voice, causing moderate laughter among his colleagues. The boys, generally, began to 'mess around'. Keith said of his form teacher and registration:

> Mrs Cornway ... sometimes we ... like answer her names to the register funny, sometimes she will laugh too, and other times she will stop the register ... stand up ... sit down ... all this ... say it properly. It is what we should expect really, because we shouldn't really. But seeing as it is only registration, I don't think it matters. ... It's not really interesting. If we are doing a lot of interesting things ... when you're a kid you want to learn, you don't want to sit there answering names and listening to other people.

The curriculum

Pupils' own interests were soon brought to bear on the curriculum itself. As the 'front' crumbled, deviance appeared, but it did not occur evenly throughout all lessons. Some subject areas – notably art and music – attracted deviant strategies earlier than others. For example, on his way to the music lesson, Pete removed his tie and hid it under his jumper. The pupils whispered and giggled as they entered the room, 'messed about' with pens and rulers, and fooled around while the register was called. Keith made a chair 'walk' around the table. When Mrs Skye asked the class what they wanted to do in music, there was a loud and predominantly male chorus of 'nothing'. Pupils talked when they were asked to work. They also chatted while they worked, and when another teacher entered the room there was a loud buzz of talk. At one point, Claire and Valerie began to comb their hair. However, this teacher gave as good as she got and retained control. For example, Keith was being especially noisy and could be heard above the others. Mrs Skye interrupted, and singled him out: 'Look, Sunshine, you had better watch your step in here'. It showed the effect of a particular teacher on events. Mrs Skye was an experienced older teacher. Miss Wright, the other music teacher, was a probationer and, throughout the year, she had extreme problems of control.

Music seemed to have low priority among pupils. Pete said openly 'I don't think music's necessary, it's a waste of time, you're not learning anything from that, nothing at all'. The opposition probably derives from the distinction Vulliamy (1979) has elaborated between 'our music' and 'their music', where adolescent subcultures take musical style as a cardinal point in their definition of an oppositional stance to adult culture. As Roy said, 'We should do things that we want, like punk rock or something'. Furthermore, the pupils identified school music as involved with the world of childhood. It offended against their new sense of adult or adolescent identity. Keith said, 'We're only doing triangles, we were using triangles at first school, we should be getting on to trombones and things'.

The pupils demoted school music in accordance with certain of their own concerns, and therefore their own informal concerns surfaced in it. For some, it tempted deviant activities. Pete, Roy and Keith discovered space for messing around and challenging the teacher and cementing their identities as 'ace deviants'. For others, it offered the space for following up friendship-building activities and the opportunity to get to know other pupils. This was aided by the physical arrangement of the classroom. Pupils were grouped around tables, and this offered more opportunity for informal talking than formal deskbound subjects (Stebbins 1975, Denscombe 1980b). The pupils made use of the opportunities. At first their talk was about work matters, then it progressed to more general but important items like 'them dragon flies in the showers' (Uggh!). Finally it moved to the outside school topics of family, pets and TV.

Art and design subjects were also marked down in the same way, and again informal concerns operated more openly. Pupils in Pete's group continued to make exploratory forays to find the discipline limits, consolidating their identities as deviants in the process. Pete forgot his pencil, Keith his art book. Pete, Roy and Keith talked and laughed quite loudly, ignored cues to 'put pencils down' and had to be publicly reprimanded. The rest of the class remained quietly attentive. Pupils were then asked specifically to work individually on a project, without discussion. Pete, Keith and Roy, however, discussed the project loudly and also talked about events they could see out of the windows. Other pupils followed into the territory that Pete, Roy and Keith had opened up. Boys like Phillip and Stewart had shown themselves to have an eager conformist orientation in other subjects. But in art they engaged in 'out of line' activities. Phillip stopped working and started making grimaces at his drawing, and discussed a better way of doing the drawing with Stewart. Carol and Pat discussed their work together, but both the girls' and Phillip's activity was quiet, and not characterized by the noise and laughter that accompanied Pete and his group.

The front of pupil conformity was also broken by gender differences, especially in the science area of the curriculum. Girls reacted to the physical sciences, boys to the domestic ones. Needlework lessons were a major arena for boys' deviance, their strategies rapidly becoming more and more adventurous. They gave silly answers, they drove wedges of illegitimate activity or talk into lesson turning points, and overplayed the pupil role (Willis 1977). The teacher managed to retain control with a mixture of firm rebuke, individual treatment (talking to some misbehaving boys quietly about their behaviour) and good humour. Miscreants were labelled 'Menace 1' and 'Menace 2', which made the boys in question smile. Such humorous titles were not altogether uncomplimentary to pupils' desired identities, especially in this curriculum area. However, despite the teacher's competence, the boys never took the domestic sciences seriously. This suggests that perceived value of the subject is basic to pupils' attitudes within lessons.

The girls were much less enthusiastic about the physical sciences than the boys, and these lessons saw their informal concerns surface (for a full analysis, see Measor 1983). Girls' deviant strategies began to show up in these lessons towards the end of the first month. One group of girls, led by Amy, made their opposition clear. They had been told very firmly, by their science teacher, who happened to be the headmaster, that they must wear safety goggles while they did experiments. These were large, plastic, unisex glasses. Amy's group made an enormous fuss about wearing the glasses, and introduced silly jokes about them. Amy stated that they didn't suit her, she would look awful in them, she refused absolutely to wear them. Amy, Rosemary and Sally spent a full five minutes 'messing around' with the safety goggles. They tried them on, rapidly pulled them off again, and rearranged their hair, very carefully. These actions were highly significant. The girls were disobeying a strong instruction given to them by their headmaster; in addition, they were putting their eyes at risk from spluttering chemicals. Their behaviour here was very different from the conformity they displayed in other lessons at this point in the year, in this 'initial encounters' phase.

The girls' deviance did not involve a noisy challenge to the order of the classroom. It went unnoticed, therefore, and consequently their work in science fell behind that of the boys, which was not the case in other subjects. After several minutes of 'messing around' the girls turned their attention back to their work, and to the experiments they were supposed to be doing. They argued for a while about them: 'I'm not going first, I don't fancy going first, which one are we making first?' By this time, Phillip and Roland had finished their experiment, most of the class were well into it, but this group of girls had not begun, and they did not finish all the work by the end of the lesson. Personal identity concerns were beginning to surface as the front crumbled.

Among the highly valued subjects were English and maths, mainly because pupils saw them as having vocational relevance. 'You need them for a job, don't you?' was a standard response. It did not mean that informal concerns disappeared entirely, but in these areas pupils' investigation was for the amount of co-operative activity permissible, not for oppositional limits. Pupils remained quiet and fully attentive to their teacher, but after they began working alone, co-operative activity began. Phillip pointed out to Stewart the question he was supposed to be doing. Janet asked the girl next to her, what she was supposed to do next. Normally the questions concerned instructions about work, and represented extremely short bursts of interaction. However, in the case of Carol and Pat, who had been 'best friends' at middle school, there was considerable co-operation also on the answers to the questions. As a result, they infringed the limits of co-operative activity set by this teacher. Carol and Pat argued about how to do a particular question, and their voices rose above the rest of the class. Mr Jones looked up and said loudly 'How's my little chatterbox getting on . . .' he paused while the girls, quietened, blushed and began to work. 'You've got a name to live down now, haven't you?' Carol worked in absolute silence for the remainder of the lesson. She had invoked the tactic that girls fear most – public embarrassment (Woods 1979).

There were genuine difficulties for pupils, because different teachers had different limits and different styles. Such testing-out, therefore, was essential. The contrast between English and maths was interesting here. Mr Ship made great use of humour to match the particular relaxed atmosphere he cultivated. This presented pupils with more space, and they correspondingly had to push further to discover its limits and proper use. Pupils quickly found they could 'get away with' talking and co-operative activity as they worked, and each day the level of noise as they did so rose. In their second week at school, however, it earned them a rebuke. Mr Ship interrupted as the noise level grew: 'There shouldn't be any need for talking or for asking your neighbour anything'. The limit was set, but he sugared it with his usual humour, 'If you want anything, ask me, that's what I'm here for, that's what I get paid for, so keep me occupied, then I won't feel guilty about all that money I earn'. Thus the pupils found Mr Ship's hidden ground rules. They had in his own words 'realised that I'm not going to kick their teeth down their throats if there's a bit of noise, provided they're working.' From then on, there was always co-operative talk in English lessons.

Pupils had to test for these ground rules separately with each teacher. For example, in science there was much excitement when it came to the pupils' setting up and doing an experiment. The headmaster clearly enjoyed this, unlike the teachers in Denscombe's (1980a) schools, who felt that any kind of noise emanating from a classroom reflected on a teacher's efficiency. The headmaster observed that 'it was work noise after all.' By definition, there is a 'non-working noise', which the finely tuned ear of the experienced teacher could quickly detect, signalling the spilling over of productive co-operative activity into deviance. However, teachers did have different ideas about what was acceptable, and pupils had to negotiate to find out what these were. The teacher's 'front' broke down as a result.

Conformity

At the same time as some pupils were establishing their identities as 'ace deviants', others emerged as adopting an especially conformist line. This differed from the automaton-like conformity of the first two days, and it involved a personal commitment, rather than a strategic response to a situation. The later conformity was a key element in the personal identities of some pupils. Giles was one example. He would enter a class in silence and take out his books, lay out his neatly named pencils and equipment on the desk in front of him and sit waiting, looking attentive. Almost all the other pupils had to be reminded of the need to have their equipment ready.

The conformists attempted to obey teacher's instructions to the letter. Phillip listened with great attentiveness and followed instructions with care. In a science lesson, he was told that the hottest part of the bunsen burner flame was at the top of the dark blue section of the flame. Phillip moved his test tube to different parts of the flame, experimenting carefully and watching patiently to see where results were best. Phillip admitted that he cared about his work and the results he got. 'You know if you've made a good job of it, if it turns out right, you feel alright'. This concern with academic results and with the appearance of one's work is one of the defining characteristics of the conformist pupil.

Sometimes, during the 'coming out' phase, conformist pupils tried to sustain the initial front of conformity of the whole cohort, possibly feeling that the group reflected on their own reputation. Phillip, for example, tried not only to influence the actions of his own group of friends but also, on occasion, the behaviour of the whole class. He insisted that Eric should put on safety glasses before beginning the experiment, while other groups were reprimanded for forgetting to put theirs on. He chose his partners in group work very carefully to ensure a good group performance. Phillip also tried to change the whole class. One rule was that pupils had to stand, when they first entered a classroom, until told to sit by a teacher. In a maths lesson, the class entered and as the teacher was delayed outside, most of the class sat down. Phillip reminded other pupils that they were supposed to stand, which they did. On entering, the teacher smiled and complimented them on remembering his instructions, and asked them to sit down. Phillip thus ensured that the class presented the right image. His behaviour is more significant if his real views on this particular rule are taken into account:

> The teachers have been alright, some of them have been not so good, some of the things that you do, not in lessons, but you know . . . you have to stand up in the class, while they're getting ready. They spend hours, just picking up papers, and moving them from one place to another, and you're standing there like a dummy . . . I can't think why we have to stand up.

Ability

We have argued that one of the underlying issues for pupils undergoing the transfer is that of identity. Pupils move into a new, larger institution, where they are unknown and anonymous. Many seem to have felt the need to re-establish their identity, as conformist or as 'ace deviant' or as the best fighter, or whatever. The irony of the situation is that the pupils came from the middle school in a clearly labelled fashion, where very little room for doubt about pupil identities was, on the part of teachers, possible. This was true of the pupils' academic ability as well as their personal orientation to school. Many of the conformist pupils were anxious to show themselves as bright and academically able, as well as interested and attentive.

The first signals of 'brightness' they gave were through oral questioning, because it was some time before any graded work was returned to the pupils. Teachers spent some time in oral questions, because it helped them to gain a picture of the capabilities of their new pupils. This frequently involved teachers asking a set of graded questions on a subject. Both teachers and pupils noted the hierarchy of 'knowers' that this strategy revealed:

> Sally: And in humanities he [Phillip] can be really good, because we were doing . . .

oh, all Romans and that, and Mr Jackson asked us what is a C, and he was
the only one who knew what number it meant . . . and other questions he was
very good at.

More subtle judgements are also involved. 'Brightness' is signalled by
getting questions right. Getting them wrong in public can severely diminish
status. 'Brightness' also involves making shrewd assessments about which
questions *not* to answer. In maths, for example, Phillip never attempted to
answer the very difficult questions. He allowed others to fall into that trap.
There was also the issue of 'finishing first'. Phillip frequently put up his
hand to ask 'What do we do, when we've finished?', or 'What do we do
next?', which publicly informed pupils and teachers about his ability. Janet
employed the same strategy, and competition between the two of them
developed rapidly.

The first piece of graded work returned to the pupils created tremendous
excitement. Normal discipline collapsed, as they called out to each other
'What did you get?' or 'How many?' Not until everyone in the class had a
sense of how the others had done did they return to their normal reasonable
quietness. After a few weeks, a sense of who was who was established for
both pupils and teachers. Alan, Bridget and Anna were all established as
'really thick', a verdict that was underlined by the public fact that all did
remedial reading. Those at the opposite end of the scale were also identified.
Nevertheless there could be shocks, for it became clear that ability in
subjects such as technical design or art also had to be taken into account,
and skills other than 'academic' abilities counted in the school, as the
headmaster had made clear of the induction scheme. An art teacher gave
substantial praise to Keith's work, and Stewart looked up from his work
sharply and stared in amazement, for such commendation from a teacher
went counter to his view of Keith. He commented on the teacher's praise to
Phillip. Thus, after about a month in school, a number of pupils had made
clear, if introductory, statements about their identity. Teachers as well as
other pupils registered these statements and signals, and read them to make
a kind of map, whereby they knew their way around the class of people. We
have also suggested that teachers revealed their identity during this period,
and that pupils found out about their styles, their characteristics, and their
demands.

By the end of their first month in the school, most pupils had lost much of
their anxiety about the formal institution. They knew their timetables, the
routines and procedures of the school, they knew their way around the
school and had lost their worries about its size. Most pupils felt settled. Sally
said, 'When I got to that open evening, all the school looked strange, now I
think "why didn't I know where that is, because now I know where it is"'.
Amy agreed, 'It seems not so big. First you think I am going to get lost all
the time, but it seems ever so small now'. However, there was interesting
evidence about the pupils' feeling of membership of their new school. Carol
said, 'You can eat the dinners here, you can't eat the dinners at *our* school,

horrible dinners, terrible, all slushy'. Carol still identified the middle school as *our* school. The upper school has its attractions, but as yet cannot claim her total allegiance or give her a sense of full membership.

Some pupils had more difficulties than others. Rosemary said, 'I am getting used to things, but I do prefer my other school'. Years of contact there had built up a credit balance in her account. 'Well, we had lots of good times there, because I have only started here, and I had all them years back there'. The new school still had to prove itself for her, and the 'front' may be important here. Rosemary was not yet prepared to trust what she had seen in her first contacts with the school, and she was reserving her emotional judgement. The importance of teachers in this was clear: 'The teachers there were nice . . . I cried me eyes out, when we left'. Another girl, Janet, was in agreement: 'It's all right now', nevertheless, 'I still miss Manor Home [her middle school]. I do more things here, but I still prefer Manor Home'. We need to know more about why some pupils had more difficulties than others, and why some chose to retard their personal transitions in this way. The key factor for these two girls was probably the fact that neither had good peer group contacts in their class from middle school.

$\bigcirc$ *4* $\bigcirc$

Making friends

In the formal area of school life, pupils had to discover the working rules, but at least there was a strongly articulated framework to begin with as a basis. Teachers set up the frame and pupils reacted. In the informal area, pupils had to make their own running in several different arenas. They had three major issues to cope with: (i) relationships with their classmates; (ii) the pressures that derived from the informal culture; (iii) cross-gender relationships and adolescent sexuality. They had no explicit formulae to guide them, only the comparatively vague intimations from siblings, older friends and, of course, rumour and myth. This uncertainty and lack of structure increased pupil anxiety in the area.

An informal front

We have seen how pupils set up a 'front' of ultra conformity in the formal area. Similarly, in the informal area, discretion governed their dealing with each other at first, and all was polite civility. There was none of the matey trading of teasing insults that had characterized the middle school, nor the aggressive physical contacts among the boys. Pupils put their 'public selves' on display, holding their 'private selves' in reserve. However, although a general civility was observable among the cohort, separate groups were identifiable within it from the beginning. All except one group, which we shall discuss later, were organized around middle school contacts, and all were single gender. Pupils made their first task the repair of social ties fractured in the transfer. They had lost these contacts just at the time they were needed most, to help cope with the formal demands of the new school, and also to provide support in venturing into the arenas dominated by the informal culture, such as the corridors, dining rooms, and of course the lavatories, where, who knows, the 'royal flush' might overcome the unwary.

As we have seen in Chapter 3, the pupils' first response to the demands that teachers put on them was to try and establish co-operative links, regardless of whether this was permitted or not. New co-operative links were discernible in a skeletal form by the second day in school. This speed is testimony to the pupils' great need of help in the new situation, but setting them up was not without difficulty for the pupils. The problem was their anonymity: 'You don't just ask anyone', Rebecca said, 'I wouldn't have the nerve to'. Subtle emotional perceptions were required. One needed an indication from another pupil of a sympathetic response, otherwise one risked a painful rebuff. Also, pupils were not yet sure whom it was worth asking help from. Amy said, 'I would wait to see if they are quite good'. The rule-based and functional nature of children's friendships that Davies (1982) has identified, are again present here. Once more it is the unknown factors that are responsible for the children's problems.

Given their difficulties, most pupils fell back on their middle school contacts and utilized them as the basis of their first co-operative groups. Even where little was known about the others, because they had been in different classes, the middle school connection provided a strand of legitimation, strong enough to bring them together in the early stages. There were two exceptions. Phillip and Keith had been in the same middle school class, but they obviously ignored each other. Rosemary had been in the same class as Marjorie, Claire and Valerie, but she ignored them.

By the second week in school, the 'front' was beginning to crumble, and it continued to do so, as pupils got to know more about each other and as their general nervousness decreased. The first indication of this was the public trading of insults, which came bursting through the initial civility. It was interesting that they all involved a cross-gender aspect, girls insulting boys and vice versa, but not members of their own sex. Pete was quite rude to Bridget. Carol and Pat complained, 'Oh we can't stand that Alan' and Jenny said of Keith, 'The way he laughs really gets on my nerves'. Soon they became more elaborate and public, and could use the researcher as a resource. One boy, David, approached the researcher and demanded 'Are you going to do a report on me today?' – this being his view of the researcher's aims and task. Sally challenged:

Sally:	No, she's not interested in you.
David:	Won't you do a report on me?
Sally:	He's a cheeky so and so!
David:	She [the researcher] won't do you.
Rosemary:	You need a face-lift too! (said with real aggression).

The public trading of insults suggested that a signalling of differentiation was going on. Statements were being made which marked out the lines of allegiances. At this early stage only very 'safe' ventures were being made. Sally knew that insulting a boy like this was part of a predictable pattern.

Rosemary supported her and, there being an adult present, at very little risk.

Building allegiances

There was other evidence that the process by which pupils sorted themselves out into different groups was beginning. The middle school groupings began to dissolve and new relationships emerged, rather different in nature and structure from those of the middle school. Although the original middle school groups had provided a temporary security, they were an inadequate base for the work of identity-construction and allegiance-formation that the pupils now had to do. The pupils did not know enough about each other to build allegiances, and yet they needed them. The issue of identity and allegiance are probably closely connected, for one's preferred identity is reflected in one's friends, especially for the girls. The first clinging in mutual support groups would not last.

The factor that really determined the informal culture's groups was, paradoxically, the formal culture. Information about identities began to accumulate after a couple of weeks in the school, as pupils revealed their different attitudes and reactions to the formal culture. Pupils gained certain academic identities also, and here the major dimension was ability. They were soon classifying each other along the lines of 'thick' and 'brainy', and by the third week of term a pupil hierarchy of academic ability had been sketched in. We have already documented the process of oral questioning in lessons, which tested pupils. Bridget conspicuously failed these tests. She failed to discriminate between an answerable and an unanswerable question, and gave replies so extravagantly wrong that they counted as silly. Anna and Alan were involved in similar incidents. Their suspected identities, like Bridget's, were confirmed by the grades on their written work.

The pupils' view of Bridget and Anna was made clear in interview, where both the quality of the categorization and the degree of differentiation was evident:

Pete: I don't like Bridget or her mate Anna.

Andrew: Bridget's thick.

Pete: She is thick.

Andrew: Should go to a special school . . .

Pete: (Anna's) thick an' all. That's why they go around together.

Anna and Bridget had at first revealed no affinity for each other, but quite quickly they found themselves shunned by other pupils, and by force of circumstance became friends. They worked together and later in the year began truanting together.

The other end of the hierarchy was fixed by similar criteria. Phillip and Janet rapidly became identified as being 'brainy'. They were both able to answer questions that the others could not. They were also seen to be able to work successfully at speed. A teacher would frequently ask 'Have you finished yet?', or 'Who has finished yet?'. Phillip and Janet would normally be those who responded affirmatively. Again, the emerging pattern of grades confirmed the basic opinions.

Pupil groups

In the first few weeks at school, three distinct forms of pupil groups emerged co-operative groups, friendship groups and 'best friends'.

The first stage in friendship formation was the building of co-operative groups. The solid middle school groupings began to fragment. Roland became friendly with Phillip and they were joined by Giles and Stewart. The group co-operated in lessons and grew more stable; in fact, they stuck together throughout virtually the whole of the school year. Similar patterns were observable for the rest of the boys. Pete, Roy, Jim and Andrew became a cohesive group. In their case, they had all been at the same middle school, although in different classes. Carol and Pat had been 'best friends' at middle school and they remained friends, while Marjorie, Sheila and Pamela tacked on to make a co-operative group. Bridget and Anna were thrown together. At first, Sally, Jenny, Amy and Rebecca had clung together as a middle school group. By the end of the first week Jenny broke from the group and began to interact with Janet. The other three girls started to get more involved with Rosemary. Claire and Valerie were friends from middle school, and were in fact cousins. It was clear that the first phase of allegiances built on middle school alliances was breaking down, and some new patterns were emerging.

The building of new co-operative links was done with care. Pupils put out 'feelers', finding out who had equipment, which equipment was best to borrow, which pupils were willing to trade equipment, whom they could ask for help, and who was most likely to have an answer worth having. Conversational overtures were important, because they initiated the new co-operative links. Conversation was also important for moving into the next stage of school relationships.

In the early days, the conversations between pupils were limited to work topics. Pupils would ask each other: 'What do we have to do next?', or 'Tell me what colour to paint this', or 'Do you like this door?', when they were building a house. If the other pupil reciprocated, the conversations widened out, and they discussed more personal matters: where they lived, how many brothers and sisters they had, or what pets they had. This move into personal, family-related matters from the impersonal subjects of school and work seemed to indicate an important shift in the strength and quality of the relationship, giving it a new character that we might term 'friendship group'. This step was followed by pupils changing seats, and choosing to sit next to each other. They occupied the spaces of the informal culture in each other's company, walking to lessons together, having lunch together. In this context, the researcher created another space for informal culture. Pupils were almost always interviewed in small groups. The choice of pupils for a particular group had to reflect those friendship groupings accurately, or sanctions could be applied. For example, the pupils who were being asked if they would agree to being interviewed refused if the groupoing went against their sense of who was allowed in their closer circle. These friendship groups involved stronger ties than co-operative groups. Interaction in them continued outside school. Girls invited each other to tea, or to spend the afternoon at their home, or to go swimming or roller skating. For boys, the 'out of school' dimension seemed to involve basically a street-based culture, playing football together, or a more general 'going around with him'. Many co-operative groups that exist in school are impermanent and fluctuate with context (Furlong 1976). But we have seen here that they can develop into more stable and pervasive groupings. It is on this issue that we might want to criticize Furlong's (1976) work, for he identified only the first kind of group, the co-operative one among the girls he examined, and assumed that it was a predominant form of grouping among pupils generally.

Both co-operative and friendship groups seemed to exist for both boys and girls, but, in addition, the girls seemed to develop an extra layer of tightly bonded relationships with one other girl. Boys were not observed to do this. The girls had a series of extremely important 'best friend' relationships, which existed between pairs of girls within friendship groups. For example, Carol and Pat were 'best friends' within their wider group, which included Marjorie, Sheila and Pamela. There was a crucial, and clearly made distinction between friends and 'best friends'. The 'best friend' relationship also extended into non-school life, and included invitations to spend leisure time together. But there were very tightly bound rules involved in this bonding of best friends that involved loyalty (Davies 1982). These rules emerged slowly throughout the school year, and we shall consider them more fully in later chapters. The crucial play for best friend status was when one girl invited another to spend the night at her home.

We have, then, identified three separate but overlapping categories of allegiance gradually emerging during this initial encounters phase. All pupils were involved in co-operative sets and friendship groups; in addition, girls had 'best friends'. Alliances and bonds made in this phase tended to last until January of the following year.

Thus, as pupils negotiated the terms of relationships with teachers, so they negotiated with other pupils. They moved through stages of blanket conformity (having a front of being nice to everybody) and utilitarian need (when help was sought to aid in coping with work demands), to more fully-fledged relationships wherein pupils identified with each other through similar interests and orientations. It is in the last formation that identity concerns are uppermost, for friends, especially 'best friends', reflect and reinforce one's self.

In these negotiations, as we have noted, the most important classification pupils made of each other was in relationship to the formal culture of the school, in terms of conformity and deviance. In Pete's terms, there was, in his class,

> one group of boys that muck about, and one group that don't, and there's some quiet girls, and ones that ain't quite so quiet.

This perspective largely explains not only the developments in the friendship patterns already described, but also the one or two cases that differed from the general pattern. Janet and Jenny provide a good illustration of this. Jenny at first associated with Amy, Sally and Rebecca, whom she knew from middle school. But she soon found they had a different attitude to school work from hers. She herself was a conformist and eventually found another girl, Janet, with a very similar perspective. They began to sit together and to co-operate. For example, in craft, they planned and constructed together a complicated Tudor-style cardboard house. Shortly after this, Jenny went to tea at Janet's, and Janet came to stay overnight at Jenny's house, so that they could go together to the school disco.

A few pupils appeared to take an unusual course in that they shunned their middle-school contacts in the early stages. Rosemary, for example, chose to associate with Amy, Sally and Rebecca, her 'attitudinal' peers, rather than Marjorie, Carol, Pat and Anna, her middle-school colleagues. The group went through the usual bonding developments, and Rosemary and Amy eventually became 'best friends'. The most likely explanation for Rosemary's initial move was that she already knew enough about the two groups in terms of work attitudes to warrant at first stage a second stage choice. Phillip and Eric also demonstrated this. Phillip ignored Keith, his middle-school contact, and Eric ignored Matthew. Finally, Phillip and Eric became friends. They knew enough about Keith's and Matthew's basic orientation to school from the beginning to know that any kind of alliance was impossible.

There is a further factor here – one of differential need. During the first month at the school there were two pressures exerting influence upon the pupils simultaneously, and different pupils made different adaptations to them. The first involved their own categorizations, which divided pupils into those who could be friends and those who could not. But then there were the pressures of nervousness and anxiety, which made pupils cling together for mutual support and which overrode the categories for a time. Different pupils balanced out those different pressures, according them varying weight. For Roland and Phillip, the need to cling to middle school friends for support was never strong enough to override their attitude to the formal culture of the school and to doing well in school. For Rosemary, her basic dislike of the girls she had been with at middle school could override her need for support from her middle school colleagues (see Power and Cotterell 1981).

Once the pupils had separated into groups, a process of differentiation went on inside the groups. This seemed to relate to the academic identities we discussed earlier in the chapter. There was a kind of status hierarchy within the friendship groups, and to be somebody who was frequently consulted was a mark of high status. Phillip had this role in his group. He had immediately asserted his own ability in every subject except art. He whispered instructions and answers to the other boys in his group, and when he was proved right his status as the leader who gave rather than received help in his group was confirmed. He also refused to accept help from any other member of his group. A similar process was going on among other groups in the class. For Phillip, it achieved two objects simultaneously – he gained the identity he sought, and a network of relationships.

Sally, Amy, Rebecca and Jenny formed a group, and their hierarchy soon became clear. Amy asked Sally for help on the worksheet. Sally in turn would ask Jenny for help, but not Amy or Rebecca. Once a particular pupil had bid for and won a particular identity, it was gradually confirmed by repeated usage. Bridget's position was rapidly established. She frequently needed help and would ask for it outside her friendship group, and where she had not established co-operative links. One incident illustrates this and shows, by a negative case, some of the rules that bound co-operative help. Bridget asked Jenny in a craft lesson, 'How do you fold this paper?' Jenny did not even bother to answer, she simply took the paper from Bridget and folded it; an action that would have angered many pupils. Sally did the same with Anna, telling her in art, very clearly, what the instructions had been. 'You're not allowed to use any letters, just drawings and symbols'. The language Sally employed in this incident with Anna was uncompromising in its instructional tone; it has a semi-authoritarian quality. The fuller significance of this pattern will become more clear in the light of incidents occurring later in the year, but it may be important to note that pupils normally employed a specific range of verbal signals and tones of voice, in this kind of situation. They would preface a piece of information with phrases that were semi-apologetic, or which discounted themselves, 'Ermm, well, I think you are supposed to . . .', or 'Well, I'm not sure I got it . . . but . . .', or 'He said that you've got to'. All of these phrases remove the pupil one step from being the instruction giver, or specifically discount themselves as having authority. It seemed from later evidence that to fail to do so brought down the label 'bossy' upon the individual's head. However, 'bossy' language, or straight instruction to Bridget, did not matter. Her lowly status at the bottom of the heap was confirmed.

Phillip formed a clear contrast to this, occupying a status at the other end of the continuum. In addition, his actions indicate another way in which identities could be confirmed and assessed, by the use of challenge and sanction. Amy once attempted to correct an instruction that she felt Phillip

was following incorrectly. He was dramatically furious with her intervention, and told her to 'shut your face!' Amy had not only challenged his status
but also had transgressed gender rules, and Phillip wanted publicly to
reassert his status and disassociate himself from her advance. Amy
responded with equal asperity, 'Oh, all right then Professor, you know
everything'. She acknowledged Phillip's bid for identity, and fixed a label to
him, but indicated by her tone that he was one of those most reprehensible
of beings, a 'big-'ead'. In these ways, academic standing and attitudes can
affect friendship groupings and identities.

Coming to terms with the informal culture

If the first major orientation was the pupils' own classification of themselves
in terms of engagement with the formal culture, a second lay in the informal
culture. For the boys, this carried a demand for toughness, and a certain
amount of bullying went on. This began to appear shortly after the verbal
insults had broken out. It involved minor aggressions by boys, pushing,
punching, shoving, and taking pieces of equipment from each other, which
were then hidden, or passed around, with a refusal to give it back. At this
stage, this behaviour occurred within established interaction groups and
was not traded between them. By the third week of term, Phillip had begun
to act in this way. On 12 September, for example, he asserted his right to use
a piece of equipment out of turn. Giles, Stewart and Eric, the other members
of the group, fell back and allowed him to bid for this superior status. This
kind of activity became increasingly frequent throughout the year in all
groups, although, in some, leadership status was more contested. In one
group, Roy gained undisputed control. He would push Pete and Andrew
and Jim around, and specialized in taking chairs away from people as they
were about to sit down. It led to Pete confessing, 'He do push people around
does Roy'. The demand for toughness and strength, therefore, applied
within the group, and a second kind of hierarchy was established, status and
power being based on physical strength and adroitness, and size. Phillip and
Roy were noticeably larger than average boys. At the other end of the scale,
Geoffrey began to gain an identity as the boy who was incapable of being
tough. He could not finish the long distance run, he could not fight, he was
persecuted by the others. His reputation, his title of 'poufter', were known
outside his own class. This had an impact on his alliances, he was isolated,
other boys shunned him, he was categorized as the 'outsider' and ignored.
We can again see two polar stereotypes of identity being constructed by the
class. At one end were Roy and Phillip, who were the models of tough
strength. Phillip was also the most academically able, and hence enjoyed
doubly compounded high status. At the other end was Geoffrey. In the
initial encounters phase it was the two ends of the continuum that were
identified and established, setting the markers for the bulk of the pupil body
to align themselves to.

These developments are an interesting commentary on the myths discussed in Chapter 1. We suggested that one of the underlying concerns was

gender demands, those being in the case of boys the need for toughness, strength and physicality. The myths had warned that awful things would happen to you if you failed in this macho culture. Geoffrey had failed and was ostracised – a terrible thing to have happen to you at such a crucial time of need. The myths, however, had missed one detail. They had only predicted persecution from older pupils, but it was clear in the event that one was at risk among one's own age peers, and that doing well in gender code terms was important within friendship groups.

The girls also experienced pressures from the informal culture. They had anticipated some psychological aggression from older girls, and they found their anxiety justified. When pupils reached the school, however, they gained additional information about their relationship with the older pupils, especially the older girls. We have already spoken of the strict age-graded regulation of status: the first year pupils perceived the older pupils as being interested in maintaining their superiority, and in keeping them in their place. The main points at issue for the girls were presentation of self, issues of fashion, wearing make-up, jewellery and nail varnish. There was, in fact, considerable opposition from the older pupils to younger first year pupils becoming too fashion-conscious, or trying to adopt wholesale the ways and styles of the older adolescent groups. Amy told how 'My sister said to me that if you try to act old, and try to be in fashion with everybody in the older years, they are just going to go against you. . . . First at school, I tried to wear something that was really old, because I tried something on and my sister said "Don't wear that, you know they'll all be making fun of you. They will think they are better, because they are in fashion", so I took that off and went in something horrible'.

In our analysis of the myths, we suggested that the issues of power and status were crucial, and that one of the ways in which myths operated was to describe the distribution of power between groups, and specifically between different age grades. This data tends to support that analysis. It also supports the suggestion that the myths offered simultaneously an invitation and a warning about entry into youth culture. This entry was not open, it was guarded, and there was a series of hurdles to be crossed. Negotiations had to be made – it seems that one of the key elements of youth culture is a skilfully mediated presentation of self. Status and security in youth culture is not won by simple assertion of self, by 'showing off': that simply signals 'getting too much for yourself'. Rather it is important to be seen to negotiate a front that is more medium range. For example, a self has to be presented that is fashion-conscious, but not extreme. We shall have more to say about this in later chapters, but for the moment it is clear that first year girls had to learn their place, and it was one which placed considerable restrictions on their appearance.

Cross-gender relationships

As far as interaction between boys and girls goes, pupil attitudes and behaviour changed dramatically with the move to upper school. When pupils entered the school there was some mixed gender groupings in the classroom, depending on the organization of the classroom. If pupils were working around large tables, for example, in the art and craft subjects, then there were both boys and girls at the same table. Alternatively, when pupils sat in long rows of separate desks, then there were both boys and girls in the same row. However, as we have noted, there was almost no co-operative behaviour between the sexes. On 12 September, in a maths lesson, Carol and Pat were working together, attempting to find an answer, without success. A boy sitting next to them joined in, and attempted to add a word or two and to set the girls straight. Carol reacted immediately, and crossly, saying 'No boy friends allowed'.

Within six weeks of attending secondary school, the gender separation had become complete for these pupils. They always sat at separate tables and on separate sides of the room. When questioned, teachers made it clear that they were not responsible for the changes, and had certainly not asked the pupils to change their seating. The amount of interaction between the gender groups also decreased. If pupils had, as a result of particular or temporary circumstances, to sit with pupils from 'the other sex', this created a strong reaction. In an English lesson, for example, Pete and Andrew had to sit next to Sally, as a result of lack of space. Sally giggled about this and the boys strongly objected.

Pupils perceived that the nature of the relationship between the sexes was different at secondary school. Sally discussed this in an interview:

> I don't get on with the boys like I used to in my old class. You could sort of go up to them and say 'Can I borrow your ruler', without them saying, 'Get lost'. You could talk to them properly as if they were another girl, but you can't here.

Part of the transition, then, involved learning the new behaviour appropriate to your gender, and the behaviour appropriate to the other gender. It was an essential element, but the rules were hidden and flexible and had to be both discovered and negotiated. Again, the quality of information in the myths was shown to be accurate, and a useful guide to the discovery of the rules.

There is, in fact, remarkably little information on the nature and characteristics of adolescent sexuality at this age. A survey study was done nearly twenty years ago (Schofield 1965), starting with fourteen- and fifteen-year-olds who were 'going out on their first date'. Clearly, a good deal happens before that stage is reached. There is a growing body of evidence to suggest that, during the years 10–12, children withdraw from cross-gender contact, thus signalling that things are changing dramatically. By the first year of secondary school, that phase was over for at least some of these children, but not for them all.

The reasons for this sudden rigid separation have to be sought within developing adolescent sexuality. Here, our pupils were undergoing yet another transition, from 'child' (a classification which counts for as much among them at primary stage as 'boy' or 'girl') to adolescence. This differentiation in the initial encounters phase is, we suggest, part of the process of identification of oneself as male or female. Strong lines are drawn between what boys and girls can and cannot do and, for a while, strong lines are drawn physically between them (Jones 1980). For most pupils, it does not last beyond their first year at secondary school.

For some, indeed, cross-gender interactions had begun by the end of the second week. There are tremendous risks in this activity at first. Pupils need to 'test the waters', to find out if they are the sort of person who is going to be successful in these adolescent sexual encounters. They thus employ strategies designed to persuade others to place them in the desired category – a good example of the social construction of identity. The first issue seemed to be to establish 'who fancies who'. The first method tried was 'writing on pencil cases', then aprons and then exercise books. The girls would write boys' names on a particular girl's pencil case. Amy went to fetch some equipment. When she returned she noticed a new piece of graffiti, and she was annoyed. 'Oooh! Who's written "Amy likes Andrew" on my pencil case? It is not true. I don't like him'. Sally laughed, and said 'No, it's Gary, isn't it?'.

From such beginnings, likings were made more public, and individual pupils took it upon themselves to acquaint others with these facts. Amy said to Pete, 'Everyone knows you fancy Rosemary'. On the same morning, Sally said to Giles, 'Do you still fancy Jenny?' At this point Stewart and Giles both got very annoyed, signalling that they were not the kind of pupils who wanted to be involved in this kind of activity at this stage. Stewart said to Sally 'Oh you're always talking about who fancies who'. Giles agreed, 'That's all you ever talk about'. Such statements made very public bids for particular identities, and Giles and Stewart here were laying claim to a wider basis to their interests than sex. Amy then passed on to territory and people who were more likely to respond with interest. She was having a party soon and she said to Roy 'I was going to put you with Nicky at my party, but now you've packed her in, I dunno'.

The next stage seemed to involve 'going out' together, although this phrase seemed to have a very indistinct meaning and varied tremendously for different pupils at this stage. Relationships based on 'going out' were made and broken with lightning rapidity, some lasting only for a few hours. Rosemary 'went out' with Pete for a while, and during that period she complained, 'He completely ignored me'. It certainly seemed that the important emotional relationships in the girls' lives were with other girls. They were longer lasting and had deeper ties. However, this was to change rather dramatically throughout the year. There was one exception to this pattern. Jenny had, in September 1979, been 'going out' with Lee, a boy from the same middle school, for about five months. Their relationship survived the school transfer. They spent a lot of time at each other's house and their parents had plans to take them on holidays together. This was an unique relationship among the pupils at this particular juncture.

Attitudes to cross-gender relationships were associated with attitudes to school. Boys who adopted deviant attitudes and 'mucked around' also 'went out with girls' (see also Willis 1977). Conformist boys were unlikely to. The line between 'going out with girls' and not was just as sharply drawn as the conformist/deviant one. 'Going out with boys' or not was a basic category also for the girls, especially the deviant girls. It mattered a great deal to their personal identities, for status was to be gained from 'going out' with a boy, and even more status if these were boys who were generally highly regarded (see also Chapter 8). Similarly, boys gained status from 'going out' with girls whom 'everybody fancies' or if they 'went out with' a large number of girls. Given this relationship between formal and informal areas, it is not surprising that Roy, Pete and Keith were the most active of the boys in this respect, and Amy, Rosemary and Rebecca of the girls, while pupils like Phillip, Roland, Giles and Janet, who adopted very conformist attitudes, appeared not at all interested.

This sexual interest soon came to exert an influence over appearances. The basic strategy was to elaborate school uniform, so that it came more closely to resemble 'fashion'. This meant that trouser shapes, skirt lengths and colours all received attention to change the symbolism from 'school' to 'teenage'. So did hair style and length. The most important item, however, was shoes, though teachers soon gave up with the girls. Boys liked to wear 'trainers', although the school forbade it. The girls also had make-up, nail varnish and jewellery. Many girls felt a strong compulsion to present an attractive front. They were frenetically interested in clothes, for example, and would comment daily on those the researcher wore. They contrasted their attitude with that of the boys:

Amy: Any time there's anything on my skirt, I'm doing this (she makes a rubbing gesture) the boys just leave it on, they couldn't care less.

Rebecca: Roy couldn't care – his face the other day . . . he had all tomato sauce, all round his lips, and he just left it there.

Rosemary: I would get ashamed if I had something like that – everyone saying 'Oh you've had baked beans' – sort of thing.

These attitudes were surfacing by the end of the first month and, with them, some pupils found themselves confronted by more conflicting demands. Firstly, the peer group demanded fashionable dress and appearance from the girls, toughness from the boys. Secondly, pupils reported parents resisting these values, both on financial grounds as far as the girls were concerned, and generally on 'growing up too quickly' lines. There were, thirdly, age-grading pressures from older pupils and, fourthly, the school, of course, encouraged conformist behaviour and appearances. As we have seen, there was room for manoeuvre, but much pupil time and ingenuity was to be given to resolving these mutually contradictory pressures over the coming months.

III

Second term: renegotiations

◯ 5 ◯

An attempted coup

Pupils continued to adapt in this style for the remainder of the first term. Most passed the psychological barrier of feeling members of the new organization, and ex-members of the old. There were fewer and fewer signs of the backward-looking perspective, the nostalgia for things past and anxiety about the future that characterized the early days.

'Settling in'

By the beginning of the second term, pupils themselves expressed a sense of 'having settled in'. They spoke as if they had passed a barrier, contrasting the two states: 'At first I was . . .', or 'When I first came here . . .' was posed against 'But now it's . . .'.

> Sally: I feel more settled in it now: this school seems part of my life if you know what I mean, like last term before Christmas, it was a whole new experience, but now it isn't it's just everyday life now really.
>
> Amy: I like it here now, because I have got to know more of the people, and I have sort of settled down. . . . It seems not so big. First you think I am going to get lost all the time, but it seems ever so small. I think it is.

Others made a similar comparison.

> Peter: It is just like it was at middle school now.
>
> Mark: Second home.

Their degree of comfort, then, for some bears comparison with 'home'. They showed their mastery of the situation by mocking their former uncertainties and anxieties, often with a touch of bravado.

Bill: Yes, I didn't know my way around. I used to get lost nearly every lesson. After about two weeks, we knew our way around, we just used to waste time, and walk about the school, and when they used to say 'Where have you been', we used to say that we had got lost. We got away with that.

Pupils' lives had fallen into a routine pattern, which they knew methodically, and this also increased their sense of security and fit.

Sally: You don't have to look at your timetable now to see what lesson you are going to – you know automatically where the classroom is, and if they change, you know where that classroom is, whereas you didn't before.

Pupils also welcomed the opportunity of contact with a wider range of teachers. They had not anticipated this as a problem, and did not find it to be so.

Emma: The first couple of weeks, having to change teachers all the time – it was hard, but then it was just . . . you just got used to it.

Pete: It's not hard getting used to loads of different teachers, but it is different.

Most pupils, in fact, despite initial task/time problems as discussed in Chapter 3, said that they welcomed the change from an integrated day into more rigid subject disciplines, which were timetabled into a routine. They were conscious of this as a difference, and again one can see a progression from nostalgia to contempt for past practices.

Jane: At Priory we just done the same old thing over and over again, we didn't do anything different, like in English we had one teacher all through all lessons. Here we have to change lessons and they don't, say, bring up the art in the English.

Valerie: I enjoy doing my work here; at my other school, I didn't used to do it, because I didn't like it. One minute you were doing a sheet of maths, and the next minute you were doing something else, all in the same class as well.

It seemed also an advance to a more adult status, for they felt they were taken more seriously, treated more professionally, by teachers with more knowledge and status than their previous teachers. Teachers who teach a 'bit of everything in the one day' are inclined to 'get muddled up', and clearly 'a teacher that specializes in that subject is going to be better in that subject.' They were 'a better class of teacher' and much more professional than those at middle school. Pamela said, disparagingly, 'My teacher just used to natter all day. Well she kept saying "put your pencils down", and then she would talk about the television programme that we were going to watch and she ended up talking about her dog'.

For some pupils it was clear that the main issue was one of friendship groups, and not the difficulty of relating to a number of different teachers. The problem was being separated from one's friends as a result of changing classes and a varying timetable. Amy made this clear: 'Swapping lessons worried me, that I would never be with any of my friends, and I might not make new friends and I would have to sit in lessons on my own'. Other pupils, after initial anxieties, welcomed the change to meet more teachers and get to know more pupils in the school as a result of changing lessons and cross-cutting separate form membership. It extended their sociability networks in the school, and reduced the numbers of individuals in the organization who were entirely unknown or unfamiliar. These sociability links insured against being overlooked and rendered anonymous. Janet volunteered the comment: 'Yes, one good thing is that you go to different teachers for different lessons. A lot more chance to meet people really'. 'Losing friends' had been the major anxiety. But from a position of entrenchment, introspection and concern, many pupils had by now become more expansive and adventurous.

Amy: Here we swap around every lesson.

Sally: Yes, you make friends that way, and get to know different faces all the time, whereas at Hayes, you saw the same faces every day. It is different.

For other pupils, it was the variety of personnel and possible relationships that appealed. Pete felt, 'It's better having lots of teachers because I got really sick of the same teacher. You see the same face every day'. Andrew chimed in, 'Yes, that's what really got on my nerves'. And Mark said, 'In our old school, we would have one teacher for everything. If you got in trouble with her first lesson, you have had it for the rest of the day, all the lessons'.

The important progression we are witnessing here is within the pupils' moral career (Goffman 1961). Pupils have become socialized into the structures and mores of the new institution and developed new conceptions of what represents normality. The basis for making judgements about their school life has shifted, and they employ different criteria. It is also as if they have reached a crucial point in the transition – a bit of high ground from where they suddenly start looking backwards with a sense that certain things, hitherto an essential part of current realities, are now past.

With regard to the nature of schoolwork, also, pupils said that in retrospect their anxiety was unfounded. Martin admitted, 'I did worry that the work would be hard, harder than what it is. It was more easy at Springvale, but it's OK'. The general feeling was that, although the work was more difficult than at middle school, it was within the pupils' general competence. Yet pupils identified a change in the standard of work set, since they had returned from Christmas holidays. This was connected for some of them with the process of streaming that had occurred (about which we shall say more later).

Mark: The work is harder than it was at middle school, but you don't notice it getting harder, because it is going up stage by stage, and you are learning more all the time.

Keith: The work started off easy, it is getting difficult now. I like the work. I like some of it to be hard, and hard to cope with, and some of it to be like what I learned in previous schools. I was expecting maths to be hard. Some of it is, I couldn't cope with all that stuff on scales this morning.

Lucy: Since we split up into groups the work has been more difficult.

In the area of discipline, pupils felt their expectations had been, on the whole, realistic. When interviewed at middle school, the pupils had expressed considerable reservations about entering the secondary school, which was perceived to be much more 'strict' and inflexibly disciplined than the middle school had been found to be. In part, this anxiety concerned the new teachers, in part it concerned new forms of punishment, specifically the cane. Pupils did feel that this expectation had been fulfilled. Things generally were tougher at secondary school.

Sally said, 'They are a bit more strict here. You have got to listen, you have got to be quiet, you have got to work on your own. You have to pay attention and you have to do your homework, it is much stricter here'. On this point there was general agreement. it was 'harder to muck about here.' John commented on 'Talking in class. Over there everyone talked in class, no one ever stopped. Here, some teachers like it dead silent, and that's hard'.

The indulgent, child-centred family atmosphere of primary school was gone in the view of these pupils. Looking back, Pat said, 'At our other school, all our teachers were like mothers to us – where they said "Do this", and we said "Oh do I have to?"'. Her friend Caroline agreed, and added 'And when you got your report, or when your mother goes to see them, "Oh she's an angel, she's a darling. She's good at this . . ."'. There was still some nostalgia over this aspect:

Ros: I do miss my old teacher – he was ever so nice. That school, it was more like a family, because you were close, but now you are all spread out.

However, while pupils had a firm impression that the new regime generally was much stricter and that 'there's a limit for each teacher', they had also, by the second term, learnt that there were considerable differences between individual teachers in nature and degree of discipline. Most pupils felt there was a gender division in the strictness of teachers. Both boys and girls agreed that female teachers were less able to maintain strict discipline control. Pete said, 'Female teachers aren't very strict, but male teachers are stricter'. Janet agreed with this: 'I think the men teachers are different, I think the men are slightly stricter'. Pamela agreed: 'Well, we really take liberties with Mrs Lines'. For Jenny, however, there was an age factor involved. One woman teacher, Mrs Skye, was older than the others mentioned, and she pointed out 'Well if you take Mrs Skye and Mr Jones, then there is no difference'.

The basic fact that the structure of lessons was the product of a negotiated relationship between class and the individual teacher was clearly accepted by this stage.

> Phillip: It's pretty tight, but in spite of this, we get away with a little bit. Yes, you're allowed, not allowed, but you can get away with something, so it's pretty evenly balanced.

The exact negotiation depended, of course, on the individual teacher, and by this stage of the school year the pupils had a fairly clear idea of them. They employed the familiar range of perspectives on teachers, 'Mr Bridges – he's a bit hard, Mrs Oates – she's really a good laugh, Mrs Cornway, she's soft'. However, whereas some other work on pupil perspectives may suggest that they become fixed (e.g. Nash 1976), it was clear during this first year that pupil–teacher negotiated agrements were frequently under threat, and were often renegotiated. It seemed that this negotiation occurred in waves, at particular points in the school year, in September, again in February, and in May of 1980, for example.

This may be related to, among other things, the structure of the school year. After a month, the pupils had negotiated a modus vivendi that lasted the autumn term. But that negotiation was made by pupils from a weak position. When they came back after the Christmas break, they could re-open negotiations from a position of comparative strength. Those interested in doing so, therefore, could possibly push the rule-boundaries back a little further – some at least thought it worth a try. By February, the pupils were ready to try out new strategies of deviancy and indiscipline, which were more sophisticated and which carried a greater challenge to the discipline frame. The basic patterns that had emerged during the initial encoutners phase held. Boys tended to have the more disruptive strategies and to push discipline negotiation further first. But subject cultures continued to exercise an effect upon this, boys being their most disruptive in music and needlework, and girls showing most resistance in science lessons. Pupils continued to behave attentively in maths and English.

A description of some of their lessons can perhaps give a flavour of the new deviant and resistant strategies which characterized the pupils at this stage. The first strategy involved challenging the teacher's 'centre-stage' rights. There is normally a part of a lesson, where the teacher gives instruction and occupies the centre stage. At the beginning of the year pupils were quiet and attentive while the teacher instructed them. The talking, chatting and other deviances occurred once the pupils were working on their own. By February, pupils were prepared to go further.

In an English lesson, the teacher asked the class to write an essay on 'Myself', whereupon Pete questioned brightly, 'On Mr Ship?'. The pupil had interrupted when the teacher was giving the essential instructions for the whole lesson. The class started to laugh, but the teacher capped the pupil's put-down, with an equally sharp 'No! On you yourself, you twit!' which received the louder laugh, and effectively contained the attempted take-over. However, other teachers were not so successful. Mrs Lines was a temporary science teacher who never managed to gain full control of the class. In a lesson on temperature, she gave instructions to the pupils to dip the clinical thermometers in antiseptic, before putting them in their mouths. Unfortunately the teacher confused her words, and said disinfectant instead of antiseptic. Pete objected loudly, 'No I won't! On the telly it said, if your mum is out, then you don't drink disinfectant "cos you can die"'. The teacher had been occupying the centre stage, getting them started for the whole lesson, and the challenge was for the centre stage. Additionally, the strategy challenged the teacher's general competence. Mrs Lines made no real answer to this. Unlike Mr Ship, she failed to gain control after the challenge. Pupils also learnt to challenge for the centre stage by asking a range of 'silly questions' while the teacher was talking, which disrupted the flow of instruction-giving and the pace of the lesson. They can be distinguished from 'real' questions, partly by their content, but also by their timing. After giving instructions, teachers usually ask 'Are there any questions?' and that is the point when genuine help for clarification of instructions is given.

The second new set of deviance strategies concerned 'mucking about' and 'messing about'. Mrs Lines's science lesson provided some good examples. The class made a whole series of 'Ugghh' and 'Aarrgh' sounds at the taste of the antiseptic on the clinical thermometers, and some of the 'Aarrghs' were loud enough to disrupt the lesson.

> While the teacher's back is turned, Alan stands up and makes a range of obscene gestures in the light of the overhead projector, so they appear magnified on the wall. There is a high level of noise and a low level of concentration. Pete starts wandering aimlessly around the room. The teacher objects and tells him to sit down. He sits down, on the floor, where he is.

Yet, there were, at this stage, limits to how far the pupils would go. Towards the end of the lesson, the teacher made it clear that she expected completed written records of the experiments the pupils had done that day. The pupils rushed to finish this, even though they had 'messed around' for most of the lesson. There was still a measure of conformity to this work norm. They would complete the task set, even when discipline was being flagrantly flouted. They had rapidly learnt the rather cynical attitude that characterizes much of what passes for education in the modern industrial society, that is that you can get by if you go through the motions. This 'going through the motions', therefore, must be done at all costs, otherwise sanctions might be employed and the space negotiated elsewhere would be lost.

'Take-overs'

In January/February, a number of further factors, which could occur in any school, accelerated a new distinctive phase in the transition. Chief among these was the absence, largely through illness, of a number of the established teachers. Supply teachers were engaged, though not enough to cover all areas, and some classes had to be 'doubled up' or left to work alone or with minimum supervision. At the same time, there were several student teachers in the school, taking lessons normally taught by experienced teachers. The result was that pupils were confronted with basically new situations in which modi vivendi had again to be negotiated. As we have noted, however, this time the pupils dealt from strength, the teachers from weakness. This combination of circumstances ushered in a new phase of threatened 'take-over' on the part of the pupils, followed by a period of 'purge' as the forces of official order reconstituted and reasserted themselves. We do not suggest, of course, that this happens in all transitions of this nature. However, it seems reasonable to suggest that, where initial negotiations are threatened by a substantial change in the power and resources position of one of the parties, the other will seek to take advantage – and that the beginning of the second term is most opportune for this. The pupils have overcome their initial anxieties and gained a foothold. They have all the exuberant over-confidence that comes from a major hurdle surmounted, and new-found status as successfully established pupils. On the other side, the teachers' ranks were decimated and the frameworks of classroom order (although they had stabilized during the first term) were not yet strong enough to withstand a crisis. It was a good moment for a challenge. It duly came in a number of ways.

A description of a lesson, taught by a supply maths teacher, can give the flavour of the disruptions. The usual negotiation was considerably disturbed, and the subject culture did not save the teacher from difficulty. None of the strategies employed by pupils are new, but the progress of the lesson shows the manner in which deviancy emerges, is tried out and escalates until a class-wide breakdown of discipline occurs:

A new teacher enters and talks to Mr Davies, and then Mr Davies leaves the room. Pete and Roy immediately begin to talk. Pete twists around in his seat and announces to the remainder of the group 'Hey we're getting a new teacher'. Within three minutes, Pete and Roy are talking and laughing quite loudly, turning the laugh into a loud and unlikely sounding cough at the last minute. They begin to talk loudly enough to be heard. The teacher says nothing. It is the usual two actors who mount the first challenge to the teacher, and she fails to answer it. The way is then clear for progress to other levels of deviance. Roy then waves vociferously at the researcher, who is sitting on the far side of the classroom from him.

There is a noisy football game going on outside the window. The noise attracts the attention of the group. The teacher says 'Never mind what's going on outside, get on with your work'.

She tells Pete to stop talking. He has been talking to Roy. Pete stops, but Roy goes on. Keith sneezes, exceptionally loudly. Alan a few seconds later does exactly the same thing. Alan then starts to sing.

This behaviour so far has all been deviance around the sidelines, in the spaces which exist within lessons, as the pupils work. The new teacher has, however, failed to spot and stop them. The pupils, therefore, were encouraged to advance beyond those normal limits and to begin to make centre-stage challenges to the teacher.

Pete marches loudly out to the front of the class, and loudly slaps his books and his pen down on the teacher's desk and demands 'How do you work that out?' in peremptory tones.

The challenge he issues is clearly directed at the teacher, the representative of central authority in the room. Yet the challenge, though dramatic, is still in a sense covert. For Peter is using the old strategy of 'overplaying the pupil role'. He is only 'asking a question', asking for help, requesting a teacher to perform her rightful duties and function. His tone, however, turns this 'proper' piece of interaction into a challenge. Nevertheless, if he himself was in turn challenged, he could claim that 'I was only asking for help'. His retreat is covered. Nevertheless, the challenge is subtle, it demands the teacher show her ability to discharge her function efficiently, prove she is a teacher, prove her right to be 'in charge'.

In fact, Pete is allowed to 'get away with it'. The teacher fails to take any public or official account of his tone of voice, and simply helps with the answer. She fails, or appears to fail, to identify the challenge as a challenge, and treats it as a legitimate question. Pete celebrates his victory, by stopping on the way back to his seat and chatting to Amy, something he would not normally do. Pete then sets to work on his sum, but after two minutes is prepared to mount another challenge, that has more bite to it. He again leaves his seat, and clatters to the front of the room. On his way he says loudly 'I don't think that's right, what you told me'. Having revealed flaws in her disciplinary powers, Pete now mounts an attack on the teacher's academic competence, the whole basis of her credibility. At the same time the attack carries another discipline challenge, for Pete breaks the rule of silent, or at least quiet, working, and makes his challenge public, and loud. This time the teacher interprets Pete's actions as an infringement. However, she underrates the seriousness of his challenge, and merely says 'Shush'. This has an effect upon the remainder of the class, and the noise level rises perceptibly. Many pupils stop working and start talking. The teacher notices this, and demands quiet.

In several respects the battle is already won and lost, for many members of the class flow into action in the territory which Pete has opened. Keith begins to whistle loudly. Mark does a kind of jig while sitting in his seat. Stewart and Allan start to fight with pens and rulers across the gap in their desk. Keith and Andrew begin hitting each other on the head. Dominic stops working and slumps bored in his seat. The girls chat and daydream. The teacher attempts to stem the tide, 'I don't remember having told you that you could break out into chatter. Get on with your work. Some of you aren't working. Like you (to Dominic) sitting there with your legs all stuck out in front of you, sit up straight and get your head down and slog on until the end of the lesson'. Her words of 'don't chatter' seem in fact rather a mild sort of reproach given the seriousness of the actions going on, certainly by comparison with the forms pupils had become accustomed to in the first term. Her cues are not therefore picked up by the pupils as rebukes, but rather serve as incentives to more disorder. In addition, she picks upon one individual, Dominic, who is normally fairly conformist, instead of tackling the ringleaders, Pete, Keith or Alan.

It could be, of course, that the teacher *had* identified them and knew full well what was necessary, but shrank from doing it in case she was unsuccessful. In the pupils' view, therefore, she was either 'foolish' or 'feeble', both arch crimes in the pupils' catalogue of teacher offences (Rosser and Harré 1976, Furlong 1977). The tactic of course failed to win her any control, and the lesson continued to the end on lines dictated by the pupils. They had staged an effective 'take-over'.

Take-overs also happened with student teachers. One such appeared in music, which, as we have seen, already had a low status among pupils.

> He takes the register. Alan answers 'Yes Miss' to the register, but the teacher lets this pass. Then he sees Janet exchanging a quick, quiet comment with another girl. He rebukes her firmly. This creates problems for him, because of the already established identity of the two pupils. He lets off the habitual deviant Alan, and attacks the ultra-conformist Janet. He then indicates that he doesn't really know the rules. Two more boys follow up the advantage. Paul and two other pupils answer 'Yes Miss'. He tells the class they will spend time working out tunes on the instruments. Pete, as always alert to a new definition of the situation, jumps in immediately with a centre stage challenge 'Can we play Punk Rock?' The teacher continues, Keith goes into a loud coughing routine. The teacher actually gets the class working, but Pete plays a Blondie tune loudly and Roy plays a manic loud tune. There is quite a wide potential for disruption. Finally the conformists join in, Giles and Phillip playing and talking loudly.

Another lesson was thus lost.

Another near take-over occurred, this time involving a senior member of staff, a head of faculty in fact, which indicates the significance of changes in other aspects of the situation. In this case, the change was in size and consequently structure of audience, i.e. the pupils.

> Two classes are put together for art and craft. The pupils are far more noisy and disruptive than usual. Ros and Nicola fight in a silly way, and pull each other's hair, and are very noisy. Whenever the pupils are given an instruction, a loud buzz of noise follows it.

Allan makes a range of silly noises through the lesson, and taps rhythmically with his pen. Someone writes the name of a pop group in the condensation on the window. Valerie combs her hair. Mark unties his tie. The disorder is general. Force of numbers has fractured part of the usual discipline frame and opened up spaces into which, rather like Parkinson's Law, disorder flows. There is no negotiated agreement between teacher and pupils for this situation. That has to be done afresh.

The teacher puncutates the noisy disruption at intervals, with demands for quiet. 'I don't see any reason for any more talking, so we won't have any'. He also isolates individual pupils like Ros for her behaviour. But it is not really successful.

At the end of the lesson the class is given detention. 'I will not put up with that general background hubbub of noise from you, when I have asked you to be quiet several times and get no real response. This is simply not good enough'.

The class leaves the room very quietly, with almost none of the usual hubbub.

The fact that this teacher had difficulty in maintaining the kind of order he wanted was regarded as significant by other teachers. There was some sarcasm. One said 'Fancy a head of faculty having to resort to detention'. This indicates a crucial difference between control and punitive measures. In the context of this particular school ethos, if a teacher resorts to punitive measures, especially on the scale of class detentions, it is regarded as tantamount to an admission of failure to control. The newly constituted class had taken-over the lesson, not in this case intentionally (as happened with the student–teacher above, where pupils reacted to the teacher) but as a kind of natural expansion, as a response to a change in their own constitution, and also perhaps as a result of their success in other situations.

Purge

This spate of take-overs and attempted take-overs led to a school-wide attempt to recreate the discipline framework with tighter bonds, and a 'purge' was launched. The staff saw the first year as 'getting out of hand'. The fact that they had previously 'settled in' meant that they were now needing a tighter line. From the headmaster down, the staff described themselves as 'having a purge'. The limits were tightened, and discipline was stressed in all formal arenas. At morning assembly the head fulminated about standards of appearance, and publicly sent three boys home to change into proper school uniform. At house meetings, the counselling staff earnestly discussed good manners, the caring community and the need to 'discipline yourself'. At registration, form teachers hammered home the same message and insisted on absolute and unusual silence and attentiveness. Within individual lessons, the liberal use and threat of the cane were woven together with demands for books to be covered, ties to be tied and homework to be completed.

The campaign was planned in advance, and comments suggested that it was not at all an unusual occurrence and was following a standard pattern. Mr Bridges said, 'It was decided last week at the counselling staff meeting that we had to have a bit of a purge, and that the school was going downhill, and that we would all work on behaviour, and uniform and politeness'. Mr Hill said, 'It's "hate the first years" time, we've decided it's time, it's that time of the year'. Teachers, therefore, have another 'front' that they will present if they adjudge pupils to be exceeding the limits.

How was the purge executed? There appeared to be five major strategies: (i) restating the rules and instituting strict enforcement of them for a period; (ii) clarifying the boundaries between formal and informal areas, and the teacher conception of the pupil role; (iii) 'exampling', that is to say making an example of one or two miscreants, *pour encourager les autres*; (iv) threatening extreme penalties, especially violence; (v) 'making a scene', or what Furlong's (1977) pupils referred to as 'causing trouble', which they tried to avoid at all costs. We shall see all illustrated in the following scenarios, sometimes several of them compounded in one piece of activity. We have selected for study here the two leading subject areas of maths and English, the art and design area because of its more informal structure, and one of the languages for especially interesting use of some of these strategies.

In maths, the pupils were not usually much of a problem. The teacher had a reputation for being 'hard', and his discipline frames were clearly recognized and observed. Keith said of him, 'He looks strict. He is supposed to be the hardest maths teacher in the school'. Nevertheless, this teacher was involved in the purge, no doubt to head off any potential challenges, and in the general interest.

> The teacher is delayed in getting to the class. There are older, re-sit O-level groups in with him and he is talking to them. He has to fetch equipment for the first year pupils and then two older girls come into the class with another issue. The class by this point is fairly disturbed, and a bit noisy. He re-enters the room and tells them generally to settle. They do not respond immediately. After a few seconds he stops them in a much more determined manner, 'OK, Stop! put your pens and pencils down and listen to me'. There is a disciplinary pause, then he goes on in an exaggeratedly calm voice, 'Now you have work to do, I don't want to hear from you, at all'. This tactic works. They are quiet. They tried to extend the normal limit, but were restrained.

The teacher took the opportunity to complain about the presentation and appearance of their work.

> I am less than happy with the degree of neatness or non-neatness that's creeping in to your work, after a very good start, especially among the boys.

There is normally a bit of space for pupils at the end of a lesson, in which they might chat once they have been dismissed. But, during 'the purge', Mr Jones insisted that the class left the room absolutely silently – without a word. He threatened to keep the whole class back if anyone talked. Half way out he stopped them and warned Pete 'Do you want to hold all the others up? . . . No . . . then do it without talking'. This was effective. In this case, the teacher's strong individual reputation was probably the most telling factor in containing the pupils. No doubt the pupils' perceptions of the importance of his subject also helped.

As we saw in Chapter 3, the English teacher cultivated a different kind of approach, involving humour and fraternization, developing a personal bond between himself and the pupils. His lessons did not escape 'take-over' attempts. He did not respond, however, in his usual style, but by threatening to move into and to enforce a more formal and harsher disciplinary framework.

> The pupils are 'in trouble' in English for a number of reasons, including non-presentation of homework. They know that vengeance is about to descend upon their heads. 'You'll see some action today' Andrew informs the researcher, and Pete adds, 'We might get the cane today'. The class is run on altogether tighter lines than usual. The teacher begins by demanding silence, and absolutely insisting on it, before he begins. Then he harangues the class for about ten minutes, on a variety of issues, non-presentation of homework, slow progress in their classwork, slovenly presentation of work, general rudeness, etc. He is obviously quite angry, says he feels let down, and threatens to use the cane.

Here, he makes the 'bond' explicit, feels they have broken this bond, and threatens the transition to tighter and less enjoyable control mechanisms. They get a taste of what this means in the next few lessons, where their usual right to 'talk a bit' provided they are working is removed. In one of these lessons, three pupils asked for permission to go to the loo, which was unusual and probably a means of creating space, when the normal areas of their own activity were blocked for them.

In woodwork, Mr Grange gave a demonstration of the technique of 'exampling'. He gave clear and specific instructions at the beginning of the lesson about precisely which tools were to be used for the task in that lesson. Roy had already not paid attention, and Mr Grange singled him out. 'What kind of blade did I say you had to use for a straight line cut? What did I tell you?' His tone was loud and angry. The remainder of the class became totally silent, stopped working and turned around to listen. They were intended to do that: the rebuke was meant as much if not more for the whole class as for Roy.

Teachers need to pick out an appropriate individual when using this strategy. If a teacher picks on a normally highly conformist individual (as the student-teacher did earlier), then their actions will be seen as idiosyncratic and carrying no message for the remainder of the class. It will suggest, further, that the teacher has defined the situation incorrectly and does not know the general rules. If, however, one of the habitual deviants is chosen, then the message carries weight and significance for them all.

The discipline frame was tightened across the curriculum – even in the low-status subjects like art and music, teachers insisted on attentive pupils and quiet, uneventful lessons. It was also tightened in some of the 'spaces' of the school day, for example in registration. The school banded together, to present one 'front' of tighter, more disciplined interaction.

Another prominent strategy teachers employed was 'making a scene' – suspending normal rules and creating an atmosphere of expectancy of reprisals. During the 'scene', normal activity is held in abeyance, adrenalin runs high, and the disciplinary message is imprinted on the pupil's nervous system. It is often accompanied by 'exampling'. Some teachers employ the technique as part of their basic philosophy, but at this school it was used as a strategy in time of need, as a very occasional stern reminder. It was employed now, as one of the battery of techniques turned on the marauding first years. One good example of this occurred in the first lesson on a Monday – regarded as a marker for the week.

> The teacher employs the now usual strictness, separating out a group of noisy boys and making them work alone. He insists on quiet as the pupils work, but at first he doesn't get it. So, Mr Brandt grabs Alan's face and grinds it into his book, saying, 'You *will* work'. Then he turns to the remainder of the class, dusts off his hands in a pantomime gesture and says, 'Do excuse me please'. After this, only the extreme deviants cause any trouble, and one of these is thrown out of the class.

'Trouble' was returned by teachers with interest:

> The teacher rebukes Keith and Mark for being noisy outside the classroom. Once inside, he rebukes Alan on the standard of his work. He announces a task and threatens to cane anyone who does badly. Quite suddenly, Mr Brandt turns to Keith, who is standing quietly listening to him: 'You've got your hands in your pockets, take them out, that's very rude'. Then he pauses for a fraction of a second and says 'Go and get the cane, and the punishment book. Go on'. Keith disappears, the class remaining silent. He returns after a few moments saying he couldn't find them. While he is out of the room, the class remains absolutely silent and still. Gary had at the very beginning of the lesson been sent on an errand. He returns to the class at this point and, uncertain of what to do and aware of the atmosphere in the room, he stands at the front of the class next to Keith. When the teacher returned with the cane, he did not question why Gary was there. He simply caned both him and Keith, in front of the whole class, and facing them. The remainder of the class were still standing. He said that if there was any further trouble from either pupil he would 'give you 6'. Teacher continued to make Keith and Gary stand facing the class, while his next discipline message was made. He asked the class questions from their homework, and kept them standing while he did it. Again there was a threat involved, but also a reward. When a pupil had answered a question correctly they were allowed to sit. Mr Brandt warned, 'Don't be the last person to sit down'. To those pupils who answered first the teacher gave house points. There were some girls left towards the end. Although official school policy was not to cane girls, this teacher warned, 'Remember, you girls are not immune from my charms'. Finally, they all sat down including Keith and Gary.

The incident caused a lot of comment, in part because the caning was public and clearly intended to humiliate as well as cause pain, in part because the teacher had raised the pupils' suspense and apprehension by making them wait while he went for the cane. Also there was no specific offence that could be seen, and which it was clear was being sanctioned. The general consensus was that Mr Brandt was 'very unfair'. Claire said, 'I hate Mr Brandt now'. They made a series of attacks on him. This teacher, then, appears to overstep the mark of teacher–pupil protocol, which allows and indeed requires firmness of control on the part of the teacher, but also discretion and fairness (Rosser and Harré 1976, Furlong 1977, Woods 1979). Clearly there is some scope for the occasional 'scene', to bring home the realities of situations in a particularly arresting way, but, equally clearly, 'scenes' have to be handled with great care if they are not to be counter-productive. Whereas the other strategies discussed are all legitimate in pupils' eyes, generally because they are reaffirming previously agreed boundaries, this particular use of scene-making is illegitimate because it goes beyond them. In doing so, far from establishing a solid basis of order on agreed terms, this teacher was sowing the seeds of future trouble for himself.

Some teachers, especially the counselling staff, sided with the pupils on this issue.

Mr Bridges: It's not on, is it, public caning.

Mr Hill: He's caned five boys this morning. What's the matter with him?

Mr Brandt later that day apologized to the researcher about the incident. 'I felt rotten that you saw that'. He explained his reasons for behaving the way he did: 'I really think things are getting out of hand in school at the moment. It had to be stopped'.

It is already clear that the length and phasing of the transition is longer and more complicated than previous studies suggest. To claim that most pupils are 'settled in' to the new school within a month, as some reports do (e.g. Spelman 1979), is true in a sense, but, as we have seen, only a half-truth, for it is not for the duration, only for a period, before a number of factors come together to cause them to try to renegotiate terms on which they can 'settle in' on a basis more favourable to them. The character of the adaptation, therefore, is cyclical, as negotiations and renegotiations follow each other according to the shifting balance of power and interest. The questions of whether, and when, they even out, we must leave to a later chapter.

⟳ 6 ⟲

Growing pains

This phase of the school year also saw changes and developments in the informal culture of the pupils. As the number of 'unknowns' dissolved in terms of the formal culture of the school, so did they in relation to the informal culture generally, and specifically in terms of one's peers. Identities clarified, and this meant friendships could be more firmly sealed and the boundaries between friendship groups hardened, which in turn altered and influenced identities.

At a general level, pupils said they felt more settled and comfortable among their peers than they had at first. Phillip said, 'It's easy to make friends. I mean even the girls, you get to know them now, so it's quite easy to make friends'. Although there were some pupils who had not found this task easy at all, Phillip's statement probably did represent an accurate picture for many of the pupils. At the same time, the fact of feeling more comfortable with one's peers, the fact of having made friends enabled pupils to feel more settled in the school generally. Rosemary said, 'I was nervous at first, but now I've made some friends and it's alright'.

Developments in friendships

Two basic developments were observable at this point in the school year. First, there were a number of shifts in the terms of relationships; some friendship groups and some best friend bondings which had been established in the 'initial encounters' did not survive that phase. Secondly, friendship group boundaries hardened somewhat, especially among the boys, and this rendered some individuals isolated. Friendship groups among the girls changed their personnel more frequently and more radically than did those among the boys; the boys' groups by comparison remained largely stable. It may be useful to summarize these changes in the girls' groups.

At first, the friendship groups were based entirely on middle school groupings. Then they moved to the position we identified in Chapter 4:

88

(Jenny and Janet)   Sally, Amy, Rebecca, with Rosemary
                                       interested

(Carol, Pat, Marjorie)   (Pamela and Sheila)   (Claire and Valerie)

(Bridget and Anna)

By February these groups had changed to:

(Jenny and Sally)   (Amy, Rosemary,   (Carol, Pat, Marjorie,
                                       Rebecca)   Sheila, and Pamela)

(Claire and Valerie)   (Bridget and Anna)   Janet was isolated

This pattern of friendship groups then remained stable until the middle of
the summer term.

The shifts in friendship patterns were observable in the day-to-day
interactions of the girls within the classroom. There would be differences of
opinion, or even quarrels between the girls, to be followed by a change in
seating patterns, and in the choice of partner for the places and spaces in the
informal culture. For example, Jenny and Sally began to sit together, and
Amy and Rosemary began to eat lunch together. These observations were
reinforced by interview data, and by confidences and comments passed to
the researcher in the school. For example, Amy and Rosemary when
interviewed did not want to talk about middle school. It was in the past.
They were, however, burning to talk about their quarrels with Sally and led
the interview in that direction. Sally confided one lunchtime to the
researcher, 'Me and Jenny have fallen out with Janet you know'. Our
argument is that as pupils 'came out' more, identities became better known
and the girls were able to make more realistic judgements on whom they
wanted to 'be friends with'. Also the need simply to cling together for
support, which had been paramount at the beginning, was no longer felt.

It still seemed to be the formal culture that was the key issue in
determining allegiance patterns. In this phase, however, it was not ability
and status in the academic hierarchy that were central, but rather the issue
of attitude to the formal culture.

The first stage of these shifts in friendship groups involved Janet and
Jenny, who began to drift away from each other. Janet's identity as the
'brainy girl' who was 'top in everything' was clearly established by this
time. She also signalled her interest in work very clearly. When the 'forest of
hands' syndrome died out after the initial encounters phase, Janet continued to show a desperate keenness to answer questions. Jenny and she
began to have a series of disputes, which became more and more pronounced, and which had some bitterness. It is perhaps significant that many
of the disputes occurred in craft lessons, which has already been identified
as an area of some importance in terms of the informal culture. Janet and
Jenny were co-operating over their set project, the building of a cardboard

house. They chose to do a large and elaborate Tudor style mansion. Janet frequently took charge of the activities and told Jenny what to do. 'That door has got to be painted green'. Jenny objected, 'No, I want to do it brown'. Janet: 'No that's not right, it has to be green'. She would stop Jenny in the middle of an activity, and do it for her: 'These lines have got to be done with a ruler, I'll do it'. Jenny slowly began to object more and more strongly, 'Don't you blooming well tell me what to do'. 'No, I'm going to do it my way'. Finally she accused Janet of 'being really bossy.'

Janet soon came to adopt the 'ingratiation' mode of adaptation – a kind of hyper-conformity to the aims and means of the official culture (Woods 1979). In a music lesson, the teacher asked for volunteers to join the school choir. The majority of the class looked disdainful at the prospect of playing classical music and singing Christmas carols. Janet, however, looked interested, and agreed to take part. In a maths lesson towards the end of term, the teacher gave the class the opportunity to watch a football game, but Janet chose not to go. She did some extra maths, while the rest of the class bustled out in high spirits. The final straw came for Jenny when Janet attempted to involve her in the same kind of activity. At the end of a craft lesson, the teacher asked for some people to help clear up the art room, which meant giving up some of the lunch hour. There was again a distinct lack of enthusiasm, but Janet put up her hand and volunteered herself and Jenny. In fact, Jenny was not prepared to be so publicly identified as having such teacher-oriented values, and she refused to join Janet in the tidying up. Jenny and Janet began to drift apart, and Janet was left isolated. Jenny had chosen the moderated norms of the majority of pupils. In these terms, Janet was the deviant case.

Jenny now moved towards Sally, who in turn broke from her middle school contacts. Again the issue of attitudes to the formal culture and its demands seem to have played a crucial role. Sally seemed to find herself in increasing conflict with Amy and Rebecca. Sally would refuse to join in chats that Amy and Rebecca had, when they could make space in a lesson. In a maths lesson she told them to stop talking and start working. In a craft lesson Amy asked Sally for help with her work, but Sally refused, 'No, I've got to get on with my work, why do you keep asking me?' Sally frequently mentioned her sense of need 'to get on with my work.' She confided to the researcher one day that she had messed around a lot at first, but now things had to get more serious, and she had to work harder. In science lessons the three girls co-operated on projects, and it was invariably Sally who worked the hardest. We have also discussed the unisex goggles the girls were asked to wear in science, and how important a symbol it became for the girls to refuse to do so. However, Sally was willing to wear them, and she additionally ordered Amy and Rebecca to wear them: 'It's for your own good', was her comment.

In short, Sally soon found Amy and Rebecca had a different orientation to the formal culture from hers. When Rosemary became a member of the group, Sally left. She confided to the researcher about her difficulty in accepting Rosemary's attitudes to work and made it clear that she wanted to do things differently:

> Sally: Do you know, we just had a test in French, on telling the time, and Rosemary she got nought and I got 10/10, and now she won't speak to me, because she said I should have helped her. I would have done, although that's not right is it, because when it comes to big tests and O-levels and that, I won't be able to help her then will I, and she won't do very well then. She says she don't like me, and that I'm going to lose friends if I go on like this.

Sally went on to object to the fact that although Ros had not known her very long, yet she felt she had the right to ask for a lot of help: 'Ros won't talk to me now'. Jenny is very sympathetic to Sally and declares it is 'Ros's own fault for not learning the stuff properly.' For Sally, the issue was clear enough. Giving help in a test went too strongly against the formal demands of school culture, and it meant transgressing some of the basic rules of a co-operative group for her. At the same time, by refusing co-operative help to Rosemary, she was signalling her wish to withdraw from friendship interaction with her as well. Sally put out a feeler towards Jenny, who reciprocated, and their friendship was to begin, based on a shared orientation toward work and the female school culture.

The three girls were aware of the reasons for the split in their friendship with Sally and knew its origins; they discussed it in a group interview:

> Amy: Sally, she's gone all serious. When I talk to her in lessons, she says 'Don't you think we should get on', and that I am a chatterbox, I can't help it.

> Ros: We like a laugh don't we, like the boys do. Sally and Jenny are doing it all right, in science, and there's us . . . they get all the results and there's us, we don't hardly get any do we.

> Amy: You see Sally and Jenny, they haven't got a name. Like I'm chief giggler, and she's Fanny Anne.

The central issue again appears to be that of attitudes to the formal culture of the school. Sally is seen to have a different orientation from Amy, Rosemary and Rebecca. She also, crucially, sees *herself* as having a different orientation. Also of interest here are Amy's and Rosemary's teacher-imputed identities as 'Chief Giggler' and 'Fanny Anne'. Though given partly in jest, they are intended as a mild rebuke for minor but persistent misdemeanours. But they are not received as a rebuke. Rather, the nicknames harden the kind of identities they wish for themselves, and that is a matter for celebration (see Morgan, O'Neill and Harré 1979). Significantly, Sally and Jenny 'do not have a name'. Their own names are sufficient for teachers' purposes, for there is little deviation evident in their attitudes.

There was a similar case to this among the boys. Phillip and Keith had been at middle school together, and yet they studiously avoided each other.

We have already suggested that this was because both boys knew that each took a totally different view of the demands of the formal culture. Phillip became friends with Stewart, and Erik joined their group. Erik had in fact gone to the same middle school as Matthew and, in addition, they lived very near to each other, but they were not friends in secondary school. Again it seemed that this was the result of quite different orientations to the formal culture. David took a mildly deviant line, but Erik was highly conformist, and seemed to feel a need to separate himself from a contact of this kind. This was certainly the interpretation that other pupils put upon it. Valerie had known them at middle school and she believed that it was their attitude to work and to being in trouble which divided them: 'Erik, he's ever so quiet. If you mix with people who get into trouble, then you will get into trouble really. He doesn't mix with people like that. If Erik knows that Matthew's mucking about I'd think he'd leave him, because I don't think he likes getting into trouble like that'. Thus the boys also seem to hold firm views of each other along conformist/deviant lines, and these come to govern friendship groups.

One of the observable effects of the emergence of these categories and perspectives was that the boundaries of friendship groups hardened. As pupils 'came out' and identities became known, it became impossible to be seen as connected with some pupils. One illustration of this was in music lessons in February, when the teacher wanted to make a major reorganization of groups of pupils. The original groups had been of four pupils, but as friendship patterns had evolved and shifted, some groups had grown, others had split, and some pupils had been left out altogether. The teacher wanted even groups again of four or five pupils. When she attempted to do this, she met with a storm of protest:

> The pupils are told to 'Get into a group of four'. Phillip, Stewart, Giles and Erik are in their customary group. Geoffrey attaches himself to them. The teacher says it has to be four people. Phillip and Stewart say 'We are four, I don't know what Geoffrey is doing here'. They are very clear as to the boundary of their group and certain who is the intruder. It is Geoffrey who leaves. Pete and Jim move right across to the opposite side of the room to work with Keith and Andrew. They make no offer to join Dominic and Mark or Matthew although they are at the next table. Geoffrey, when he leaves Phillip's group, moves to Pete's table. He is again decisively rejected, Roy telling him to 'Get out of here'. The teacher's attention is attracted by this loud display of aggression and she insists that he is allowed to stay, but it is under sufferance.

Geoffrey is as much an isolate among the boys for his perceived excessive weakness as Janet is among the girls for her perceived excessive conformity. It is not only seating patterns that are involved.

> In an English lesson, sun is streaming in the window and Pete and Andrew move tables to get away from it, they move three tables down, so they are sharing with Phillip and Stewart. However, they do not interact or socialize with Phillip and Stewart at all. They turn around and talk to their friends at their usual table. Phillip goes on working, while Pete and Andrew talk and generally mess around.

Identities are by now well enough established, so that these pupils know there is no point of contact, they have nothing to share. In fact, this can on occasion be made very clear. The tracks of enmity are laid down at the same time as those of friendship.

> (Pete is telling a joke. Phillip happens to be standing nearby.)
>
> Pete: What do four elephants in the back of a mini play?
>
> Answer: Squash.
>
> (Phillip does not laugh at all. Pete gets annoyed.)
>
> Pete: Oh go on, then, laugh
>
> Phillip: I only laugh when things are funny.
>
> (They glare at each other. There is clear tension between them.)

This could work in cross-gender terms too:

> Bridget asks Pete to move. He refuses very aggressively. The teacher overhears and says 'Be nice to your friends'. Pete gets a deeply shocked expression on his face and says 'Friend!' in a scandalized tone as if it were a preposterous suggestion.

By this point in the year, the boys' allegiances and alliances are fairly clearly laid down, and there are quite hard-and-fast lines, even barriers between groups of boys, which are not crossed.

This was true to a certain extent for the girls, but there were the major fluctuations in alliances, which have been described. When the teacher attempted to reorganize the girls' groups for music lessons there were protests too. Amy, for example, objected strongly to the fact that Anna had been included in her group and Rebecca left out. But we have already suggested that by now there were signs that this basic middle school group of Sally, Jenny, Amy and Rebecca was fragmenting. Ros joined the group and Jenny drifted out of it when she could. They found it almost impossible to work together by this point in the year, which gives interesting insight into the ways that friendship ties are necessary for proper co-operative activity to function and for work to get done.

Best friends

We suggested in Chapter 4 that, at least for the girls, there was another level of friendship, that of best friend bonding. As the general shifts in friendship groups occurred, so did changes in the selection of a 'best friend' from out of the friendship group. It was clear that the 'best friend' tie had strong emotional content for the pupils by this stage. When Jenny pulled away from her friendship with Janet, the latter expressed a deep sense of sadness about it. Her language when she described the fact is interesting. She said 'Me and Jenny have broken up'. It is the language of adult, or adolescent, heterosexual partnering. She said she felt very upset by the loss of the relationship, and showed in a number of ways that she resented it, and in fact attempted to win Jenny back. One of her tactics involved an attack upon Sally. Janet tells Jenny, 'Sally has taken your ruler'. The use of the word 'taken' is crucial here, for the implication is that of 'without asking' you first. Jenny, however, responded, 'It's OK', thus giving a clear signal of her loyalty to Sally. Janet by implication is excluded and rejected. The implications may go further, because the right to borrow equipment 'without asking' is one of the factors in 'best friend' bonding. Janet's attack was then in no way random, Sally had borrowed a ruler, and had not asked, recognizing her right to do so as part of the new bond with Jenny. Janet challenged the fact that Sally did have such a right, Jenny confirmed that she did, and so confirmed and strengthened the bond between herself and Sally.

Another new 'best friend' bond, which developed between Amy and Rosemary, seemed to involve some new qualities. There were elements again of intensely felt emotional ties, but also it seemed that questions of mutually shared identity were becoming important. The relationship was not based on a middle school tie and the elementary need for mutual support. Instead, Amy and Rosemary had sought each other out, recognizing that they shared more than attitudes to schoolwork. Amy and Ros always sat together in lessons, and walked to and from lessons together. They spent lunch and break times together. They were separated for some lessons, and on these occasions lay detailed and precise plans for exactly where and when they would meet after lessons. They would point to the exact spot where they would meet at the end of a lesson. The friendship spilled over into 'out of school' activities. For example, they went roller-skating together, and to the school disco, spending hours discussing what they would wear. They spent evenings at each other's houses, and occasionally stayed the night. They borrowed tapes and tape recorders from each other, and enthused over the same rock groups. They also borrowed clothes from each other. Amy said one day, 'I'm lending her my silk blouse to go with her pencil skirt' (to go to a Valentine's night disco). The girls also bought exactly similar clothes, and dressed in the same style. They had their hair cut in the same distinctive style, which involved the hair being swept back behind the left ear and held by a coloured comb. What these girls are doing is growing closer together to the extent that they actually share an identity. One girl sees herself in the other. They share beliefs, attitudes, property, appearances. They jointly reinforce the kind of selves they wish to be. Again, therefore, we suggest that identity concerns lie behind the 'best friend' syndrome, for in fashioning personae through these difficult passages (including that of puberty) it is helpful to have an 'alter ego' to reflect one's image to aid the work of self–other perception (Cooley 1902).

There was one other significant development. In the initial encounters phase, few insults or statements of aggression were traded within gender groupings, especially among the girls. Clearly this situation had changed somewhat by the second term, and the girls as well as the boys were making their likes and dislikes of others more obvious, yet still not very public. Sally confided to the researcher, and to Jenny, that she felt offended by Rosemary. Amy, Rosemary and Rebecca discussed Sally's departure among themselves. They did not challenge her openly about it. Disputes were still non-public for the girls.

The macho hierarchy

There did not seem to be any parallel best friend bonding for the boys, who remained in 'matey' larger groups of friends. The demand, predicted by the myths, for increased toughness on the part of the boys continued to be an important issue. We have suggested that a kind of 'macho hierarchy' was present in the secondary school culture, and that it exerted a range of pressures on the first year boys. February was the first of about three occasions when large-scale fights took place among the boys. On each occasion, there were many fights, one succeeding the other. There was a kind of 'fights' fever'. Some of these fights involved boys from other comprehensive schools, especially Mayorfields, the rival school. A large gang from that school marauded down the lane to Old Town, and there were rumours of axes, chains and other weapons being used. The fights in February mostly involved the older lads, and in 1979 they established one boy, Graham, as the best fighter. He happened to be Keith's brother, which brought reflected prestige to Keith. The boys whose own identities were largely invested in the informal culture took a great interest in these events. Pete told the researcher about a fight the previous evening after school, which had involved older boys. One boy got stabbed, albeit with a blunt knife, so that it made only grazes – but it made 'a load of grazes' – he personally saw them. Watching the fights could bring penalties from the school, which took a severe line on fighting. However, Pete, Roy, Andrew, Keith and Jim had all watched a selection of the fights, and knew the results of them all. Doubtless their witnessing these activities reinforced their own sense of male identity, and signalled their own interest in this aspect of the informal culture.

However, this 'macho hierarchy' had implications for what went on within the class, as we indicated in Chapter 3, and a kind of status network based on toughness evolved within the classes. This continued to exert an effect at this phase of the school year. The pattern of one individual asserting his dominance within a friendship or co-operation group continued. Phillip, for example, was consistently hitting Erik, and stealing Stewart's pencils, and pushing Giles around. Roy continued to do the same thing in his group. By February, however, another development had begun as status hierarchies *between* groups, and especially between the leaders of groups, began to be tested and established. Keith one day used a pencil belonging to Phillip 'without asking'. They were not part of a co-operative

group and it represented a challenge. Phillip acted decisively and aggressively. 'You didn't ask!' he bellowed, and 'You better do so!' He had walked
right up to Keith and stood looking aggressively at him, as he said this.
Keith backed down, apologised and did not repeat the offence. Again,
Phillip is challenged by Mark, who is only semi-literate, and clearly at the
bottom of the English class, in direct contrast to Phillip. Mark insulted
Phillip and pushed him. Phillip swung around and hit back very hard. Mark
backed down. On another occasion at about the same time of the year, Roy
challenged Phillip in rather a different way. Roy took Giles's eraser and cut
it into two pieces with the Stanley knife he was using in the craft lesson.
Giles protested. On other occasions when pupils teased Giles, which
happened frequently, Phillip had stepped in and protected him, telling
pupils to 'leave him alone' and 'give that back.' On this occasion, however,
he did not do so. He seemed to accept Roy's claims to toughness, and, as in
lessons when he refused to volunteer answers he was not sure were correct,
so here he ignored a challenge because he was (presumably) not entirely
sure he would win. Instead, Phillip joined in the teasing of Giles, snatching
one half of the eraser from him and throwing it around the classroom, over
Giles' head, refusing to give it back. So, there seems to be an attempt to
establish some sort of status pattern in terms of toughness between as well as
within groups, by this point in the school year.

Growing up

We have noted that pupils welcomed the transfer to secondary school, as a
vital step away from childhood and towards a more adult status. In
consequence, certain activities, language and behaviour became virtually
proscribed, as being 'childish'. For example, Jacqui, Christine and Barbara
saw a group of boys in their class playing a game in the playground. It was a
chasing game, sometimes known as 'sticky toffee' or 'stick in the mud'.
These girls teased the boys quite unmercifully for this activity. 'What
babies!' 'Ughh! we stopped playing that in the second year'. 'Oh why don't
they grow up?' Another group of girls commented during an interview:

> Amina: At our other school, we used to play just running about with the boys and
> that, but you don't do that any more. . . . Well you are getting older, it is a
> bit silly now to do it.

Organized games and games more befitting to adult status were acceptable
– but you did not go out into the playground to 'play'.
    This demand had implications for curriculum and school practice. Pupils
welcomed any situations in which they were able to feel older, trusted,
responsible, and denigrated vehemently those which stimulated the reverse
feelings. It was another point at which the formal and the informal merged.

Christine: You don't get told what to do as much as in the middle school, and there they used to ring a bell, and you had playtime, and they used to blow a whistle or ring a bell, you know a handbell, but they don't here.

The way in which certain objects, in this case a handbell, can come to have heavy symbolic weight and meaning is of interest in this context. Formal school practices also became important, for they gave the pupil a sense of moving into personal responsibility for the self. They could do things for themselves, be trusted to cope; they no longer needed looking after.

Ruth: At dinners here, you are responsible for your money.

Jacqui: Over there, you had to give about 25p and you had to go for dinner every day, didn't you. That was it for the week. Here you bring your money, separate every day, and you can decide for yourself.

The reverse was clearly true as well: if the school involved pupils in activities or attitudes that were seen as 'too childish', they were liable to object in a number of ways. This seemed especially to be the case in craft lessons. For example, the class was asked to make stick puppets, using ping-pong balls for heads. Jacqui objected quite strongly to this activity. 'These puppets are so babyish'. Marie also objected to the objects they were asked to make in the lessons, and also to the slow pace of the lessons. This was especially true in needlework, because her mother had taught her to sew and had shown her many short cuts. She said crossly 'We only make stupid things in here'. Amy made exactly the same kind of comment: 'We made a skirt at my old school, and now we have to do this'. They were matching lines, curves and corners on sheets of paper. Activities in art lessons could create the same kind of reaction:

Stewart is doing the simple painting exercise he has been set, which is designed to extend pupils' ability, control the movement and the colour in the mixing of paints. But he is not doing it in the careful, conscientious way he has been asked to. He makes his objections vocal, 'Boring in 'it?' It's baby work'.

This desire to acquire a more 'grown up' status, to be treated publicly in a manner that signified the change from childhood, vitally affected the way pupils viewed and reacted to particular teachers. There were a number of factors involved here. One was just general treatment, a sort of general style on the part of teachers.

Mark: Mind you the teachers don't forget that we are . . . but they do treat us in a more grown-up way.

Peter: Yes but some teachers like Miss Blanche, she still insists on calling people 'First-years'.

His resentment at this practice was clearly transmitted in his tone of voice. The point perhaps needs explanation. The school's practice was to call each year by a letter of the alphabet. The years under research were T and V years. The letters used corresponded directly to the car registration for each year. That meant that pupils were never called first years or fourth years, it was always V years or R years. This made Miss Blanch's practice stand out by contrast. It also suggests that the school's policy on this matter accurately reflected some pupil attitudes from their informal culture. In a sense, teachers like Miss Blanche had themselves failed to recognise the pupils' transition, for they did not appear to see that the pupils' status had changed, and called for different responses.

Many pupils wanted to be granted more responsibility from teachers. Some succeeded in fulfilling these aspirations, some did not.

Pat: I like the Headmaster's lessons, because he tells you what to do, and then he says 'Right, get on with it'. . . . Adult, that is really the other way you feel is childish. Our other teacher for science, she doesn't give us any instructions, she just says 'Write this out' and then she goes, 'Right, just do what the question says'. He don't tell you to write it all down, he just says, to jot things down, so you will be reminded what to do if you get stuck. And he says like 'Watch this acid, remember it is this one, it was a dodgy one'. And that is sensible. But that Mrs Fields, she don't give you any precautions'.

Pupils had a sense of doing something dangerous in their science lessons. Many enjoyed the responsibility of looking after dangerous substances and coping with the new situations, but they needed to feel confidence in the teacher in charge, so that in turn they could feel confident about themselves.

Another factor indicating adult status was trust in their competence to do things:

Carol: What I like about the senior school, they trust you, don't they? In the other school, they wouldn't hardly give you a pencil, because they said, Oh you lose that, it's the end of you.

Yet there were threatening aspects to this treatment too:

Sheila: The teachers, sometimes they use long words.

Pamela: Our middle school teacher said if you don't know, ask, and I will tell you again.

Sheila: No, you can't do that here, because they have already told you.

The need to 'put childhood away' was also reflected in the implements and equipment of the school day. Valerie had to borrow her sister's pencil case. it was made from cardboard, and covered with pictures of red tin soldiers. The first day that she brought it to school, she continually apologized for having such a childlike thing with her: 'I nicked it from my little sister'. Later in the day: 'It's horrible, it's really awful'. Finally she admits, 'Well it's really babyish'. She contrasts the object with Rosemary's pencil case, which is made from lilac fur fabric. There was a dramatic change in the kind of presents they asked for, and Easter eggs, for example, were quite unacceptable. They were not only childish, but unfeminine, for 'Easter eggs make you fat'. Instead there is a new, more appropriate present, 'I've asked for clothes'.

This age-grading principle extends outside school activities, to leisure pursuits. Tina's father commented wryly at this, 'Have you noticed, the thing that's changed most, what she does with her spare time', and he gave a solemn wink. The exact details of these changes were summed up rather effectively by some rhymes, which were written into another girl's (Sheila's) autograph book by her friends:

> When Sheila was a little tot
> She liked to play with toys,
> Now Sheila has grown up a bit
> She prefers to play with boys.

> If all the boys lived in the sea,
> What a good swimmer Sheila would be.

> If all the boys were fish and chips
> Then Sheila would have greasy lips.

Reading interests underwent a change. Joy was still able to say, 'I read quite a lot, books like *Little House on the Prairie*, or *Winnie the Pooh*, I love that'. Other girls would not have agreed. The comics the girls bought and read during this year changed quite substantially. Commercial interests cater for this shift, and produce basically three age-graded groups of comics. There are those for younger children, like *Beano*, or specifically girls' paper, like *Bunty*; then there are comics produced for this 12+ age group, like *Pink* and *My Guy*; in addition, there are comics for the older age group, like *True Love* and *True Romance*. At the beginning of the year Christine said, 'Yes I like reading comics, I like reading comic books, things like the *Beano* books. I like them sort of books'. This changed and most girls seemed to get involved instead in the girls' teenage type of comic, like *Pink* and *My Guy*, and came to look down on children's comics.

On one occasion, the researcher brought a range of these comics into an English lesson, which had been given over to the project. The girls made unerringly for the comics of their own age grade, and showed some disdain for those intended for the younger group. However, it is equally significant that they showed some degree of embarrassment at working with and reading the comics intended for the older age group, with their stories of explicit sexual encounters, failed marriage and divorce, and incidence of illegitimate children.

As far as activities went, it was unacceptable to have 'a party' for your birthday – you had 'a disco'. Jacqui described one she had: her parents worked at the Youth Centre, running a variety of activities, so she was able to use that building, and invited about forty friends.

R: Did you play games, or did you dance, or what?

The response was as expected, and the emotional content clear. Jacqui stared reproachfully at the researcher and said in disparaging tones, 'No, we danced of course'.

This data supports the analysis made of the myths, which point to birthdays as marking something significant about personal identity. Jacqui here is indicating her sense of being older, and of choosing activities which signify that sense. Her thirteenth birthday marks her as a teenager, and confirms her new 'older' status. She must act her age. However, some girls got left behind in their progress through this area of the transfer, and the others were quick to apply pressures on them. Pat said in her English lesson to the group at her table that she was going to a party for a birthday. Sally picked up the word 'party' in a scandalized tone, and said, 'A *party*, at your age!'

On the other hand, there were pressures holding the girls back from too rapid an advance, which insistently reminded them that they were at a half-way stage and had not yet won full entry into the teenage culture. The pressures came from parents and from older pupils within the school.

Claire: My mum thinks I'm too old for my age, and that I'm growing up too quickly. My parents are going away for the weekend, and I don't want to go with them. I've got two little brothers, and it's no fun. My mum says I act like I'm 31 and not 13, and that I should want to do things with them.

Clearly parental pressure could be at direct variance with the individual pupils' desires and interest, and the sense of urgency in cutting away from childhood.

As for older pupils, we described in Chapter 4 the pressures on these girls against indulging in fashion and make-up. By February, some of the girls at least were willing to resist these pressures. They began by manipulating their school uniform in the direction of fashion. This involved style and length of skirt and type of shoes particularly. Rosemary, Amy, Rebecca, Janet, Bridget and Anna, for example, were all wearing high-heeled and fashionable shoes by February. Jacqui, Janie, Christine, Vivien and Barbara also wore fashionable shoes. The rest continued to wear shoes that they had worn when 'children'. There were some girls who had begun to experiment with make-up at school, and this negotiation was a particularly difficult one. The rule seemed to be that girls at this age and stage could wear eye make-up, but nothing else on their faces. The same girls who wore fashionable shoes were also experimenting with make-up. The rules were clear.

Vivien: Sometimes I wear eye shadow, but lipstick and that looks horrible.

Jacqui was in agreement.

> Jacqui: I only wear eye shadow, but I wouldn't wear that blusher stuff and all that.

The nature of the sanctions for transgressing these limits had become clearer to the girls by this point. Early in the year they had seen the penalties as getting 'beaten in'. Now they had a different set of ideas.

> Kerry: You get a reputation, 'She wears make-up. Look at her', and all that. It is like this girl in this school, she wears great black eye shadow and blusher.
>
> Jacqui: Yes, they call her horrible names, and say 'She's easy to get' and things like that. 'Look at that slut, look at her waiting on the corner again'.

The same rules governed particular kinds of clothes:

> Amy: I want a pencil skirt, and some of them tights without feet, but my sister says 'No, not at my age. They're too tartish'.

Again the mechanism is clear: the girls are negotiating against two separate perceived pressures: one that urged them away from childhood, and one that held them back from full participation in adolescent routines. The other interesting factor is the way that minute details of dress and appearance gain quite massive symbolic weight within the viewpoint of these girls. There may well be similar issues and symbols for the boys at this stage, but we were not able to gain such detailed knowledge of their progressions.

Relationships between the sexes

In the area of cross-gender interaction and adolescent sexuality, the pressure to put aside childhood patterns was also growing intense at this point in the year. There is a clear sense for these girls that 'things are different now', and that many areas of their lives have to be dealt with under a new set of rules.

> Amy: I used to go out with a boy when I was only eight but it was only nothing . . . when you played kiss-chase, things like that.
>
> R: Why is it different now, and how?
>
> Claire: Well you are older; you don't kiss (like you do your mum and dad), things like that. It is different. When you were eight years old, you didn't care, if you did a handstand, and they saw your knickers or whatever . . .
>
> Amy: You have got to look decent.
>
> Claire: You didn't wear make-up when you were eight either.

Sally discussed her family. She had two younger sisters, and had taken care of them during a recent half-term holiday. She told how her little sister had wanted to 'play a game of doctors and nurses'. She agreed she had wanted to play games like that when younger, but 'You don't want to do that sort of thing at our age, when you are older, do you?' She displayed an intense degree of embarrassment at this incident, which was told only to her group of friends.

The girls disavowed certain of the tactics by which attraction had been signalled. One boy, Paul, was very immature physically. He had been teased systematically by the girls for his willingness to continue playing games like 'sticky toffee', which they considered too childlike. He also continued to engage in behaviour condemned by some of the girls as too childlike in terms of sexual communication.

> Janie: You know Paul Masters, well he sent me a love letter (laughs) ... Jacqui gave it to me, and I just looked at it, and then I opened it, and then he smiled at me. I just turned around, I mean ... I was nearly in stitches.

The basic rule of the new approved sexual signalling was ambiguity, involving a series of covert messages, which made the fact that 'Jenny liked Bob' both clear and unclear at the same time. The situation carries tremendous risks, and these need to be covered. 'If a boy know you "like him" but does not reciprocate at all, then the girl is in trouble, for major ridicule can result from the boy. This is a situation to avoid at all costs'. If possible, therefore, a number of subterfuges and partial cover-ups need to be negotiated, allowing the girl to withdraw from the commitment if there are no reciprocated feelings, and to pretend that she was not really interested at all.

The following example reveals very clearly the sanctions and penalties that could result if a girl failed to negotiate effectively.

> Christine: There's a boy in our class I like at the moment. He's nice he is ... I didn't want anyone to tell 'im, I wanted it to be a secret.
>
> Amina: Someone wrote a letter to him, and signed it for Christine, and he called her names.
>
> Jacqui: It was somebody in our class, every girl in our class knew who it was Christine liked, and that letter was made by stencil so you couldn't tell who wrote it. He really called her names, and his mate Matthew Plumm, he wrote a note with horrible names on it and gave it to Christine.

Everyone in Christine's class knew about the situation,, and many of the girls laughed at her. Matthew himself was furious and constantly referred to Christine as 'a stupid bag', and systematically ignored her when he was not being insulting.

At the beginning of the year, the girls had in fact done a lot of passive watching, sighing and dreaming over the boys they felt attracted towards. Ros sat watching Bruce out of a window: 'Oh, I think he is lovely, I really fancy him', she would repeat in soft, sentimental tones. They also spent a lot of time discussing rock stars and poring over the pictures of them they brought into school.

By February, however, more action was needed, and there had to be new tactics appropriate to the girls' emerging needs. The style of these, again, was to allow enough information to filter through to the boy involved, so that he could act if he so chose, but equally to allow the girl a retreat without embarrassment. This permitted the girl to test out the water, and in fact to test out her identity, to find her place in the hierarchy of sexual attraction.

> Claire writes a boy's name with a heart in the palm of Rebecca's hand, where it cannot be publicly seen as it can on the back of a hand.

> Jenny has 'I love?' written on the back of her hand. So has Amy.

Both girls can then communicate in a range of other ways with the object of their fancy – for example, they can stare at him, walk close to him, comb their hair and giggle when he enters the room – but very little is being committed to public knowledge.

> Amy and Jenny write the names of particular boys on each other's craft aprons. The activity involves a good deal of giggling excitement. Amy won't write 'Amy loves Martin' on her own apron, but is prepared to allow Jenny to write it on hers. The point is she can always then make a public disclaimer and say, 'Oh Jenny wrote that'. Yet she also insists that Jenny must keep the apron secreted away. 'Don't go around wearing that, will you'.

> Ros wants to go out with a particular boy, in everyone's agreed opinion. Nevertheless she is not prepared to admit she wants to. Amy says 'If you want to go out with him, why don't you admit it'. But Ros is covered as long as she does not 'admit it' openly.

This gives an insight into the role of girls' friends here, for Ros in this incident is absolutely dependent on them not to tell the boy involved.

In the classroom, where the gender segregation was at its strongest, the main emphasis was on covert, ambiguous signalling. If a girl sat near boys, they might overhear conversations or read the notes and names on her rough book or ruler. Then the secret would be out, and problems could arise.

> Ros was discussing Simon, whom she had noticed at the disco the previous evening. 'Do you know him, he's in the second year, he wears polo necks all the time, he's really nice. They stop abruptly as they realise that Pete, who is sitting at the next table, is clearly listening.

Pete once borrowed Valerie's ruler without asking, and she responded with explosive anger. This may in part be because he broke the co-operative rules, but the strength of the reaction may have arisen from the fact that there were several boys' names written on it, and she was conscious of the risks if that information became public. If a girl actually did sit next to a boy, then a lot of teasing occurred, the assumption being that she 'liked him'. Sitting next to people is a crucially important signal of attitude toward them, whichever the sex.

For most of the year, the gender segregation was preserved totally. Both sexes objected very strongly if they were made to sit close together. Special circumstances could make this clear. For example, in a science lecture, when four forms were taken into the lecture theatre to see a film, the usual sex segregation broke down. Girls had to sit next to boys, and both parties objected, quite strenuously. This had nothing to do with likes and dislikes. At this point in the year, individual pupils who were publicly attracted to another of the opposite sex would make no connection with each other in class; they would systematically avoid any public signal of the kind. Thus Karen and Roy sat nowhere near each other in lessons, although they were 'going out'. However, when she unexpectedly came into a classroom where he was, they exchanged looks.

At middle school, observation suggested that the great amount of physical aggression that went on between boys and girls at this age might have been connected with covert communication of a sexual attraction. A physical involvement is suggested by the aggression, but it is rendered ambiguous by the aggression, which signals hostilities and anger rather than interest or warmth. This kind of behaviour stopped by and large at secondary school, but it sometimes persisted among particular pupils. It was the pupils themselves who gave an insight into the meaning of the aggression.

> Amy was walking up the stairs. Alan continually touches her in a marginally aggressive way. He would touch her on the back of the shoulder then move rapidly away before she could hit back. She says to the researcher: 'He is really mithering me' and expresses annoyance. She goes on to acknowledge, 'It's only because he likes me, I know that he fancies me'.

She is mostly, but not entirely, saying 'this is a joke', and the double meaning of the aggression becomes clear. This kind of signalling would seem to be a matter of some complexity that has to be learnt, and clearly pupils learnt at different rates.

There was for the girls a strong sense of being at a half-way stage. They were beginning to emerge into the life of adolescent sexual interaction, and were trying to find their way in, but there were many pressures on them. It would seem that downward age-grading pressures are operating with some strength in the perspectives of these girls, separating them from childhood, but holding them back from fully-fledged teenage status.

> Tina: I'm too young really [said very seriously] to go out with boys. My mum doesn't like it, 'cos she thinks I'm too young. I will when I'm 14 and over, but now I'm a bit young.
>
> R: Isn't it difficult though, when most of your friends are going out with boys?

Tina: Yes . . . but . . . er . . . I won't go out with them, 'cos I know my mum wouldn't be very happy and I said to her that I wouldn't, and I don't want to let her down.

Other girls identified a chronology, almost an hierarchy of development, and they specified their own place in that phased development. Things were, they had made it clear, very different from when you were eight, but:

Claire: With my cousin Lisa, she's 16, it's different again. They go round each other's houses. They bring somebody round home, they might bring their boy round or whatever . . . and they stay for tea alternate nights and things like that.

Amy: I wouldn't do it at my age now. My brother [aged 18] brought a girl home once, and he was embarrassed at first, but then it was alright.

Claire: . . . They are steps higher than what we are. . . . When I am 16, and going out with somebody, I won't be like I am now. I don't think I shall be as embarrassed.

This sense of being at a half-way stage was acted out in an incident, recorded in field notes in February of the year. Janie and Jacqui had deliberately chosen seats, in a double lesson where they could watch, and see, older pupils moving between lessons. Janie was satisfied, because she had seen Colin, the boy she was interested in, so she started to play with a small doll she had brought with her. She cut out and carefully coloured a paper dress for the doll, and became utterly engrossed in the activity of making the dress fit the doll. This was all done on her lap, where the teacher could not see. But the activities are a mixture of age-graded activities, and indicate the overlapping currents of development. Some pupils were able to articulate this feeling of 'half-wayness'.

The age and the stage was experienced as a very difficult one by many pupils, who disliked the waiting sense of being not one thing, yet not quite another. Sally said she 'hates this age, you like keep going through stages and you get spots and everything. I wish I could just grow up really quickly.'

In summary, identity concerns continue to be uppermost. We begin to see three clear stages in the development of friendships: (i) security, during the initial encounters phase, when pupils associated together for mutual comfort on the slightest indicators of common characteristics and suppressed their own individuality; (ii) identification, when they began to 'come out', realizing their individuality and seeking firmer evidence of like-mindedness in their friends, predominantly in the area of attitude to school; (iii) growth, where, particularly in best friend relationships, pupils appear to feed, and to feed off, each other's desired identities, and hence seem to grow together. We have seen how the pupils in some senses are pushed from below to become new people, with new statuses, appearances and concerns, but checked from 'going too far' by those further ahead of them. They may be 'seniors' and 'adults' compared with their previous school, but in their new school they are still 'first years' and only 'embryonic' teenagers, still under informal tutelage. They are learning that there is a lot to learn in both formal and informal areas.

IV

Third term:
consolidated adaptations

Making space

By the summer term, there was a more realistic branching out and flowering of identities. Earlier, in the first term, the 'rules' had been stipulated. The pupils had responded, and 'tested' for elasticity. In the second term, they had attempted 'take-overs', and brought on a 'purge'. They had discovered differences among teachers, subjects and situations. They knew how far they could go, in most cases. It remained for them to work out *within* these perimeters more consolidated adaptational modes that were in line with their own interests. As school demands began to bite, some found they could not, or did not wish to, meet them; or they began to work to a selective system, accepting some demands, rejecting others. We begin to see, therefore, a *conformist–deviant* divide appearing even before the school's streaming policy is brought into play. This supports the earlier work of Hargreaves (1967), Lacey (1970) and Ball (1981). But, as we shall see, there is scope within these general adaptations for considerable personal refinement, and this suggests that the 'interests' approach of Furlong (1976) and Hammersley and Turner (1980) is relevant, though our data suggest that 'interests' can be generalized and lead to generalized adaptations.

They are, however, the result of active engagements by individuals. Pupils are not passive recipients of organizational imprints. The demands of the organization have to be monitored in accordance with personal aspirations. We find attempts, therefore, to transform reality, to legitimate accommodations, to acquire a little more control, in short, to redefine the situation in accordance with their interests. Prominent among these concerns are the desire for *status, competence,* and *relationships,* linked by the need to re-establish identity. We have seen, for example, the anxiety about friends during the transition; the probings of the 'honeymoon' and 'coming-out' stages; the establishment of co-operative groups and (for girls) 'best friend' relationships; and we have noted how these not only function as counselling and succouring agents but also minister to one's identity concerns. The final phase of the transition, in which pupils eventually come to terms with the new institution, involves working out in more detail the

108

conditions of these relationships and the rules of group membership.

By the third term of the first year, pupils are on their way after the trial runs and false starts of the previous two terms. During this phase, they become more sophisticated and more complex beings. They have learnt one of the most valuable lessons in life – the art of adaptability, how to maximize one's interests in an environment where some of the elements, at least, are not always conducive to their realization, while others help to shape those interests.

Their successful negotiation of the passage is symbolized by the preparations being made for the imminent arrival of the next cohort. The cycle encapsulated within the process of transfer is about to begin again. Soon they will cease to be 'first years', let alone new arrivals, and anxiety and perplexity will give way to new-found confidence. This cycle is matched by developments in the school year, though the two do not coincide. For in the second half of the summer term, there is a general air of relaxation in the school, especially after the examination period. Sports' days, field trips, camping excursions leaven the more serious academic pursuits, and add to the sense of 'end of season'.

It remains to substantiate this argument. In the next two chapters therefore, we shall consider aspects of pupils' consolidated adaptations. We have foregone the formal/informal separation that we have undertaken hitherto, for, by this stage, we feel they have become inextricably linked in certain important respects. This matches the logic of this transition, for successful passage through it involves, above all, resolution of dilemmas set up by the interaction between formal and informal orders.

What, then, are the characteristics of this final phase? Chiefly, this is a matter of firmer knowledge and attitudes, and increased sophistication in deploying strategies to secure one's aims. We see the latter particularly in bids for status and control, in the use of joking, in the creation of personal space and time, in adjusting to work or work-avoidance strategies, and in the accommodation of symbols such as school uniform. The pupil cohort becomes increasingly distinguished by divisions as individuals and groups make their adaptations. We shall consider boys and girls in turn, because the gender factor leads to one of the most distinctive divisions.

Boys

Deviance among the boys is clearly shown in attitudes toward school and teachers. Among those who had taken an oppositional stance, their attitudes had hardened. School was 'rubbish', 'boring', 'dead'. Teachers were 'boring', some you 'got tired of' or 'couldn't stand', some 'yacked on and on.' This can be contrasted with the more tolerant line taken by other pupils who felt more happily involved with their teachers. It is, also, a more advanced kind of relationship than they have enjoyed with teachers hitherto.

Mark: I have got to know my teachers better than the ones in middle school.

Simon: Yes, I mean we are getting older now, we are starting to mix in with the
          adults. . . . When you are younger they tower over you and you are sort of
          scared of them. I tower over Miss Smith now, she is really small.

By contrast, pupils like Pete and Roy felt that some very troubled and
negative relationships had been established.

Pete: In technical studies, that bloke hates me. . . . Rubbish teacher. Our humani-
          ties teacher, he's a bore out he is. I ain't never done any homework for him in
          my life.

Roy: Mrs Gales has us for reading, fat cow!

Pete: She's too old – ain't she – too old to be a teacher. So's Mr Granger. I hate him,
          he really is old-fashioned and I hate old-fashioned people . . . Mr Jones, he
          needs winding up.

The pupils engaged in some new strategies of deviance in this summer
term. Perhaps the most extreme was 'skiving' off from school generally, or
from particular lessons. This is a strategy that did not appear very
frequently among the first year pupils, and only the most deviant attempted
it. Roy was the only boy to do so, and Andy successfully told a lie to cover
his whereabouts. More popular was 'homework avoidance', usually by
doing it very quickly, which met the rule while disregarding quality. Pupils
continued to employ centre-stage challenges, some of the boys becoming
more adroit at timing them, and more daring in their use of them. These
challenges now were used against permanent teachers, who had revealed
themselves exploitable in discipline terms.
   Jokes became a popular centre-stage challenge. Boys learnt how to inject
them into the flow of classroom discourse. So when a giant named 'Bogey'
appears in a humanities lesson, Dominic dubbed him 'Green with envy'.
The joke is an astringent weapon for pupil resistance (see Beynon 1984,
Willis 1977, Woods 1979). In skilful hands, it can successfully divert the
general direction of a lesson.

T: What is a river?

Matthew: It's got water in it (class laughs)

T: So has a tap (class laughs). Is that the same?

Matthew: Just about.

T: Well, what can you tell me about the Thames?

Matthew: It's wet.

In this example the teacher wanted to discuss the life history of a river, and
the changes it makes in its path from source to sea. The jokes made it

difficult for the teacher to keep the class's attention to the line of thought she wished to pursue. It was, therefore, a successful centre-stage challenge.

In a French lesson, pupils had to do a 'shopping expedition' exercise. Bill sat bored at the back of the class. He snored loudly, which gained the full attention of the class. Everyone laughed. The teacher decided her best strategy was to attempt to involve Bill.

> T: Alright, you come and do the shopping.
>
> Bill: I don't need nothing.
>
> T: Then be quiet in your corner.
>
> Bill: In my corner! That sounds like I'm mental.

Thus do pupils sharpen their powers of repartee. It is one of the chief survival mechanisms – some of these pupils will literally 'live by their wits'. Some boys in fact developed a particular skill in joking, and they were accorded a certain status. Like all jokers, they were people of special worth, particularly if they had a strong line in repartee (Klapp 1949). If the joke has a slight sexual connotation, and the teacher is a woman, the status is even higher.

> T: Make a knot in the end of that string.
>
> Sean: How do you get knotted, miss?

But the jokes serve other functions as well as winning status for the individual perpetrator and neutralizing the power differential. For they can also transform reality. Jokes can transform a boring lesson into an interesting one, or they can bring what the pupils might perceive as pretention down to earth in the common elements of their own culture. For example, one teacher, in a humanities lesson, was speaking of the difficulties Scott and his expedition had experienced, on their journey to the Antarctic, in keeping their teams of animals well fed and healthy.

> Stuart: Feed them on Pedigree Chum.

In the French shopping expedition, the teacher asked pupils the names of the packets and jars she had brought into the classroom.

> T: Qu'est que c'est?
>
> Bill: That's Sugar Puffs!

This amused the rest of the class greatly.

The jokes also represent the attempt by the pupils to assert their own, twentieth century, adolescent, media-oriented reality against an alienating and irrelevant subject. It may be viewed as a demand for relevance.

One day the teacher asked me where we got our groceries – in French, that is – and for a laugh I said 'Sainsbury's'.

Some teachers could manipulate jokes to their own advantage, others could not. The latter might find their position in the classroom eroded by pupil jokes. One teacher, for example, explained a mathematical theory. She explained it very thoroughly, and it meant she occupied the centre stage for a long time. She finished brightly:

T: So you could go on doing the square of numbers for ever and ever and ever.

David: Amen.

His timing was perfect, and the class collapsed into sustained laughter, after which it was difficult for the teacher to restore the situation.

Pupils, especially the deviants, had refined their 'work avoidance' strategies by this stage. They continued to exploit and extend the space around lessons in various ways. It was an especially fruitful tack if there was a lot of equipment to get out at the beginning of a practical lesson.

Sean Carpenter was especially good at this, and used it frequently. Sean in a needlework lesson, shows the teacher his hands, which are filthy from playing football in the mud. He asks permission to wash them, but takes so long he earns a reprimand. When asked what he thinks he is doing, Sean acknowledges 'dossing around'. Sean asks if he can open the window one July day, when the weather is hot. He is given permission, and this gives him the space and time to move from his seat and the window. He can fuss around opening it, and then really elaborate the procedure by pretending to fall out of it.

Allan would be systematically slightly late for lessons, always the last to enter the room, taking his time on the walk to the next classroom, gaining a few extra minutes. Usually he has a good sense of just how long he can afford to take. Allan mistimes his entrance to a science lesson, he is always slightly late, as we have said, but one day he gets it wrong, takes too long and is cautioned, 'Where have you been?'. he makes an excuse, but the form of the teacher response is interesting, 'Well, I think you had better do that in your own time'. School seems to be creating a new division of time for the pupils: time that is their own, and time that school has a claim upon.

The end of a lesson could sometimes be used in a similar fashion by some first year pupils. Pete, Roy, Allan and Keith most usually would look at their watches, and stop working and pack up their books and equipment a few minutes before the end of a lesson. This was especially noticeable at the end of the afternoon. Alan tried another strategy sometimes:

Three minutes before the end of the lesson Allan asks for permission to leave the room to go to the loo. The teacher refuses, making a joke out of it 'You can hang on three minutes. Remember you are British'. Allan would presumably not have come back at the end of the lesson, simply creating extra time of his own around the lunchtime break.

Pete, Roy, Andrew and Keith attempted to take this strategy further. One day a supply teacher took a craft lesson. They heard the bell, and under cover of the confusion and noise in the metalwork room, they took themselves off. The supply teacher discovered their absence, and as she happened to be the head of the craft department's wife, she reported this to him. This brought a far more serious reprimand than usual. The pupils concerned were threatened with the cane, received detention, and were never seen to attempt it again. The teachers generally objected very strenuously to this pupil tactic. As the humanities' man said, 'They got into packing up before the end of a lesson. I wasn't having that. About every three weeks they need pulling up sharply about something or other'. Thus, although there were no more attempted take-overs on the scale of those of the second term, probes for further purchases of time and space were made regularly.

There were also attempts to gain space and time outside lessons:

> In an English lesson, the class was asked to describe a typewriter. Pete insisted with great strength and sincerity that he had never seen a typewriter, and could not therefore describe it. He asked to be allowed to go to the commerce rooms of the school and look at one. Andrew asked to be allowed to go with him, on the same grounds. The commerce department was in fact on the very opposite side of the school. They were both allowed to go. When they finally returned, Pete said to John, 'Yes, course I've seen a typewriter, me mum's got one'. His strategy has allowed him 'time out' of the lesson, of the work activity. In this context, the researcher could be useful too. Pupils were pleased to be taken out of humanities lessons for interviewing. Usually they chose the lesson they liked the least.

Pupils continued to disrupt the official reality and redefine situations by 'mucking about' in lessons. Inevitably, the opportunities were greater in craft lessons. In an art lesson, for example, the teacher brought in a number of unusual objects for the pupils to draw – animals' teeth, bones, and a dried chicken's foot, which Pete took, pulling the sleeve of his jersey down over his hand so that he appeared to have a chicken's foot instead of a hand. He then lunged around the room, clawing near the girls' faces and producing screams of disgust.

Some strategies are viewed as being far more seriously challenging than others. Kevin placed 'mucking about' fairly high on this scale. He commented, 'We just have a laugh, we never really muck around'. Roy made a comment on the joking activity that goes on. His assessment was, 'Allan just sits there and makes a joke, that's about it. He didn't ask for it, he didn't do nothing to get caned'.

'Skiving off' is seen as a far more major act then joking. As we have noted, too, there are curriculum variations here. Pupils were far more willing to be deviant in foreign languages, music and craft subjects than they were, for example, in maths or English. Status of subject, therefore, affects the seriousness scale. Mucking about in home economics might be far less serious than 'talking a bit' in maths, for instance, and a pupil who went so far as to skive off maths or English as opposed to music would be making a very definitive statement. It was also a fact that more deviance occurred in lessons run by women teachers than by men, although clearly the curriculum affects this. A woman teaching maths is likely to meet less resistant strategies than a woman teaching home economics.

Mostly, it was the deviants who employed these work-avoidance strategies. The conformists, as we have noted in Chapter 3, by and large behaved differently. For example, in the top stream maths group, no centre-stage challenges were made, despite the fact that the top stream was over-populated and made for a very crowded room. Nor was there any mucking about. There was some talking, but mostly about the task while the pupils were working alone.

The conformists continued to show a high level of interest in their work and in doing well. They went on answering teachers' questions throughout the school year, when the 'forest of hands' syndrome had long died away. They were the pupils specified when teachers commented, 'Always the same hands going up'. Conformists handed in their homework, on which they had spent time and effort. They maintained their concern about the appearance and presentation of their books and their work. The contrast between conformist and deviant was illustrated while the pupils stood outside waiting for their French lesson. Phillip and Matthew rehearsed the new verbs they had learnt the previous lesson. Pete and Roy discussed records and clothes they had bought during the weekend.

We have seen how a competitive ethic developed among the 'conformist' boys about work. But there was more than status within the group involved – competence at work was also a matter of self-esteem. They wanted to do well irrespective of others' work. There was a general concern about work, about getting things right, about doing things properly. Phillip talked of his desire 'to get things right, you know you've made a good job of it, you feel alright'. In the third term of the year, Phillip was asked how the year had been. His response dealt firstly and in a most detailed way with the issue of work. 'It's been easy, because what we did in Hayes, we haven't done some of that yet – in maths especially'. Phillip was asked if he was happy with how he was doing:

> Phillip: I wasn't happy with that last maths mark, 90 per cent. I think I should have
> done better, got higher, but I didn't. My dad always expects something like
> 92–94 per cent, but it is hard to get up to it. It's mostly my dad. When I
> come home and said I got 90 per cent, I said dad won't be very pleased, and
> she goes, 'I wouldn't mind getting 90 per cent, I never got anything like it at
> school'.

Strong parental influence is clearly indicated here.

Other pupils showed a willingness to put their work first, and even to give up doing things so that their work should not suffer. Roger, for example, gave up playing the trumpet, because he was afraid that it took too much time away from his work. When questioned about this, he admitted that trumpet practice usually took about a half hour each day. We shall have more to say about conformists in the following chapter.

Girls

No girls expressed the same kind of total opposition to school as did some of the boys. Much of their opposition to school showed up in different forms from the boys, and it rarely brought 'trouble' to them (see Llewellyn 1980, Fuller 1980, Spender and Sarah 1980). Most of their strategies can be listed under 'work avoidance' categories. Girls could quietly daydream and chat a lesson away, unchecked by a teacher, who might be preoccupied with some of the boys' disruptions.

Some teachers made this semi-official: 'You can have a little dream, but not a little talk'. Some girls would stop and daydream, work for two or three minutes, stop and chat, work, sit and draw pictures, examine contents of pencil cases, discuss a new hair style, discuss things they could see out of the window. None of this would bring any rebuke from the teacher. In one maths lesson, Ros never concentrated for a longer time-span than 45 seconds. The average length of time that she 'worked' was 30 seconds. At other times the girls would sit apparently absorbed in what they were doing. But they were not working. In one lesson, Valerie sat quietly drawing a very elaborate pattern, which she then carefully coloured in.

Like the boys, girls tried to 'make space' for themselves in lessons. Rebecca, for example, was usually late for French lessons. Bridget got up to throw something in the waste-paper basket, but stayed on her feet for a long time, talking to people at different desks, and wandering up to the teacher to complain of toothache. She made no disruption to the whole class, received no reprimand, and again a girl had very effectively created space for her own concerns. Another popular way of doing this was 'going to the loo'. Valerie, for example, was once gone for over twenty minutes, yet was not challenged when she quietly re-entered the room, resumed her seat, her chatting and her daydreaming. An important feature of girls' work-avoidance strategies was to get a modicum of work done in order to avoid trouble. If a pupil fell too far behind the others, it could lead to disciplinary measures being taken, and comments like 'Ros you are trailing behind the others', or 'Bridget, sometimes you don't get anything down in your book at all'.

Getting enough of the work done involved a range of sub-strategies – usually getting other people to do some of the work for you. This depended either upon established friendship links or upon manipulation of those who were academically able. Amy became very good at this. She managed, for example, to get her new friend Claire to cut out all her work in woodwork. Ros also told the researcher that Rebecca did all her maths homework for her in the course of a needlework lesson. It was clear that the 'best friend' bond enabled pupils to break the normal rules of co-operative activity. Best friends did 'copy' homework from each other, five minutes before the lesson began, and shared answer-giving telephone conversations in the evenings. The other strategy involved using those who were high on the academic hierarchy and known to be conformist. Janet, for example, sewed Rebecca's rag doll for her, while Lucy finished off her puppet.

Sometimes a teacher did the work for them. If a pupil fell too far behind the others, it could make it difficult to keep to the teacher's whole timetable for the class. Sometimes the easiest thing to do, therefore, was simply to complete the work for the girl involved. For example, Mr Davies finished off Bridget's sculpture so that the whole class could begin the next new project together.

The passive nature of much of this work avoidance was complemented by the display of a quality of shy quietness. In a German class, for example, Mr Brandt asked Amy and Valerie a question, based on their homework. Neither of the girls had done the homework, so could not answer the question. They sat, silent and looking shy and demure. The teacher sighed and asked someone else. The girls had 'got away' with it. This was the teacher who had caned another pupil, Bob, for not knowing the answer, and for not having done his homework. Shy embarrassment is signalled as an acceptable quality for girls, to such an extent that it obscures their deviance, at least with male teachers.

We suggest that the presentation of a passive front, which was common among all the girls, was in fact an active statement in the construction of a feminine identity. Centre-stage challenges, loud disruptions and class-wide jokes seemed to be exclusively a male preserve, as did the noisier forms of 'messing around'. There were a few girls who attempted such activities and who, in consequence, faced sanctions not only from teachers but from the boys, who viewed such behaviour as non-feminine. In one instance, Christine and Valerie took out a mirror with a picture of Elvis Costello on it, and discussed it, although they had just been asked to begin some new work. The boys noticed, but did not comment on the activity, suggesting that for them it was unexceptionable female behaviour. Later in the same lesson, Christine and Valerie began flicking pen-tops around the room. This did bring comments from several boys: 'Oh, that's stupid'. 'What's that supposed to be?' Thus the boys denied the girls' right to muck about in this fashion.

Lynn Davies (1978) asserts that girls see their level of deviance as being as great as the boys', but they also clearly see it as different. Pupils identified the differences. Emma reported: 'In science the boys get told off more than the girls – they just chatter and giggle'. Janet agreed, 'Some of the girls in our class, whisper and giggle, but the boys are the ones who make remarks out loud . . .' In a year of observing pupils, there were almost no examples of centre-stage challenges by girls. The one example that came to the researcher's attention is instructive. In reply to the music teacher's 'Come along, have you all finished?' Janie replied loudly, 'I don't know till I have a look'. But Janie only brought sanctions upon herself for such acts. The boys described her as 'having a big mouth' or as 'mouthy'. Several of the boys stated, 'I can't stand her' or 'She gets on my nerves'. She had exceeded the bounds of feminine propriety as the boys saw it (see also Llewellyn 1980 and Spender and Sarah 1980). Needless to say, such sanctions act as powerful socializing agencies on girls in general, and contribute towards the tendency for girls and women to withdraw from the public verbal arena and to be seen as overdoing things in the private arena by talking and gossiping too much. Jenny Shaw (1980), for example, has suggested that girls will respond to such sanctions, but again passively: 'Girls withdraw from the danger zones, where their presence simply invites abuse' (ibid, p. 73).

Teachers did little to check girls' work-avoidance strategies. We have suggested that this was mainly because, by comparison with the boys' more ostentatiously disruptive tactics, the girls' strategies were practically invisible. The effect of contrasting tactics by boys and girls became clear in the French lesson, where the boys really did disrupt the class. The teacher was forced to address all of her direct method style questions to them to keep the quiet. The tactic was effective. The girls sat and talked quietly, daydreamed – and were ignored. All of this supports the view on girls, that:

> Their non-participation can take many forms, few of which are disruptive. They rarely seek to impose their dissatisfaction on the whole class, but will elect to withdraw in a variety of unostentatious ways. Girls are less likely to create chaos, if required to endure something they are not interested in.
>
> (Spender and Sarah 1980, p. 152)

As Spender and Sarah (1980, p. 105) note, 'Boys are the source of fun and laughter, but also the confusion. The dynamics of the classroom are radically affected by the presence of boys. Even a seasoned teacher can be dictated to by the dominant elements of the class'. Denscombe (1980a) has noted how teachers are predominantly concerned about 'noise' and many have observed the lengths to which teachers will go to 'avoid confrontation' (A. Hargreaves 1979, Stebbins 1970, D. Hargreaves *et al.* 1975, Bird *et al.* 1981).

There may be an additional reason for teachers doing little to check the girls' strategies. Girls 'get upset'. The headmaster commented: 'One is always picking up the bits'; he also said, 'You get flocks of girls going round to complain to the Head of House about Mr X and Mr Y'. Teachers tried hard to avoid 'upsetting' the girls. For example, when Rebecca was, for once, challenged by her teacher for walking aimlessly around the room, she showed signs of distress, claiming that she had lost a book. Not only did she avoid a reprimand, but captured the aid of the teacher, who appealed to the rest of the class for help!

If a teacher failed to placate an upset girl, the pupil might take things a stage further and complain to the counselling staff.

> Pete Brandt told off a girl yesterday, of course she was in here, hysterical, couldn't speak, had to be calmed down . . . now he didn't realise it was just the fact she had

problems and 'Light the blue touchpaper and ... he forgot to stand back basically'.

Women teachers were, on occasions, equally culpable. Mrs Gates, for example, in one lesson challenged Christine's passive resistance and persistently nagged her. 'You haven't done much today Christine'. 'Will you start working'. 'Will you stop talking'. There was a stream of such comments, to an increasingly flushed and angry Christine. The pupil began to 'answer back', supported by her friend, Barbara. Finally, Mrs Gates lost her temper with Christine, who kept wandering around the class with a number of vague excuses. Mrs Gates eventually smacked her, as she would a small child. Christine was furious. Later, she complained to the counselling staff, and the relationship between the two was very difficult from then on. this illustrates another feature of girls' resistance – the 'insolent answer' or 'insolent silence' if the initial passivity is challenged. We only observed this kind of insolence in *response* to such a challenge.

The other major area of girls' deviance was organized by intruding subjects of importance within youth culture into the formal setting of the school. School uniform was adapted in accordance with current fashion. For example, Ros one day wore a blouse that had only a tenuous association with school uniform regulations. It was the right colour, but it was elasticated around the neck, without the requisite collar, and was a peasant style, with embroidery. On warm days, Ros was to be seen wearing the blouse pulled down on to her shoulders. School equipment was also subjected to such influences. Pupils like Janet continued to use standard equipment, plain dark-green pencils, and simple ball-tip pens. However, many girls selected from a wider range of equipment commercially available, and when anything new was brought to school, it roused great interest. There were rulers with Mr Men figures. Mandy had a pencil with a koala bear head, whose furry ears caused much comment. Barbara had some bright red and orange pens with curved ends which tapered to a point, and with animal faces painted on. Another girl had a pen in the shape of a bright orange plastic carrot. Mandy drew a face on one end of it. Ros had three pencil sharpeners, one in the form of a Pepsi tin, the other a globe, the third a piano. We have already indicated that pencil cases were significant objects. Fur fabric seemed to be the most popular thing to use, closely followed by blue denim. The denim ones often had two patch pockets on the outside in a mimicry of jeans.

A very important item in the teenage girl's identity and relationships was the 'rough book'. Special subject exercise books were not at this stage 'messed with', but rough books were. Girls wrote all over their rough book covers, and also inside it. Later, when the covers were entirely obliterated by graffiti, they covered the rough book with a poster of some kind, which gave it a fresh surface. This meant that the graffiti could change fairly rapidly, mirroring the shifting relationships and interests that occurred. The two most popular topics were boys' names and rock groups. Ros's rough book, for example, was covered with a poster of Blondie, and the inscription 'Blondie Rules O.K.' The possession of a decorated rough book was a signal perhaps of interest in the informal culture. Ros attempted to involve Sally in this activity, and wrote 'Sally likes?' on her rough book. Sally looked cross and rubbed it out, signalling perhaps a wish to be 'out' of such activities.

Some of the girls staked out strategic sites in the classroom, from which they could view fashion, boys and other objects of interest outside the room. On one occasion, the class had a double period of music. The music room was at a crossroads in the school buildings, so that when the first period ended, a number of pupils had to pass by the windows of the music room. Amy and Ros left their friends and positioned themselves at the table next to the window. There they watched and commented on the older pupils, especially the boys, as they passed. The clothes and shoes of older female pupils were also discussed. This was a frequent activity. In science, Amy, Rebecca and Rosemary sat near the window. They noticed a boy they were all interested in, and pointed him out to each other, 'Look, there's Richard'. they gave him their full attention, totally ignoring the lesson. This could in fact lead to 'trouble' from the teacher. When Christine, Barbara and Kerry did the same thing in humanities, and waved exuberantly to their friends, Mrs Gates gave them a detention. Barbara explained how they had gone too far: 'It was because people waved out of the window to their mates'.

The girls, in fact, had a range of devices to secure their ends. In an art lesson, for example, a girl from another form came in briefly. She whispered to Amy, 'I only come in here to see Roy'. She had an official excuse for an unofficial purpose, which often counted for more among the girls' interests. The informal culture, in fact, often provided consolation for the unwelcome demands of some of the school's formal culture. 'Oh, boring maths' signed Amy. 'It's the disco tonight, though', she chirped.

The growing pull of the informal culture was also reflected in changing attitudes towards food, and especially to school dinners. While at middle school, the pupils had reacted favourably to the school meal they had eaten when visiting the secondary school, but this view changed fairly rapidly for many girls once at the upper school. By the middle of May, girls like Amy, Ros and Rebecca, who were most interested in the informal culture, were refusing to eat 'school dinners'. Ros said it was like her dog's dinner, and her dog's meat was 'horrible'. Instead, despite their parents' expressed wishes, the girls bought food from the ice-cream van which toured the school playground each lunchtime. Amy told how Rosemary and Rebecca came to her house for lunch, her parents being out. They each had an ice-cream and a Mars bar from the ice-cream van, their usual midday meal.

There was *one* area in which some girls were most deviant than the boys at this stage. By the middle of the summer term, some girls had begun to truant from school. To begin with, pupils simply did not 'turn up' for things. One example was when Anna, Kerry and Bridget 'were supposed to turn up for an extra humanities lesson, we had detention, and me, Kerry and Anna didn't turn up – we went down Kerry's house first.' These pupils had in fact been threatened with 'the slipper' by one of the senior staff for their actions, but had not been given it. They shortly went on to fully fledged truanting. One day, for example, Anna and Bridget went home at lunchtime and threatened not to return for afternoon school, saying they would watch the Derby on television. Bridget did so, though she was caught. 'I skived, but I got caught, this boy brought in a note for me, but there was too many mistakes'. Truanting caused severe 'trouble' with teachers, and it was much too extreme for most pupils. Amy, for example, commented, 'I can't stand Anna Dean, she skived off school, and her sister helped her do it'.

By and large, the girls' perspectives on teachers were the same as the boys. They liked teachers who could control, have a laugh, were understanding and so forth. But there were some additional issues that were important to the girls, deriving from their informal culture. Mr Brandt, for example, was unpopular with all pupils for a number of reasons, but the girls had additional cause:

> Pat: I don't really like Mr Brandt. He makes you feel horrible, do you know what I mean? . . . He is always on about sex, he is always talking about it; when you get up and say ein, zwei, drei, like that, and he goes 'Oh this is my favourite number 'sex', and he is always talking about it. This girl came into our class yesterday, and he said 'I don't think you are dressed properly' to us, and 'she is' to her. She had a low neck on down to here, and the other girls all had buttons high up to here, and I just . . .
>
> Rebecca: He's really dirty, he's always on about sex and that. My sister went on a German exchange with him and she said he was always in the pro-houses.
>
> Amy: He's always on about page 3 in the 'Sun' an' that, and girls. My dad, he'll make comments about things, just for a laugh, he don't go on and on about it like him. I don't like it.

There are some very clear notions about sexual propriety and morality involved here. Yet Mr Brandt was contrasted with Mr Hill, who although he did some very explicit flirting was forgiven for it. Mr Hill always addressed one sixth form girl named Erica as 'Hey Erotica'. He would walk with his arm around the shoulders of a younger girl who was upset, but there were no sanctions on him. Mr Hill was 'one for the girls' but they 'had always liked him'. He was young, and good-looking, had a good sense of humour, he flirted with them, and they responded. In a sense, he was an 'honorary' member of their culture in a way that Mr Brandt could never be.

Some girls formed a strong feeling for a particular teacher. Joy blushed furiously when Mr Namier entered the room, and all the girls at her table looked across at her. He came into the room several times during the lesson to pick up equipment and Joy had the same reaction each time.

Girls would sometimes use their own sexual attractiveness to win their way out of trouble and to practice their developing femininity, as when Janie lost her German book. She adopted a certain pose, and eyed her young male teacher coyly. 'Please don't tell me off, I've lost my German book. I've searched high and low for it. Do you want 10p for it?' Janie produced 10p, but was given a new book and 'let off'. The boys, by contrast, did not practise similar strategies with their female teachers, nor did they acknowledge any sexual attraction for them.

Some male teachers seemed to minister more to the boys' informal culture, with a certain confidential mateyness, which bade perhaps for 'honorary' membership of 'the lads', with considerable earthy humour. The boys may have appreciated this, but the girls certainly did not. One teacher, for example, told them once how he was ill, he had diarrhoea, could 'spew up' all over them. He was a laugh, but sometimes took things too far.

Vivien: (He told us) he was swearing and had got a headache . . . fancy telling us that. We don't want to know his private life and what he's got.

Tina: He goes – Oh I have had my hair cut today, have you noticed?

Another time, Mr Saxon dealt with a poem in which a boy caught worms. He went into a long, graphic description of the symptoms of the disease, which made the boys laugh. However, the girls were embarrassed. Tina nudged Joy, and they both turned around to nod meaningfully to the researcher about the incident.

The girls equally had expectations of their female teachers, who above all, they considered, should be 'properly' feminine. When Miss Blanche on a snowy, February day wore a frilled, yellow cotton skirt, with a primrose roll-neck cotton sweater, a darker yellow Indian cotton waistcoat, and yellow open sandals with stiletto heels, Rosemary giggled and observed, 'She looks like a walking banana'. Miss Blanche also wore a great deal of eye make-up, and the same strictures applied to her as to them. Her appearance led to allegations of a range of sexual activities on Miss Blanche's part. Carol thought she was having an affair with Mr Davies. She said they were always together, always holding hands. 'They make it really obvious', and 'He is married with three kids'.

Yet, equally, a teacher who disregarded fashion and seemed unconcerned about her appearance could also meet with sanctions. As Delamont (1976) has pointed out, all the clothes-consciousness of the adolescent girl in school uniform will concentrate on the style of dress and physical appearance of teachers. Mrs Lines, for example, taught science, and was very generally disliked by the pupils. For one thing, she 'always wore trousers', no doubt taken as an allusion to the masculinity of the stereotypical female science teacher (see Ebbutt 1981). As for 'that lady we have for metalwork, she wears anything for a laugh.' Interference with what the girls regarded as legitimate behaviour might also be put down to feminine inadequacy. Thus Janie was very irate at a remark from Mrs Gates to 'stop flirting with the boys' when she was just being friendly to Paul. The reason, as Janie saw it, was that 'boys don't talk to her.'

Miss Blanche, on the other hand, was ultra-feminine – on the right lines mostly, but she could take things too far. It was clear that there had to be a middle way. Issues of sexual modesty were crucial.

Pat: I asked Mrs Cornway if we could make dresses in needlework and she said No, and one of the reasons is because you have got boys in the group, and if you made dresses, you would have to come in, in your bra and knickers and just try on bits of dresses, and even if you went to the toilets to try it on, you would still have to come back, and you'd have the dress off, unpinned, and you'd be embarrassed by it.

The curriculum and pupil identity

As we have noted, not all subjects attracted an equal amount of deviance. Pupils were far more willing to be deviant, and to engage in the strongest actions, in the low priority areas of the curriculum, for example, music. Maths and English always saw less deviance. By the end of the year, it was possible to map out an explanation of this. Pupils needed to balance formal and informal concerns. Subjects such as maths and English were seen instrumentally by them as being of high, marketable value; hence the formal concerns predominated. It seems that when a subject is rated as being of low value, then the informal concerns surface and are played out. This does not mean that a subject like music is of no value for pupils. Conversely, it is a useful resource for the playing out of pupil's informal interest. Objecting to school music enabled pupils to signal their interest in adolescent subcultural music, for example.

Pupils could use areas of the curriculum to make statements about their priorities, and their preferences for the informal as opposed to the formal culture of the school. Identities were established in these ways. This can perhaps best be illustrated by reference to data taken from pupils about the science area of the curriculum, where gender-based identities are much involved. Boys objected to the domestic sciences, and girls to the physical ones.

We have already illustrated the deviant actions that occurred in home economics lessons. Pete and Roy described the 'real rolics' they had in that lesson. Clearly their activities there were far beyond mere 'mucking around'. The girls saw the boys' activities there as worth describing:

Rebecca: The boys don't like needlework.

Sally: They always muck around more with a lady teacher, they are not as strict as the men, like in cooking, they can get away with a lot more. Pete and Roy, they are always mucking around with Amy in there.

Amy: In cooking they got moved; we had to make cheese on toast, and set the table, and we got marks for it (so it was a more serious activity). Their table was everywhere, and they all had this sauce round their mouths.

The boys were willing to engage in more extreme work-avoidance strategies there than elsewhere. Pete, for example, boasted, 'I ain't brought my fabrics money, I have paid for art, that's all.'

R: Why haven't you brought the money for fabrics?

Pete: Come on, it's rubbish. Look, we have to bring our money in for it, don't we, and we have to buy our own material as well. I never use anything – I only get round to drawing it, and then go on to something else. I ain't doing my mum out of 75p for a load of rubbish.

Pete basically removed himself from real participation in this lesson.

Our suggestion is that the boys' deviance was related to the fact that they were asked to do something they did not regard as appropriately masculine:

Roy: I can't sit for an hour and watch a woman making pastry like that, it's boring, isn't it?

David: Boys don't do needlework.

Keith: It's cissy.

Ian: Girls have got better hands.

Keith: I don't really like doing needlework, as much as other things like cutting up rats.

It is interesting that Keith chose the notorious and symbolic rat for his example of a 'properly' masculine phenomenon. The boys made clear proscriptive statements about domestic science: it contravened their sense of gender identity.

On the other hand, a subject such as home economics does offer considerable opportunities for the expression of gender identities in the informal area. There are taps to turn on loudly, and elecrical switches with buzzers attached to set off at inappropriate moments. There is food to steal and eat, cake mixture to throw around and daub on other boys' noses and hair.

The girls did not find themselves drawn to the activities in their physical science lessons. Throughout the year their animosity to science intensified. It is important to understand what their objections were. The girls protested about the nasty smells in the science lessons. One day, their experiments involved smelling chemicals. Jenny reported, 'I felt sick', and claimed she could not finish the work. Sally said the project gave her a headache, sufficiently bad for her to miss the disco that evening, which was serious indeed. Others found the activities unappealing and abhorrent:

Valerie: In science, we had that thermometer thing, and when we had to stick it in our mouths. . . . That was horrible. I was sick that night . . . I think I stuck it down me froat, too far, it was 'orrible.

The other dominant reaction was fear. The girls admitted to feeling fear, when confronted with the range of equipment and dangerous chemicals. Acids were especially threatening:

> You have got all of these acids, and you have got to remember which ones are harmful, and what they do to you. It is quite hard to do things, because I am scared of fire, and when I put on the bunsen burners, I am really scared of them, I always think I am going to go up on fire . . .

The fear of fire and of the bunsen burners was a recurrent theme.

Amy:　　　I think Ros is scared of the Bunsen burner.

Rebecca:　She is, when I had her for a partner, I did everything, she was too scared to do anything.

Once, when dealing with alkalis, the girls stood fearfully at arms' length from the experiment.

The girls also objected to the fact that they got very dirty in those lessons. In one experiment, they had to drop carbon into a solvent, and it produced a black substance that got all over their hands. It led to protests: Sally said, 'It made us really dirty'. The others agreed, with expressions of real disgust on their faces.

Ros:　I was scared it was going to burn right through my fingers, like some awful acid or something.

Another afternoon, pupils were working with eye droppers and Indian ink. Ros spilt some on her hand. She inspected it anxiously, complaining:

Ros:　Oh no! Look what I've done!

T:　　Oh, that'll come off in a few days.

Ros was not in the least appeased, and explained to Amy:

> Tonight I have to serve sweets at this little bazaar my mum is running. This won't look very good to people, will it?

The girls also stated that they felt squeamish and disgusted by some of the things they saw in science. The teacher showed the class a brain, preserved in a jar of formaldehyde. The girls displayed a really strong reaction to the brain, demonstrating again a sense of what was 'not nice'. The rat, which had a starring role in the stories told at middle school, was to make its appearance in the middle of the summer term. The girls displayed a squeamish sense of disgust and indignation at being asked to witness such impropriety.

Janet:　Just cutting up an egg made me feel ill, because it is a cell, and you see all the nucleus and the membrane. It's revolting. I haven't eaten an egg since.

Such activities are not only disgusting and objectionable to girls, they are labelled as specifically masculine as well. Girls signal their differences.

> Jane: I think science is a boy's subject, most of the science teachers are men, aren't they? I think the reason why they are male teachers is because of cutting up rats. I don't think a woman could face that.

Girls also commented on the difficulties they had in handling and controlling some of the scientific equipment. Ros just could not cope with the microscope. She insisted repeatedly, 'I just don't understand this, just don't'. She spent the entire lesson, floating round the room, seeking aid and assistance and, incidentally, ensuring that everyone knew she could not deal with this piece of equipment. Yet such hesitancy was not evident in all subjects. In domestic science, in her needlework lessons, Ros, despite her incompetence with microscopes, was one of the first pupils to grasp the workings of the double-needle electric sewing machine. Similarly, there was no evidence of the fear of 'fire', and the bunsen burners that characterized physical science lessons, when it came to lighting the gas in cookery lessons, or dealing with hot ovens and sizzling frying pans there. It appears that girls have difficulty with some machinery. The difficulties are pronounced in curricular areas that are perceived as masculine.

The girls thus had a strong reaction to science. They had a clear perspective that it involved them in things that they did not feel it was appropriate or pleasant or inviting to do. The girls signalled their objections to the dirt, fumes and smells of science and also to being asked to look less attractive, for example when having to wear unisex goggles or tie their hair back. They displayed themselves as squeamish, frightened and weak by their objections, and as somewhat incompetent in relation to complex machinery as well. These activities in science contravened conventional views about what 'proper girls' should do, and therefore girls resisted doing them.

Both boys and girls read gender-related characteristics into domestic and physical sciences. Their response helps to make their sex-based identity clear to those around them. Our suggestion is that pupils actively used aspects of the school curriculum to construct their gender identities. They were not simply responding passively to the formal culture, but using these arenas as a resource in the informal culture. Expressing fear and revulsion was one strategy – they could also practise 'feminine' deviant behaviour to excess in these lessons. They were not, for example, 'melting plastic' and 'making excessive black fumes' as the boys did when messing about. Rebecca balanced a bottle of Tipp-Ex on Ros's head. Amy painted lip gloss all over Ros's face, then they tickled each other. Ros frequently took out a comb and did her hair in this lesson. Pamela reported that 'we just suck polos in science lessons.' Girls also included a lot of 'chatting' in these lessons, often on subject matter far removed from school science – perhaps what they would wear to the disco that evening.

Teachers, perhaps subconsciously, encouraged these gender identities, at times when they were manifestly trying to do the opposite. This was most apparent in design work, to which the girls objected as strongly as they did to science. The pupils were asked to solve some design problems during the course of a year, using a range of materials: paper, wood, plastic, metal and fabric. Apart from the fabric lessons, some of the girls resisted doing these problems on the grounds that they were not suitable for girls. The teacher attempted to deal with this by ntroducing an element of competition between boys and girls. However, later, another teacher entered and teased one girl over the tower she was making: 'That's the leaning tower of "Old Town" over there'. Here the girls were receiving two simultaneous, contradictory messages, one urging them to attempt the tasks, the other carrying heavy implications about their unsuitability for it. This was not an unusual occurrence. Even the design teacher, who tried to encourage them to develop attitudes to the subject comparable to those of the boys, later that week asked the girls specifically to move some delicate and fragile models, because girls were more careful than boys. Another design teacher, who taught technical drawing, pointedly made a loud fuss about the girls doing well in his subject, insisting that they could and should do so, and that there was no reason they could not do better than the boys. Yet, at the same time, this teacher made jokes about female incompetence with any type of machinery, and he frequently joked and made aspersions specifically about women being 'dreadful drivers'. Again two messages are being communicated to the girls. It indicates the extent to which teachers, whatever their intentions, are steeped in a gender-divisive culture.

◯ 8 ◯

Deviance, conformity
and knife-edging

In the summer, we noted a certain hardening of pupil identities along the lines of academic ability and orientation to school. Simultaneously, allegiances became more tightly knit, and more firmly differentiated, and, by this stage, outside-school interests were coming to have an increasing influence on them. The pupils had worked out, too, a concept of 'the normal (to them) pupil', and deviations were savagely derided. While this is true of both boys and girls, their personal and social development does differ in some important respects, and we shall therefore consider them separately.

Boys

The academic hierarchy

By this stage, pupils clearly knew who they were in terms of ability and knowledge – two of the main criteria in pupil status. Reputations for good or ill had been gradually built up over the year by the accumulation of grades and teacher comments. There were a number of key events that affected the perception of this academic hierarchy, which seemed to harden basic identity. 'Parent's evening' was one of these. The school chose not to give termly written reports. Rather, it had one evening in the year when parents were invited to the school to discuss their children's progress. Teacher comments were traded about between pupils and this was one way in which pupils acquired labels. However, the most serious development affecting the hardening of (academic) identities was streaming, which by the third term had taken place in maths, science and foreign languages. The pupils themselves were in no doubt about the meaning of streaming. For example, when the teacher indicated the streaming in German it produced a lot of reaction. The teacher attempted to smooth it out: 'The first group is for people who have worked a little bit harder'; Jack said loudly, 'And whether you are thick!'

Phillip reckoned he had a clear sense of everyone's placing and position in the class and as a result, he welcomed streaming.

If somebody is better than other people, and if it is just pot luck, you, you and you all in one class, which it is at the moment. There might be two, three, four bright ones and the rest are pretty dim and you are doing this work and you finish, and nobody else has finished, and the teacher won't have a lot of time to help you, when there are those others. At first in maths, things didn't go fast enough. Some people were pretty dim really, and you are on worksheet eleven, and they are back on seven. You are probably held up a bit.

On the whole, pupils had a shrewd idea of who fitted where in the academic hierarchy. For example, when the teacher announced the new streams for German, Alan said loudly 'Am I in the top group?' The whole class laughed. But pupils equally label themselves. Mark said 'Ten to one, I'm in the bottom group'. However, sometimes pupil assessment of other pupils could be at variance with that of their teacher. Erik and Giles were two examples of this. Pupils expressed surprise that they were not in the top group for anything. Phillip said of Giles, 'He always seemed very bright'. Pupils at the other end of the hierarchy agreed. Keith said of Erik:

Keith: He probably slipped out, there weren't enough room, but he should have been in there . . . because the work he is doing now is really easy for him. He is bored with what he's doing.

We have already suggested that the other major issue in terms of identity was that of attitude to school. Again, it was clear by this point what the major categories were and where individual pupils were located among them.

Phillip: There's gangs. There's Roy, Pete, Jim, Andy, Keith and Allan, that's one group. There's me, Stu, Nigel sometimes Erik, that's about it.

Phillip's group were 'pretty good', but as Pete said of his group, 'I suppose we are the kids that go to discos, and have a laugh and that aren't we'.

Academic identity and relationships

What effect did these now clearly established identities have upon inter-actions between pupils and relationships within groups of pupils? Co-operative groups continued to function for the class. A design teacher testified to their importance. 'I had a lad in my class this morning – very upset – in tears in fact. I pulled him up for not doing any work for at least three weeks and he said it was because he had no friends to work with, he had tried to work with two other boys but they wouldn't let him'. The basic rules that governed co-operative groups continued to operate without much change.

As facets of identity became ever more clearly established, then variations were observable. Phillip or Erik, for example, had for some time been seen to have ability in academic lessons, and were accustomed to being asked for help. However, both boys were self-confessedly 'hopeless' at art and design subjects. There, someone quite different might be given status and asked for help. Thus, to some degree, status within groups varied with different kinds of subject. Bill Stoop had low status in academic areas. However, he liked woodwork 'because I usually finish first, and I can help other people, and well most people come up to me and say "Come on help us", so I do.'

Nevertheless there were changes in the interaction that took place within these co-operative groups, largely caused by streaming. Streaming had two major discernible effects. In the first place it fragmented some alliances, so that pupils no longer had their established network upon which to rely. This created some problems. If a pupil had to ask for co-operative help from other pupils with whom he did not have proper links, then he employed a range of other tactics. Thus, in German, Simon came across to Erik from the other side of the room, and sat on Erik's desk. He picked up Erik's keys, and played with them. After chatting for a minute or two, and only then, he asked, 'What does No. 4 mean'? But Erik was aware that the rules were being broken, and prevaricated:

Erik: Yes well, you know, that's what it means. It means that. Yes, that's what it means.

Simon: Oh come on, what does it mean? Tell us.

Erik: (Hums and hahs, then finally he translates it.)

Although Simon again clearly needed help later in the lesson, he would not actually go and ask Erik again. Rather, he asked a number of other pupils.

Streaming put strains on many friendships. This was particularly true for the group which included Phillip, Erik, Giles and Stuart. Phillip was the only boy who was placed in the top stream for all subjects within this group. This led to a slackening of his relationships with the other boys, especially with Erik, who had previously always worked most closely with Phillip. Now in the top stream, Dominic, also there for all subjects, drew closer to Phillip, taking Erik's place.

There was one other unexpected effect of streaming. A perception of shared academic standing seemed to be able to overcome the rules on gender exclusions. There was an increased amount of interaction between boys and girls in the top stream. In one lesson, Lucy tried to borrow a pencil from Darren. He recognized that it broke the normal rules, therefore it could not have a simple answer: 'Yes, it's 10p an hour', he said, but he did give it to her. By June, there were new areas of cross-gender interaction, sometimes amounting to co-operation. For example, Phillip asked Emma if he could borrow some equipment, and she agreed. Elsewhere, Stuart and Janet discussed the length of the stories they were writing in English, and Lucy joined in. They were all in the top streams and all from fairly middle-class homes, except Phillip.

This kind of cross-gender interaction rarely happened in lower streams. One instance shows the differences rather clearly. In a needlework lesson,

Ian repeatedly asked Kerry for help with his work, thus going directly counter to the cross-gender rule. Other pupils were not slow to comment on the interaction between Ian and Kerry. 'Look at Ian, he's always asking her for help'. In fact, this action denoted the growing relationship between the two, which culminated in their 'going out' together.

In other instances, aid between members of different groups was traded on some hard bargaining terms and not in the matey spirit of the co-operative group. For example, Ian England and Don Cape discussed answers in a music lesson. Ian asked, 'What have you got for number two?'. Don replied, 'Give me number four first'. Sometimes the rewards were of a more subtle nature, involving power and status. For example, when John needed to borrow an eraser, and no one in his usual co-operative group in English had one, he was forced to venture outside the group. He asked Phillip, who began to play a kind of power game with him:

John: (points to the eraser) Can I borrow it?

Phillip: What? (although it is perfectly clear)

John: (picks up the eraser) Can I borrow it?

Phillip: What else?

John: Can I borrow your rubber – please?

He gave in to Phillip's demand for subservience but put a sting in the tail to register his own point: 'Your Highness, Sir'.

Some boys won the right to break the co-operative rules, as a result perhaps of their standing in the alternative status network we have called the macho hierarchy. There may have been something of this in the exchange noted above between John and Phillip. Roy was also able to use this to advantage. For example, Roy recognized that Barry was good at German, and on several occasions he leant back and looked at Barry's book, although in fact they were not members of the same co-operative group. Nevertheless, Roy felt he was strong enough to insist on these rights for himself. Barry was unlikely to accuse someone as large and tough as Roy of 'copying'. Keith also managed to establish a similar prerogative for himself. He acknowledged his own difficulties with maths, and said 'I ask Erik, he's a whiz kid, he tells me the answers'. Keith and Erik were by no means part of the same group, but Erik was unlikely to challenge Keith, and Keith knew it. Allan attempted to achieve the same position, but failed. He was regarded as highly deviant but not at all tough. When he looked at Martin's work and emanded an answer, Martin responded with anger and told him to remove himself, giving him the title 'Superbrain'. Clearly there were risks involved in the attempt to adopt this identity. It is interesting that, while Keith expected help from Erik, he was not willing to give anything in return. When Erik failed to understand something in a woodwork lesson, and asked Keith for help, Keith angrily refused: 'Oh go away Brainbox, you're always supposed to know everything. Do your own!' Clearly, these relationships were not based on any 'co-operative' principle.

The boys' friendship groups continued to be fairly stable throughout the year, in marked contrast to the girls'. The groups seemed in the view of the boys to be dependent upon shared and mutual interests. They continued to insist that they didn't have 'best friends', applying the term exclusively to the girls and giving it a feminine connotation. For them, the term would have to be 'best mate'. Even then, some boys saw objections to the idea of having a best mate, which were based upon elements of their new identity.

> Keith: It's not the best way to go about really. . . . They feel left out, and say you've
> got a girlfriend, how can you be with your best mate and your girlfriend at
> the same time.

At the same time that allegiances were more tightly forged, enmities became stronger. The boys separated into groups based on their attitude to school and the opposing claims of the adolescent culture. The groups were basically those identified by other research as conformist and deviant pupils. Boys sometimes expressed hostility towards others who had taken a different orientation. Pete, for example, said, 'I can't stand Phillip'. Sometimes there was actual aggression, especially involving highly deviant boys and those they considered too conformist. Certainly, by the third term, pupils with different orientations could no longer tolerate working together. Allan was placed through lack of space on the same table as Phillip and Erik. They were at the opposite pole of the academic hierarchy from each other and had contrasting orientations to school. Allan tried many of his repertoire of tricks, pulling silly faces and making silly noises. Erik looked blankly at him. Then Allan tried to start up a general conversation, without success. Phillip and Erik left Allan out completely. Clearly it cannot be easily assumed, as liberal educationists have tended to do, that the strong will help the weak in these situations.

The major objection the deviants had to the highly conformists was that they worked too hard. Andy, for example, said of Erik, 'It's just that he sort of loves school work – just keeps on doing it. I don't bother. I mean I do what they ask, and he does two times more'.

The other notion was that conformist boys were 'soft'. Roy made this explicit.

> R: What do you think of boys who work really hard?
>
> Roy: They're soft.
>
> R: What?
>
> Pete: I couldn't sit there and work all day.
>
> R: You worked quite hard in maths today.
>
> Pete: I don't strain meself!

The notion that working hard and doing well at school meant you were regarded as 'soft' also perhaps helps to explain some of Phillip's tough stances. He was in danger of having that identity foisted upon him, because of his academic standing and interest in the demands of the school. This meant he had a real need to present a tough enough front to keep himself out of trouble. Even so, he was seen as different by the deviant group: He 'never goes out after school . . . just plays golf.'

> Andy: None of that lot go to the disco even.
>
> R: Do you think they ever go out with girls?
>
> Andy: Not at all.

So the issue is not simply one of attitude to school work. The style of a boy's leisure time interests are clearly crucial as well. The desire to go out a lot after school and an interest in discos and girls and music seem quite crucial elements of identity for some. Phillip's 'style' was contrasted by Pete and Andy with their own:

> Pete: I went for a fag with my friend Warren the other day.
>
> R: What's he like?
>
> Pete: He's the sort of kid that goes to discos and things like that, and does things, mucks about in school and that. I suppose it's what a lot of us are like, ain't it. But you don't think we are 'one of the lads'.

The girls seemed to share this perception. The sexual element was clearly present in the comment Amy made one day when Phillip had angered her over some matter. Amy said viciously to Phillip, 'You don't have any girls going out with you'. Phillip retorted quickly, 'No, and I don't want to have either!'

While Phillip was seen as too conformist by boys like Pete and Roy, it was Geoffrey who was seen as the stereotype of this identity and was virtually shunned by other pupils as a result. He seemed to have taken on all the teacher values, although he did not do particularly well in academic terms. There were several 'key' incidents here.

Bob had already been caned by Mr Brandt for not knowing an answer in German. On another day, soon after that event, Mr Brandt again had Bob on his feet, and while the rest of the class sat, grilled him for an answer. The rest of the class watched, a bit grim-faced, for Bob was well liked, while Mr Brandt was not, and they had already witnessed several public canings by him. Geoffrey, however, laughed with the teacher when Bob got his first attempt at an answer wrong. He tried to engage the researcher in sharing his amusement. The teacher clapped when Bob finally found the right answer, and Geoffrey alone of all the class joined in. This kind of response was repeated frequently enough to make Geoffrey highly unpopular during the course of a year. Given that he was already seen as 'soft' as a result of his non-performance in games and the cross-country running, it led to a great deal of bullying and teasing.

Much of this squares with the views of Willis's 'lads'. They, too, saw conformist boys (the 'ear'oles') as non-masculine, non-sexual, and 'soft' (Willis 1977). But, in some respects, our data suggest a different model of pupil adaptations than that proposed by Willis. He described two broad stereotyped groups of deviant 'lads' and conformist 'ear'oles' with pupils identifying with one identity and differentiating from the other (see also Hargreaves 1967, Lacey 1970). For the majority of first year boys at Old Town, there seemed to be two polarities to which they reacted: 'too conformist', and 'too deviant'. The outer markers were specified and personalized, and most boys reacted to both in some measure or another, not just one. In this respect the pupil culture was a dimension, and not a collection of different sub-cultures.

It was not merely orientation to school that was at issue in the 'too deviant' identity: elements of academic ability were also involved. It was crucial not to be seen as 'too thick'. Such an identity invoked sanctions. We have already seen that Bridget and Anna, for example, were shunned socially. Those publicly identified as 'too thick' could encounter insult, teasing, and also aggression. They were frequently labelled by insulting nicknames. Pete, for example, always addressed Mark as 'Hey Goofy Teeth', and those pupils who took remedial reading were known as 'spastics' or 'spassies'.

> Mark gets attacked in English one day when the teacher is out of the room. He is barely literate and has serious academic problems. Some other boys laugh at his work.
>
> 'Look at it, it's so untidy, it's terrible'.
>
> 'Has he started that work yet?'
>
> 'No, he's only done the contents'.
>
> 'No, no, miraculous, he's only done half a page'.

However, the stereotype of extreme deviancy was Jack McIntosh. He was not a member of the class which forms the main subject for this research, although these pupils occasionally had lessons with him. He was in bottom stream, remedial groups for all subjects, and was notorious among both staff and pupils. Although Jack may not have been in their class, all the pupils knew about him. By June, he was being caned regularly once a week to try to make him produce some English work. He had gone through the whole repertoire of school punishments by this point. Jack had also exhausted the resources of the counselling staff of the school, who admitted defeat and called in the educational psychologist. Again, the pupils knew about this, and it added to their sense of his danger. He was not popular, had few friends and the girls all agreed, 'We can't stand him'. As a side issue, it is interesting that he alone out of all the pupils showed interest in the National Front. His rough book was covered in swastikas and NF slogans and he systematically persecuted Vivien, the only black pupil. Clearly, Jack was an exceptional case, but, we would submit, a useful marker for pupils to negotiate their own identities against.

The essentially different chartacter of such people is illustrated by these comments:

> There is Jack McIntosh, he is really queer that boy. He is sick, he shouldn't be at this school. All he can say is 'Do you want a fight' or 'Looking for a kick in the head?' or something like that.

For many pupils, boys like Roy and Pete showed a far too deviant attitude. Yet they did not occupy the same kind of outrageously deviant position that Jack did. He had lost all equilibrium. This further illustrates the concept of 'the normal pupil'. Deviations were mercilessly punished.

Knife-edge strategies

Sometimes, to appear 'normal' calls for special techniques, and we have termed these 'knife-edge strategies', by which pupils balance on the thin line dividing two undesirable options. For example, deviant boys did not wish to appear clever, but they also shunned being considered 'thick'.

> Bill: I don't want to be top all the time, but I don't want to be bottom. I just want to be in between.

A particular incident in the course of the year made this clear. When the class was streamed for maths, Roy was placed in the bottom group (the remedial group) with Allan and Geoffrey. This reflected his low marks and his general 'mucking about' in the subject. Within two weeks, however, he had worked sufficiently hard to be promoted two groups to the middle group, where many of his friends were. Doubtless the fact of being separated from his friends may well have motivated Roy, but that was not the way Pete and Andy saw it. Andy started to tell the researcher about Roy being put into the low group. Pete very uncharacteristically stopped him. 'Shut it, And!' he said loudly, but Andy failed to get the point. Pete again intervened, 'Just shut up, will you', and he would not allow Andy to finish. However, when Roy gained promotion, Pete thought it worth telling the researcher about it, and the language he used was interesting. 'Roy has got into our maths group now. He was too good for that other group. That was the group for the dummies'. We have noted the importance of the subject area of mathematics to pupils. Had it been needlework, it might have been a matter for celebration to be placed as low as possible. Roy had thus worked his way clear of the dreaded label of 'too thick' in an area where it mattered. In the same week that he gained promotion, he had a skinhead haircut, as a symbol of his basic allegiance to deviant values.

Several other strategies were employed by the deviants to maintain this knife-edge image. For one thing, you could be seen to be not very good at some things but good at others, such as practical subjects. Bill, for example, was very good at woodwork. We have mentioned already the issue of 'finishing first' and the signals it involves in terms of conformity and the academic hierarchy. Yet Bill Stoop was ready to acknowledge that in woodwork he always 'finished first, then I have to wait.' Pete was 'pretty good' at art, especially at the kind of graphic design that enabled him to employ symbols drawn from the punk subculture. Roy was exceptionally good at all sports, and was in the school teams for almost all of them.

Pete made another issue clear. It was unacceptable in his terms to be seen to be working hard and doing well. On the other hand, it was equally important that one should not be thought of as incapable of doing well, if one should so choose.

> Pete: I got a really bad report in maths, and I'm meant to be clever. . . . I don't want to be bored stiff though. Kids like Phillip sit down and work all day. I just can't do that.

Incidents recorded in classroom interaction confirmed this view. In maths, Bruce put up his hand to tell the teacher, 'I've finished'. The teacher responded, 'That's good'. Pete then said, 'Finished before him'. Teacher, 'You didn't put up your hand'. Pete, '*I* didn't want to show off'.

This reinforces the point that mathematics is generally important to all pupils, including the deviants. Secondly, it shows another property of normality for the deviant pupil – not 'showing off'. Pete is also worried about being seen to be good at or too interested in his work. On the other hand, in maths, he actually is concerned to do fairly well, and that others should know he could do well. It is his choice, not his ability, that is being exercised.

Teachers were sometimes held responsible for putting pupils at risk of appearing 'thick'. Keith, for example, made this comment: 'Allan is not very good at German, you know, not because he doesn't listen or anything – he doesn't understand it. They shouldn't do things like German and French, for people that can't do it – just can't do it – sit there all through the lesson and get shouted at'.

This fear of being labelled 'too thick' is in part responsible for some of the co-operative activity that we have emphasized is such an important facet of school life. We have seen that pupils were reluctant to ask for help in front of the whole class. If the others in the class have understood the point it could lead to their thinking that the pupil asking the question was 'too thick'. It could, of course, also lead to the teacher's discipline sanction of 'You didn't listen', and that was to be avoided too. Bill would not ask a question because 'they would just think you were a bit simple, or you haven't been listening, so I just ask my mates.'

Knife-edge strategies were employed to avoid being seen as 'too deviant'. As the school year progressed, many of the boys began to alter their attitudes somewhat, seeming to feel that increasing maturity brought increasing responsibility. Again, this may have something to do with their grasping the concept of 'maleness'. David, for example, did some 'mucking about' at the beginning of the year, but by the third term had stopped doing so and was working hard. He had achieved top stream status in maths and science, and was motivated to do the same in languages, because 'it is your last school – you have to carry on pretty well'.

Some noted deviants have had second thoughts:

> Keith: I am trying to get a good report, that's why I am trying to be a goody-goody. If I come out of this school, it is my last school, and I haven't got no degrees. I won't get a job and I will have to come back in again at nights. I don't want to do that, because then my dad will take the mickey out of me.

The gender side of the issue is expressed by these pupils:

> Ian: Boys are boys aren't they, they muck about more than girls, but when they realise they have got to start learning to get a job, then they start working.
>
> John: And girls always have boy friends on their minds.

If some boys' deviance was tinctured with signs of conformity, some conformists were not averse to the occasional misbehaviour. This we see as yet another kind of 'knife-edge' strategy. The identity of super-conformist was not one they wanted. They had seen that it led to isolation and to some harassment. On the other hand, they were concerned with school culture, with doing well and with making use of what school had to offer. Their occasional deviance, then, was not a rejection of school; rather it represented an acknowledgement of the rules of the informal culture (cf. Fuller 1980, Lambart 1976, Prendergast and Prout 1980). These 'knife-edge' strategies on the part of normally conformist pupils only really developed in the third term, the pupils concerned being anxious up to that point to establish their academic standing with the formal culture.

These strategies are deployed in the spaces that have already been mined by the ace deviants. These boys know they are 'safe' in committing deviant acts there. It signals their 'normality' as persons to the other pupils, but runs minimal risk of bringing retribution. As we have seen in the previous chapter, low status subjects provide good opportunities for the expression of gender-related behaviour. They also provide good opportunities for knife-edge strategists. For example, in home economics, Phillip and Stewart – usually conformist boys – engaged in a range of 'mucking about' activities, stealing and eating raisins, smearing each other's skin and clothes with cake mix, turning the gas off and on, opening the oven at the wrong moment, and so on. Phillip actually 'got sent out' of the home economics lesson for misbehaving, but whereas in some situations this would have been very serious indeed, here it didn't matter very much. Many people had been 'sent out' and nothing more had happened to them, the teacher was known to be a weak disciplinarian, and the subject was of low importance. For Phillip, in fact, it was his last few weeks of doing the subject. Phillip's interests in this situation, therefore, were much better met by deviant behaviour (see Hammersley and Turner 1980, Turner 1983).

Craft and design was another area of the curriculum inviting deviance from basically conformist pupils, either because, in their eyes, they had low marketability, or because they felt they had no talent and no investment in the area. In one typical lesson, for example, Phillip, Erik and Stewart had all finished their work ahead of the rest of the class. Phillip said, 'We've finished, we can just mess around all lesson'. Stuart responded with, 'Go and beat some poor little bugger up'. In another craft area, using plastic materials, Phillip and Dominic threw plastic discs around and made up a game flicking them with their rulers. Phillip kept a careful eye on the teacher, making certain that he did not get caught. On another occasion, he propelled Giles's pencil out of the window with the aid of a ruler. Phillip usually ate sweets, a forbidden activity, throughout the art lesson, but took care to escape detection. He frequently chatted to neighbours, neglected to pay attention to his work, and received poor grades. All these are 'knife-edge' strategies – they are deviant in character, are a qualification for membership of the informal culture, yet are carefully engineered not to threaten one's basic identity and interests. The contrast with 'real deviants' is nicely shown when pupils were required to bring in a fruit or a vegetable to draw. Phillip brought an apple, and ate a good part of it during the lesson, although they had been specifically told not to do so. This evaded rebuke, but the 'ace deviants' Pete, Roy, Andrew and Keith, had all forgotten to bring anything to draw, a much more serious misdemeanour, which in fact got them into actual 'trouble' with the teacher.

Another place for knife-edge behaviour is in lessons taken by temporary teachers, or by a teacher who is not the regular person in charge of the class and thus not responsible for their grades and their identity. On these occasions, there is a loss of the rule-structure negotiated with the regular teacher. Such lessons became interstices wherein otherwise straitjacketed identities can be readjusted or refined. We have seen earlier how these lessons provided the sites for attempted take-overs in the second term. By the third term, pupils are using them for the less rebellious 'knife-edging'. In one design class, for example, a teacher was forced to put two first year groups together when one teacher was away. Phillip engaged in extra 'mucking about' in that lesson. He cut up an eraser with a Stanley knife, and threw the bits around the room. Some of them were returned, and as he dropped one catch, he said 'Look, I'm Botham'. He actually received a reprimand from the teacher, on two occasions. However, these reprimands carried no weight in terms of his proper identity with his own teacher, yet they do signal Phillip's interest in doing things that are certainly not conformist. On another occasion, when a supply teacher had taken over, Phillip was talking loudly to his neighbour. The teacher walked up to Phillip and stood by his desk. He ignored her completely and went on talking loudly to Stewart, a fairly major challenge to any teacher's authority, and the sort of challenge he would not normally make. When she asked, 'Are you finished?' Phillip responded, 'Not quite'. Here, Phillip very cleverly exploits the ambiguity in the teacher's question. Was it 'work' or 'talking' that she was referring to? There was little doubt that the majority thought it was the latter, in which case his answer was extremely rude. But there was just a chance it could have been the former, in which case his reply was perfectly respectful. Again, the knife-edge quality is well revealed.

That knife-edgers use subtle judgement was revealed once more in a maths lesson. Matthew and his friend, Dominic, were catapulting paper pellets around when the teacher went out of the room. Later, they talked together when they were supposed to be working. But they shut up, and listened carefully when the teacher told them she wanted to give them some new material, and needed their full attention. It is this ability to discern the rhythm of a lesson and to judge the appropriate point for the play of their own concerns that is important.

By the middle of the summer term, despite knife-edgers' delicate balancing acts, much of this activity was beginning to be noticed by some teachers. Some of Phillip's teachers, for example, began to comment on his behaviour. The art teacher said, 'He was good, but he's starting to be a little bit silly these days'. His identity began to change, but Phillip did not mind this in these limited areas. When interviewed on general issues he wanted to talk about some of the 'mucking around' he and Erik had done. He was interested to identify himself and his friend as capable of 'mucking around' in certain situations, for example when a relief teacher took over a science lesson for the headmaster:

> Phillip: Were you there when Erik and I dissolved those things? We put them in water and over heat, and they were supposed to be in two separate beakers, well Erik got one and he went like that, and poured them together, and one was a blue substance and one was clear, and it went all frothy and bright blue and coming out of the test tube!

When it was pointed out that Erik did not usually muck about, Phillip expressed great surprise at the suggestion, and commented, 'He does muck around quite a bit really. Not as you call mucking around like that, but a laugh'.

Again, the location of the deviance followed the pattern we have identified. It occurred in a science lesson, with a temporary teacher, who could not keep effective discipline. The fact that it was important to have friends who had the same orientation to school culture as yourself was also emphasized.

Phillip had, in fact, a fairly clear picture of his own position. He worked quite hard, but not as hard as he could. Furthermore:

Phillip: I feel I have matured, gone down a bit. I felt I was a bit more responsible before, because I mess around a bit, not as much as other people, but have a laugh. I didn't before.

There is a sense here that getting older and becoming more mature involved, indeed almost demanded, more deviance. It reflects more independence, more self-assertiveness, a necessary feature of growing up. Some of the 'deviants' also stated that as they got older it was possible to 'doss around' more, that discipline became less tight. There is a hint of a perspective shared between conformists and deviants. Phillip's comment on working, but not really trying too hard, shows his concern with not being viewed as too conformist or 'showing off'. He had a clear recognition of the pressures operating on anyone doing really well. Thus, knife-edge strategists learnt to keep quiet about their academic successes. They also adopted a series of tactics which guyed the appropriate response to doing well, and served to defuse the incident. They used a number of pantomime gestures to cope with the situation of getting an answer right and being publicly praised. Ian England, for example, praised in a music lesson, which is especially embarrassing given the subject's inferior status among the pupils, blew on his finger nails and polished them against his chest, in an ostentatious manner. In a science lesson, Matthew, when praised, smiled and did an exaggerated smirk. Stewart, if he received any public recognition for his work, would raise both arms above his head in a boxer's salute of victory, and bounce around smiling and bowing, and declaring 'I'm magic'. All of these strategies had one element in common – they derived from the informal culture of the pupils, and specifically from the media input to that culture. It showed that the individual concerned was acquainted with the adolescent, informal culture. It was the pupil's way of managing the identity projected on to him in certain situations by the teacher. He was not just a quiet little conformist, who gave all his time and attention to work.

This was shown, too, in their appearance. While on the whole they maintained a 'proper' appearance far more closely than the deviants, not being drawn towards the demands of adolescent fashion, they did practise deviant infringements such as tying enormous knots in their ties, or leaving ties three-quarters undone. They also embroidered some of the graffiti of youth culture in places where it did not really matter. For example, Matthew's exercise books were of the proper neat appearance, but his rough book was covered with posters, scribbles and slogans advertising the virtues of 'Liverpool FC'. Stewart's apron, which was worn for design lessons, had slogans about QPR on it, although it was not emblazoned to the full with the emblems of punk rock as Pete's was.

Girls

As with the boys, there were three broad categories among the girls – conformists, deviants, and those who walked the thin line in between on a 'knife-edge'. We shall examine them as we observed them, and as they observed each other.

Conformists and deviants

Janet (a conformist):	Laughing
	Chattering
	Asking for help
	Doing work all day
	Stopping for lunch
	Packing up
	Walking home
Ros (a deviant):	Sit down
	Work all day
	Boring subjects
	Which you have to do
	Don't talk, just work
	All the day
	Go home
	School

(Poems written in June 1980)

We have seen in the behaviour of Janet reported in Chapter 6 how keen conformists were to work. Sally was similar, though she 'used to get really fed up with homework', now 'I just get really interested in it, and I do it. Yes I am really interested in it, I don't know why'.

These girls also displayed a desire to do well academically; in fact, they were at times desperately anxious to do well. One day Janet stayed off school with a bad cold. When she returned she said, 'I do feel a bit ill' but 'I had to come back because I missed so much yesterday'. She knew that her class was doing a whole new subject area in maths, and she was anxious not to miss it. There was also an interesting contrast in the length of time taken off school when Janet, the conformist, and Ros, the deviant, caught chicken pox, with Ros staying away for twice as long. When there was a French test to help decide how they would be streamed, the conformist girls complained bitterly that they had had no advance warning. Usually docile and co-operative, they were driven to protest here, for they knew what hung on the results and it was a matter of great importance to them.

These girls acknowledged their interest in the formal culture. Their dedication to the formal task could lead them to reject areas of the curriculum that they felt distracted them from the important activity. Jane said in a woodwork lesson that she 'really got down to some work in English' and didn't talk at all. She objected to doing the woodwork lesson, and wished she had two hours of English so that she could have finished her work.

Maths was a crucial area of the curriculum to them. Pat was already anxious about 'her maths' in middle school. When the form was streamed and she was placed in the second stream, her anxiety was all the greater. Her parents finally went to the counselling staff, for Pat was not sleeping properly and having disturbing nightmares about the maths she was doing. Once the pupils had been streamed for maths, those in the top stream described their reactions:

> Emma: It is a sort of privilege to be up there, you have got to be properly brainy, but you have got to know what you are doing sort of thing. When we got there, and he was giving us the work, like that algebra, I didn't think I would last.

It became increasingly clear that, while many girls had the resources to meet the requirements of being 'brainy' and conformist, there were problems attached to their *choosing* that particular kind of identity. Social isolation and teasing were common penalties of conformist behaviour for girls. Janet described her sense of being 'left out' for most of the year, and Jane agreed.

> Janet: The girls all go around in sort of gangs and it is not very nice for the person who is left out, because they feel they are talking about them all the time . . . I have been with some people when they have taken the mickey. But I think it is not fair for these people who want to work, to have the mickey taken by those people who don't want to work.

There were occasions when this general hostility could spill over into violent verbal exchanges between the girls. On one occasion, for example, Jacqui sat in the waste-paper basket, and asserted noisily that she was stuck. Jane told her to protest more quietly. Jacqui replied furiously, 'Shut up Jane, you snob!' On other occasions the drama could involve virtually the whole class. One day, there had been an exceptional amount of badgering and hostility addressed to Jane, and when she went home she complained to her mother. Her mother then spoke to the form teacher. The following afternoon, Mrs Gates called Jane back, after she had dismissed the rest of the class. Jane entered needlework, her next lesson, very late, and the remainder of the class wanted to know why. Many of the 'deviant' girls got very angry, and Vivien accused Jane directly, 'It was about us, wasn't it?' Jacqui walked up to Jane and said loudly, 'Well you get a transfer to another class, 'cos we don't like you!' The verbal assault on Jane continued in a worsening atmosphere, finally reducing her to tears. A properly conformist orientation to school put real social pressures on a girl and had implications for her friendship patterns. She could find herself isolated and shunned by the majority. Such incidents were frequent and brought great pain and unhappiness to the conformists. This again raises questions about the comprehensive school, and the pressures on the academically achieving, conformist pupils to under-achieve.

It is in the hostility that 'the conformists' faced that we may be able to find an explanation for occasional interaction between them and girls at entirely the other end of the academic hierarchy, when they were asked for help with schoolwork. The 'conformists' were aware that this broke the co-operative rules, but perhaps gave the help as a kind of trade for less harrassment. It also showed that they were useful and enhanced their status as people who 'knew things', who 'got things right' and were 'worth asking'.

On the whole, however, deviants were critical in their outlook on conformists. They saw them as being 'good', or 'good little girls' or 'goody-goodies'. In charades, one girl had to act out the title 'The Good, the Bad and the Ugly'. They pointed at Janet to signal 'The Good'. Conformists were defined chiefly by attitude to schoolwork. They 'do everything perfect and get praised for it'. They also did 'very neat work'. Anna, for example, was quite appalled that Sally wrote so neatly in her rough book.

Doing so much work left them little time or inclination to have any 'fun'. Moreover, they often spoiled it for others:

Ros: Janet goes around, all grumpy and that.

Amy: She don't have a laugh or nothing.

The deviants, on the other hand, enjoyed a laugh and 'muck about'.

Another difference between conformists and deviants is illustrated in an incident where Jenny and Sally were discussing the recent tests they had had and the streaming that had occurred. They were interested in identifying very clearly which pupils had gone into the 'top groups'. Amy, however, almost immediately returned the subject to friendship, who was friends with whom, and who was going out with whom. She was thus asserting the importance of sociability and patterns of informal culture over that of the formal culture.

The conformist girls were also seen as being 'bossy'. We have seen an example of this with Janet, in Chapter 6. On occasions, as we have shown, the whole class could be disrupted. The 'conformist' girls hated this, and deprecated the teacher's lack of control. Sometimes they would try to influence the whole class, 'hushing' them, or reprimanding other pupils – another instance of spoiling their 'fun'.

Conformist girls were also held to be 'boastful', thus transgressing the basic rule about 'showing off'.

Amy: In maths, Janet and Jenny used to work together, and Janet used to go 'I'm bound to get them all right'. Jenny used to hate that, because she used to say 'she thinks she knows it all'.

Several incidents were recorded in field notes, where pupils signalled their dislike of this kind of activity, and of those who engaged in it. In one, in a crowded classroom, Janet said, very loudly to Sally who was at the opposite end of a long table, 'I can't hand in these six before tomorrow anyway'. Sally asked 'What six?' 'These six house points'. Several pupils exchanged looks around the table.

Deviants can be very critical of others. Rosemary thought Janet was 'stuck up' because 'if you say a wrong answer, she says "don't be stupid", and she thought she "knew it all".' Janet was 'a class up', 'brainier' than they were, and took delight, apparently, in emphasizing the difference.

> Jacqui: She won't mix in with us. If we have a game, she will just sit down and do her homework.

Our observations supported Jacqui's point. One lunchtime the researcher entered their classroom. Janet sat at the front of the classroom, alone, copying up homework from the board. The remainder of the girls sat in groups, reading comics like *My Guy* or comparing nail varnish or discussing boyfriends and writing their names on books and equipment.

There were clear differences in appearance between conformist and deviant girls. 'Deviant' girls were much more interested in fashion and make-up. They engaged in subtle manipulation of school uniform, as we have seen. They contrasted their interests with those of the conformists:

> Amy: When we used to come in, in the mornings, I would speak to Rosemary and Rebecca, and we used to be talking about the clothes we wear, and that, and I don't think Sally liked that.

The different priorities given to different areas of interest were issues of importance. This was signalled in other ways too. In March the class had to choose a topic in English and write a project on it. Rosemary chose 'Fashion and beauty'. Pat chose 'Buster Keaton'.

The conformists were just as critical of the deviants' appearance:

> Sally: Well, they don't work very hard, they wear make up. Yes, and boys. Oh Gawd! especially Amy, she always comes in and tells you about the weekend she has had with some boys. Rosemary is always putting lip gloss on in lessons.

> Jane: You can tell them, those girls are always reading magazines about their health, spots. I don't go out and buy them, I think it is a waste of money really. I read more, sort of books, and they don't.

Deviants and conformists had different interests. One day Amy, Ros and Rebecca sat discussing different flavours of lip gloss, the most effective deodorants, and the kind of perfume their mothers used. Janet discussed the hockey match that she would play in that evening for the school. The girls were asked to keep diaries of their activities over the half-term holiday, and these also revealed a difference. The conformist girls spent the majority of their leisure time with their families. The deviants' activities centred around their peer group.

We have already suggested that food had all kinds of importance for girls of this age, and that the deviants systematically refused to eat school lunch and seemed to gravitate towards 'junk food'. By contrast, the conformists still were prepared to eat school lunch. Jane especially expressed attitudes to food that were at variance with the others'. She objected to eating snack meals: 'It's not good for you'. She and Janet agreed on a distaste for the junk food the others liked: 'It's all chips, they should eat proper things'. Jane even refused sweets: 'No, I don't like to eat them, it's not good for your teth'. These remarks further confirmed the 'goody-goody' label.

We have seen that one of the key issues for the deviants – separating them from the conformists in their own view – was that of sex, one of the manifestations of which was involvement with boys. What was the conformists' view on the deviants' outlook on this subject?

Jane: Christine, they think a lot about clothes, and boys and that. I don't think that is happening to me much really. I don't care too much, because though I might want new clothes, I know I couldn't really have them, because there is a family.

Emma: Well, the girls, they think they are grown up, and they think about themselves and boys.

Janet: Well they talk about all the girls problems, and who they hate, and who they like.

Emma: They talk about boys, which they like, and which girls are tarts and everything.

An interest or a lack of interest in 'boys' was one of the clearest and most important criteria in this area.

Jacqui: Jane wouldn't go out with a boy, I don't think.

Amy: Emma and Lucy and that lot wouldn't go out with a boy.

When Janet finally did start going out with Michael, a top stream boy on the fringes of Phillip's set, this simply brought a change in the charges made. It was unexpected, yet could still be explained away by denying Janet's sexuality:

Amy: Janet, and she goes out with somebody, and she hasn't even kissed him once yet, but I mean!

Claire: She has been going out with him for about three months.

The conversation of the deviant girls centred around boys, those they met, those they were interested in, those they were bored with and were about to leave. Status in the informal culture seemed to derive from a lot of boys wanting to take you out. Jacqui attempted to put the research project to good use: 'Yer, write a book about us, so I'll become famous, then all the boys will come round my house' (see Burgess 1984). When the whole of the first year was taken on an educational visit to the zoo, Rebecca was late returning to the bus. 'We was chasing the boys along by the river'. Chorus of voices: 'Typical of Rebecca!' Teachers sometimes referred to this: Mrs Gates, for example, said in her report on Ros 'Too many boys'.

Going out with boys was not the only aspect of the sexuality theme. There was status to be won or lost in terms of knowledge about matters of a sexual nature, regardless of experience. Again, the same pattern had characterized the boys. Those who were seen as too conformist were viewed as sexually unknowledgeable. Amy and Claire described the little clutches of girls who sat around at lunchtime discussing matters sexual. Both girls stated what they would do if they did not know or understand something in such a discussion:

Amy: I wouldn't ask, I would pretend I knew

Claire: If we were in a group of girls and they said a word and I didn't know what it meant, I would pretend I knew.

R: Do you think you get teased if . . .

Amy: (before R had time to finish the question) Yes, she doesn't know, she is stupid, whatever.

On another occasion, Sally and Jenny were discussing Caesarean section operations, and the way they are done. A friend's mother had just had such an operation. It illustrates how this kind of knowledge is passed around and gained, and it is all dependent on friendship networks. Janet looked interested and asked what they were talking about, but Amy replied, 'Oh, you wouldn't know'. Later, the same three girls were discussing Jenny's brother who had recently married a woman who had been divorced. She was pregnant, and the girls were discussing who the father of the child was. Jenny was quite certain it was her brother. She said indignantly, 'Well, it wasn't the milkman'. She then told a joke about 'not waiting for the milkman, because he never comes'. Sally looked puzzled, and Amy teased her for 'not getting it'. Sally crossly asserted that she did. Then they both accused Pat of not getting the joke. The girls seemed more concerned about establishing their status in respect of having sufficient knowledge of sexual matters to understand the joke, rather than in enjoying the humour of it. Jane showed herself incompetent in this area of informal culture. She talked of a friend who had managed to 'get in to see' the uncut version of 'Saturday Night Fever'. She said she was disgusted by it. 'There was so much sex and swearing in it'. She added, 'She learnt a whole load of words she has never heard before'.

Jane fails here through association with a friend who not only has the attributes of a 'goody-goody', but also did not understand many of the terms used. Expressing disapproval of sexually inappropriate behaviour is not in itself frowned upon – and indeed is to be expected in some instances of excess, which might bring the dreaded accusation of being a 'tart' – but confession of ignorance is unforgivable. In other words, the right kind of knowledge is necessary in order for a proper moral judgement to be made.

If boys were so important in deviant girls' perceptions of conformist girls, what did the boys think of the conformist girls? Other work would have us believe that male influence acts as a check on girls' abilities and achievement (for example, Sharpe 1976). Certainly, the boys in our study did not see 'brainy' girls as desirable objects.

> Ray: Who wants to go out with a brainy girl? It would make you look a real idiot, a real brainbox. I wouldn't fancy that anyhow ... I wouldn't want to marry a girl who told me what to do, all the time.

These data have similarities to those provided by Willis (1977). They show a direct parallel between boys and girls, for in Willis's study the conformist 'ear'ole' boys were seen as less sexual and also as less sexually competent than the deviant 'lads'. Clearly the same is true for girls who are placed in the highly conformist category. Their sexuality is in question, and their very identity as feminine is suspended as a result of academic success and interest. The boys confirmed the general prevalence in this school of this popular stereotype.

> John: Boys are boys, aren't they? They muck about more than girls, and when they realise that they have got to start learning to get a job, then they start working.

The boys supported the deviant girls' views on womanhood. None of the boys welcomed the idea of their wives working, and said they would agree to it only if it was absolutely necessary. This view seemed to be held most strongly by boys whose own mothers worked. Fundamentally, the boys saw it as their responsibility to work to earn enough to maintain a wife and family; girls were not to share that responsibility, but to run the home. This meant that for girls to work hard at school was irrelevant.

> Keith: Not as much, because half of them are going to turn out to be housewives.

> David: We have got to go out, and get the money, so we have got to get a job. We have got to work for results to get a job, that is why.

Boys perceived sociability as crucial for girls.

> Keith: Some of the girls still act a bit like a woman's meeting, stuff like that – talk a lot – all girls do, because they do when they get older, don't they, a neighbour comes round, a cup of tea ... quick chat, 'Have you read this

book? . . . it's good!' . . . they all start looking at the book, they are always talking, aren't they. It's a good idea that they should get together, it keeps with them all their life; in school, they are always talking . . . always talking.

Here Keith relates the girls' deviance at school directly to their likely life-styles as adults and condones it as necessary socialization.

As with the boys, the girls see these differences as being underpinned by social class:

Jacqui: She thinks she is better than us: her mum and dad work, she's got two cars and that, she thinks she is better than us, so she treats us like mud. Jane, she just don't like mucking in with us.

A typical incident occurred in an art class, in a general discussion about travel and summer holidays. Janet said she had been to America, and lived in Canada. Sally answered sharply, 'Well, I've lived in this town all my life!' raising her eyes heavenward, and sighing with irritation.

They spoke different languages:

Janet: When I say certain words, Rosemary keeps repeating it and saying I am posh. My mum thinks I speak terrible.

Jane: Well I try not to speak poshly, but I don't speak commonly, but people still say a bit you know.

For all girls, therefore, a certain relief was to be found for their imediate problems of peer relationships within streamed groups, which promoted friendship groups where their values were shared and there was less biting opposition from those who held different values.

Sally: I think it is right to put people in groups [stream] because then they can get on. Janet can get on really well with it, and I can get on with it, and then there's Rosemary, she sort of looks at mine, 'How did you get that' sort of thing, she doesn't really know how to do the French, she gets upset.

There was virtually no indication that friendships were made across the boundaries of ability sectors. The conformist, achieving girls jelled into a friendship group, and found it a relief from the social problems that had existed outside it. Thus, Janet, Jane, Emma and Lucy, for example, became firm friends within school, and their relationship spilled over into outside activities such as ballet classes and flute and viola playing. All of these girls who chose to be conformist came from homes which, by the father's occupation, would be traditionally defined as middle-class, while others in the four forms did not. Emma's father was a local architect. Jane's father was a lecturer in a teacher-training college and her mother lectured in further education. Janet's father managed an insurance company. Janet explained:

> I think it is good really to mix with somebody like Emma or Jane, because I think they are much better than, say, someone like Shirley. She took half a bottle of pills the other day. They are much better. Living on my estate they speak terrible, because you know they are all Londoners, but since I have mixed with Emma and Jane I have spoken better, but it all depends on who you mix with I think really.

Whatever the social-class influence, however, there is clearly a fairly pervasive culture of femininity exerting strong pressures on all these young girls. The deviants appear to be strongly influenced by this, the conformists less so – possibly their social-class background has some degree of neutralising effect – though this is not to say they will not be more deeply affected later, or that they do not experience difficulty in coming to terms with their own sense of identity. Some girls handled this, like some of the boys, by taking a middle way and employing 'knife-edge' strategies, which enabled them to avoid the sanctions that fell upon the 'too conformist' but still to do tolerably well at school.

Knife-edge strategists

Like the boys, these girls indulged in occasional deviant acts, but at times and in places where they either would not get caught or it didn't matter if they did. Supply teachers provided good opportunities. Diane once spent part of such a lesson shouting loudly across the room to her friends. Julie engaged in a fair amount of general 'mucking around', for example, throwing rulers across the room when someone asked if they could borrow them. They made full use of the opportunity to chat and gossip. In a humanities lesson taken by a supply teacher, Sally and Jenny ate bubblegum and blew large bubbles, which came to some sticky ends, and called Amy's name loudly to attract her attention.

Registration was another arena for strategic deviance. One day the class was exceptionally rowdy. Christine, for example, was throwing polo mints around. Julie, a typical 'knife-edger' was not doing anything as provocative, but she was, under the cover of all the other noise, shouting across the room to someone else. Yet she deliberately chose a point when she was unlikely to be detected by the teacher. To some, even this would not matter if the teacher had discipline problems anyway and was not generally respected. Thus, Diane did not seem unduly perturbed when, after she had laughed very loudly during registration, Mrs Gates reprimanded her with 'I don't expect bad behaviour from you'. This 'teacher-certificated deviance' may have been useful to Diane and this was a safe place to get it. Mrs Gates would not take the matter further; her opinion was not respected anyway in the school. The class already knew that Mrs Gates would not be their form tutor the following year.

Probationary teachers provided other situations. With one such teacher, while the boys kept her fully occupied with a series of centre-stage challenges, Diane talked to Julie and played around with scissors and her pencil case. Then she turned right around and talked to Elaine. The really conformist pupils like Jane went on working steadily through all of this.

As with the boys, some areas of the curriculum lent themselves more readily to strategic deviance than others. In one language class, for example, the discipline frame was constantly being challenged. Sally used the cover given by this to make a small paper plane and send it flying around the room. Woodwork and metalwork were 'safe' to ignore. Sally stated her dislike of these subjects and her view that they were a waste of time. She and Jenny did no real work for the entire lesson, but sat and talked to the researcher. In a technical design lesson, which many of the girls characterized as being 'really for the boys' anyway, and in which supervision was lax in the large room with big tables and a lot of activity, Diane and Julie 'mucked about'. They took the waxed paper straws they had been given and had a sword fight with them, and then made moustaches out of them, holding them over their top lip. Nevertheless, they did not actually damage the equipment they would have to work with. These knife-edge strategists were all placed in the top group for maths. Diane and Julie went into the top science group, Sally and Jenny went into the second-from-top stream. Both girls frequently talked of their shared, appropriately feminine attitudes to science, emphasizing their dislike of the smells and their anxiety about the bunsen burners, yet they had clearly managed to achieve a certain competence in the subject.

The knife-edge group also took a middle line approach to the areas of youth culture that carried significance. For example, Diane and Julie later in the year both wore nail varnish, but not make up. Jenny one day borrowed Mandy Queen's new shoes. They had extremely high heels and were very fashionable. Jenny herself did not usually wear shoes like this, but she made sure that many people knew about it on this occasion. By the end of the summer term, Diane and Julie were wearing shoes with high heels. But they were not otherwise making any innovations in their school uniform, whereas the 'deviant' girls had moved toward these and other 'fashion' items far more rapidly.

We have noted the importance of adolescent sexuality, and the problems involved for the girl aspiring both to some academic success and to femininity. Jenny solved it by going out with only one boy, Bob, for almost the whole of the first year. Sally did not actually 'go out' with anyone, but she let it be known that she was not averse to the practice. Jenny inscribed 'I love Bob' with a heart, suitably embellished with arrows, on the front cover of her rough book. The inside pages, however, were full of very neat working out of her maths. As we have seen, the 'rough book' was an important symbol of girls' identities, and the knife-edgers compromised here, as elsewhere.

Sally, for example, did not have boys' names on her book, and rubbed some off that Amy put on. But she did have pictures of pop groups on the cover, though it was interesting that these were 'middle-range' groups like 'Abba' rather than heavy rock like 'The Sex Pistols'.

Some of the knife-edge girls played around on the fringes of the deviant

groups in a whole series of ways. Friendship ties were one of these. Jenny
and Sally maintained their co-operative links and some friendship links with
Amy and Rebecca, who had been at middle school with them. Diane did the
same with Jacqui, who was one of the 'ace' deviants in her class. Sometimes
they were prepared to extend such links into out-of-school activities. For
example, by the summer term, Diane was meeting other more deviant girls
in the evenings. Kerry actually said, 'Last night me and Diane went out for
a muck about'. While maintaining weak, but still useful friendship ties with
the deviants, the knife-edge girls could also decry the conformists and hence
disassociate themselves from any possibility of being identified with them.
On occasion, they might do this more directly by making fun of the
conformists. For example, Sally and Jenny were talking and giggling in an
art lesson, while Janet went on working very hard, totally absorbed in her
drawing. They pointed at her mockingly, signalling the fact that they placed
informal issues higher on the list than Janet. The fact that their values were
seen to be shared helped show up their middle range position. Another
technique was simply to distance oneself publicly from extreme behaviour.
Thus, Sally complained about Janet: 'In English she wanted everything her
way, she wouldn't let anyone else have any ideas, she really annoys me. She
is always going on about her ballet exams, especially at dinner times. Even
Jane, and she's her friend, says she goes on about it too much'. Sally thus
publicly announced her disapproval of these attitudes and actions, and
simultaneously signalled her shared perspective with youth culture which,
as we have seen, deprecated 'bossiness' and 'boastfulness'.

These strategies were partly designed to win acceptance within the
informal culture, and they seemed to succeed. During the summer term, for
example, when both Julie and Diane began to indulge in knife-edge
behaviour, it was rapidly acknowledged by their peers:

>   Vivien: Julie and Diane . . . are dropping out now, and aren't as good because
>   they've started to go around with Jacqui and she mucks around and that.

Jenny was known to be going out with Bob, and of Sally it was said 'She
used to go out with Jimmy' and she 'just isn't going out with anyone at the
moment'. Interestingly enough, the real conformists also recognized the
position:

>   Jane: Diane and Julie, they're more on the other side, like me, only a little bit into it.

Knife-edgers, who had previously run the risk of being labelled with the
conformists, themselves indicated the extent of change such strategies
meant for their identities.

>   Sally: Some people called us snobs, last year, when we first came . . . because . . .

Jenny: Bridget thought we were as well, because we never said anything the first couple of weeks, but she knows now we're not.

Sally: We're in between . . . we are not bad exactly, but we are not good exactly, we are in between.

For one girl, Diane, there was a role model available in her sister, although she recognized that for many people her sister did appear too conformist. Nevertheless, she identified with her sister, and felt encouraged by the way she managed to hold both sides of her life in balance. 'Everyone thinks she's a goody-goody, and never goes out, but she goes out ever such a lot, and she gets her work done'.

The other side of the 'knife-edge' was to do well at school, and this they also managed to achieve. They were consistently awarded high marks and were eventually placed in the higher streams. They saw themselves basically as positively oriented toward school values. Diane admitted she was quite 'good' at school. She was discussing the issue of teachers using corporal punishment on girls: 'My dad wouldn't care [if the teacher hit her], but he knows no one would hit me 'cos I'm good'. There was a time for 'mucking about':

Diane: I don't think it is right . . . you should get on with your work and then have a laugh, when it is the right time.

Knife-edgers generally tried to avoid appearing 'good' by keeping a low profile on their academic success, as opposed to the conformist's tendency to 'boast'.

Sally: I don't tell the people in my class anything because some of them are at a lower standard than me, and if I told them, they would think 'snob, she got 80 per cent for maths. Why should we want to know her high marks?'

Thus by a careful mixture of strategies and presentation of self, these girls managed to survive, and indeed prosper, in a way the highly conformist could not.

Nevertheless, the conformists were not the passive receivers of the label that much of the research on them has implied (Willis 1977). They were proud of their own achievements and identities and disapproved of the deviants. They did experience pressure in a comprehensive school, but once they were streamed they found friendship groups, which gave them support. Both conformists and knife-edgers saw themselves as different from the deviants, and were able to articulate the values and attitudes that separated them:

Sally: Rosemary, she likes talking, and mucking around more than anything.

Emma: Well, we have got lots of people who muck around in our class, lots of people who think they are at school, just for the sake of being at school. Some people who really try to work hard.

They objected specifically to the deviants' experiments with smoking. Jane told with horror about Christine and Barbara smoking in the classroom at lunchtime, leaving the windows open to clear the smoke and smell. Then they went to Barbara's house, while her mother was at work, and smoked some more there. In the other form, the same thing was seen to be going on, in school and out.

Jenny: We just went to the toilets now, and we went in there, Cor! There was all these girls in there smoking, you could hardly breathe.

Sally: Like some people smoke at this age and that. My dad keeps on kidding me about it. You know Amy and Claire, well they came to knock for me one Saturday and I went out with them, and one of them got out some cigarettes and offered them round, and I wouldn't have one. We were going to go out again after tea, and I didn't want to go. I sort of made up an excuse that I was cold, but I didn't want to go in case they sort of said I was a chicken, something like that, not smoking.

In the data on boys we suggested that most pupils had two stereotypes, which they reacted against: that of the 'too conformist' but also one of the 'too deviant'. The same pattern existed for the girls. The 'too deviant' were those who had 'got a bad name' or 'had a reputation' or, worst of all, were seen as 'tarts'. This became clear because of shifting friendship patterns between the girls. Amy and Rosemary had become 'best friends' in the 'provisional adaptations phase', but it did not survive the third term at school. Amy moved decisively away from Ros, it seemed because Ros was 'too deviant'. Ros did not do well academically, and she put so much emphasis on the informal that Amy became unhappy with her association with her. Amy made a catalogue of the problems:

Amy: The other day, these girls called me and Ros over, and just because we had eye shadow on they said, 'Tarting themselves up for nothing'. If Ros would act more grown up, and cool down a bit. She can start getting you a bad name if you're not careful, she started getting me a bad name . . . OK. I used to go around with her, and I used to put lip gloss on with her, and just walk around. She would just sit there, doing her hair and putting make-up on, and everybody thought that I would do the same. And she's always giggling, that makes it worse. I've got a pencil skirt, but I don't want to wear it at school, but Ros does. They all say 'Showing your legs and that'. Ros, she is called names, and everybody started saying I was a tart as well and everything that's why I don't go around with her any more. She got me a bad name.

Amy's comments give a comprehensive catalogue of attitudes and behaviour that rated disapproval in the informal culture, and made her 'too deviant'. Ros's sexuality was an additional, serious problem.

> Amy: Well, Ros came to my disco. She really threw herself at Pete, she would do anything to have him, and she was letting him do things just because she wanted him, she got off with him, as if she was going out with him, but she wasn't properly and now the boys think, 'Oh she will go with anybody now'.

Amy clearly felt that she would be tainted with the same brush if she associated with Ros. She could not simply change her own behaviour, her identity was tied up with Ros's, and she had to break out of the friendship.

If Ros was seen as 'too deviant' by many of her class mates, her identity remained far short of Shirley's, a girl who occupied the stereotype of the extreme deviant. Ball (1981) described one girl, Beverley, who had this kind of role at Beachside Comprehensive. Shirley and another girl, Sylvia, were well known by both pupils and teachers. Many of the complaints against them were similar to those against Ros – they wore too much make-up, were too concerned with their personal appearance, and wore clothes seen as inappropriately fashionable for their age-grade. But there were far worse things as well. Shirley and Sylvia were 'hard', a characteristic usually attributed to boys, and they would 'go out' with boys much older than themselves.

> Valerie: Shirley, she goes out with the fourth years, and they all think they are really hard.
>
> Claire: She is one of the worst girls I have ever known.
>
> Jenny: She is really disgusting.

Shirley had the graffiti of youth culture not only on her school equipment but also on her own body. She wrote the name of the rival comprehensive in orange felt-tip pen in large letters up her arm: M.A.Y.O.R.F.I.E.L.D.S. R.U.L.E.S. O.K.? On the bottom of her bag, she had a series of moderately obscene pictures of one of the counselling staff. She was known to swear also, and to use obscene language with teachers. Within one month of being at the school she was suspended and sent to a truancy and trouble institute. During the first year at school, she became pregnant and had an abortion. At the end of the year she was involved in an incident. She had been assaulted by a group of boys by the tennis courts. They had stood around her in a circle, and made her take off most of her clothes, while they engaged in games of touching, teasing and threatening her. At a local disco, she was again surrounded by a group of boys who made her remove her clothes. The kind of sanctions that can be applied to a girl who entirely loses her reputation are graphically illustrated. She was a person to be entirely avoided.

Knife-edgers and conformists on the one hand, and deviants on the other also had different attitudes towards the future. All of the girls questioned said they wanted to be married, and that they wanted children, yet while the deviants spoke only of that, the knife-edgers and conformists also wanted some kind of reasonable job and career. They wanted to work at something interesting at least before they were married, and perhaps after their children were grown up. Their whole motivation in working hard at school was to ensure them a proper entry into the job market, a situation which they viewed as being balanced against women.

> Janet: I think there is more jobs for boys really, because if you are out of work, then ladies have only got little jobs like Avon and things like that, but the men have got all factory works, milkman and everything. So I think you have got to work harder if you are a girl to get a better job.
>
> Jane: I don't think women can drive aeroplanes, some can drive buses, but I think that's worse than anything. So I think women have not got much choice.

This can be contrasted with attitudes of the deviants, expressed typically in the following statements, where jobs are not a prime concern, the whole focus being on babies and marriage:

> Janie: I want some children, loads of them now ... a couple of little babies, all cuddly.
>
> R: Do you ever think it would be boring to have kids and just be at home all day with them?
>
> Janie: No, you can play with them, and that, they can help you do the cooking ... like jam tarts.
>
> Jacqui: I should think they would be ever so sweet.

The intensity of their feelings on this matter is well illustrated by their reactions to the researcher, who was married, female and without children. Claire, Amy, Rebecca and Ros were discussing with her the issue of careers for women and the job the researcher had. Claire said heatedly to the researcher, 'You are really, really selfish, aren't you?' Ros agreed: 'I think you are very selfish', said with the same intense disapproval in her tone. Amy chimed in, 'You should have children, it keeps a family together, it's important for that'. The conversation progressed, and an intense opposition to the idea of women choosing jobs and careers instead of children became abundantly clear.

The deviant girls saw their position as being directly in contrast to that of the boys. It was not as important for girls to have jobs when they left school as it was for boys, 'because girls can do housework' and boys 'have got to get the money'.

We asked the girls to write an essay, in which they imagined that they were 80 years old and that they were looking back over their lives and describing what had happened to them. All of the girls described getting married, as a matter of course. However, there were some differences in the age and point at which they married, and in what they had already done with their lives. Both Julie and Diane described themselves as getting good qualifications from school, and entering higher education to gain other qualifications before their marriages. Both envisaged a career with animals, before marriage, which continued in a diminished way after marriage. Jane also saw herself obtaining good school qualifications and then good secretarial qualifications. The majority of the girls saw themselves as having some sort of career before marriage, which they gave up at marriage. However, there were exceptions to this. Ros, Rebecca, Janie and Jacqui had no career. The age of marriage also varied dramatically. Jacqui saw herself marrying at 20, Emma at 29. All of the girls saw their marriages involving children, and there was a remarkable incidence of twins. Perhaps this reflects a kind of defiant assertion of sexuality and fertility on their part, at a time in their lives when they were beginning to adopt sexually differentiated identities.

V
Conclusion

$$\text{\reflectbox{\Large$\mathcal{O}$}}\ 9\ \text{\Large$\mathcal{O}$}$$

Theoretical and policy implications

Generalizability

It remains for us to draw out some of the educational implications of the study. First, however, some might query the soundness of making recommendations for policy and seeking to refine theory on the basis of a single case study. However, generalizability does not reside within the case study itself. In the first place, the material is made available to others to add to their knowledge and apply to their situations as they see fit. In this case, the generalizing is done by others. Whatever aspects of this study rest on a common basis with others, to that extent will it be applicable. The case study does not, of course, cover all instances of transfer at 12-plus – in fact, no more than one. But, inasmuch as there was a high degree of typicality about the school and its environment, we suspect that the processes we have observed are fairly common ones.

Secondly, generalizing is done from the *theory* to which the case study relates. Throughout, we have referred to a number of theories, relating to, for example, myth, pupil perceptions of teachers, pupil strategies, identity construction, cultural formation, socialization, and so on. We are following an inductive path here, which works from the particular to the general and holds that any developing theory must encompass all instances. Thus, we feel that this study adds to our theoretical knowledge in these areas, and it is from this collective knowledge that we must take any recommendations for policy.

There is an additional point that is intrinsic to the case study. One of our criticisms of many of the other studies of pupil transfer is that they have examined only partial aspects of the pupil experience. No matter how thoroughly such research is carried out, it must remain suspect if such partiality is not recognized. Any strengths that our analysis possesses derives mainly, we feel, from its wide-ranging perspective on the total pupil experience. In this sense, there is an internal generalizability contributing to the validity of the particular aspects within.

What, then, is the relevance of the study for theory and policy?

Status passages

The notion of a status passage is potentially very useful for our understanding of pupil transfer within the pupil career. The concept originated from Van Gennep's work, *The Rites of Passage* (1960), and was later developed by Glaser and Strauss (1971). It refers to transitions in life wherein people undergo a change in status, whether it be from being alive to being dead (Glaser and Strauss's own example, 1968), from being a childless woman to becoming a mother (Oakley 1980), from being married to being divorced (Hart 1976), from being a naïve recruit to becoming a trained bread salesman (Ditton 1977). It may seem that this is rather a grand concept to apply to primary–secondary transition. For many pupils, it might be thought that the transfer will appear a continuous, natural process, stepping off with eager anticipation from one status with easy assurance on to the next in one movement. But, it is in fact, vastly more complicated.

Van Gennep (1960) examined the structural features of status passages, arguing that they needed to be closely regulated for the smooth functioning of society. From his study of pre-literate societies, he identified three main stages in status passages: (i) separation; (ii) transition; (iii) reincorporation. It is not difficult to see how these phases and the rites associated with them apply to pupil transfer. The pre-transfer induction ceremonies, the purchase of new uniforms, the rehearsal of myths, may be regarded as rites of separation. The pupils are being separated from the 'junior' cohort of which they have been a part for a number of years. They were in transition during the summer, and in the first few days at the new school. This phase is characterized by 'marginality' or 'liminality' (Turner 1969). Pupils had left one status, but were not yet fully secure in the other, 'neither here, nor there, but betwixt and between' (ibid, p. 95). There were extensive anxieties in this phase, which were expressed and sublimated in a systematic and coherent body of pupil myths (Chapter 1). There was a highly developed and wide-ranging induction scheme used by the upper school to try and smooth the transition and to win the pupils into the school's particular ethos (Chapter 2). There then followed a series of stages, from an initial presentation of formal 'front' wherein pupils appeared hyper-conformist (Chapter 3) through 'coming out' with truer identities and attempted 'take-overs' (Chapter 4) to negotiating for a modus vivendi acceptable to both sides (Chapters 5–8). Ultimately, after much negotiation with teachers, pupils are 'incorporated' into the society of the school, roughly at the point where the cycle is beginning again for a new intake.

Transfer between primary and secondary schools is therefore a very good example of a status passage. Study of the transition might add something to the general formal theory of status passages, which in turn might inform educational policies. For example, our data suggests that status passages contain more significant phases than previously identified. Van Gennep's three broad stages are hardly adequate for an understanding of school transfer if the pupils' experience is taken into account. Our study indicates a number of phases and sub-phases that embrace the whole of the first year. For example, during the 'reincorporation' stage, we detected three sequential stages which we term 'initial encounters', 'provisional adaptations' and 'consolidated adaptations'. Within these are sub-phases. For example, in the 'initial encounters' stage we identified a 'honeymoon' and a 'coming out' phase. Progress in the formal area was matched by developments in the pupils' informal culture, where the emphasis on clinging to a group for security during the initial encounters stage gave way to 'identification', as the pupils 'came out' and realised their individuality, and ultimately to 'growth', where pupils appeared to feed and feed off each other's desired identities.

Furthermore, our study makes clear there are mini-status phases to be negotiated within the major ones. We have seen how teachers, particularly through the use of humour, might increase the desirability of the passage into their area; while others, through the excessive use of power, might reduce it with respect to theirs. Thus pupils undergo a number of mini-passages to different situations, individualized by factors such as subject and teacher. Similarly, some pupils undergo individual status passages. Not all pupils advance through the transition as a cohort, going at the same pace, employing the same style and going through the same phases. With such a perspective, we may be able to identify individual teachers and pupils who, for one reason or another, are having particular difficulties.

There are educational implications here, for previous studies of pupil transfer have suggested a fairly rapid 'reincorporation' into the school. Our study suggests, however, a longer time-perspective is necessary. After a short period, pupils had made 'provisional adaptations' to the school. Some studies of pupil transfer, we feel, have missed the 'provisional' nature of these adaptations and have assumed that the passage has been made within the first term. Changes continued to happen throughout the whole of the first year. Furthermore, the notion of 'incorporation' is rather misleading, for the adaptation that pupils make is clearly a complex process of negotiation, with give-and-take on both sides. We have seen, for example, how pupils made space for their own interests, both within and around the formal culture.

While Van Gennep looked at status passages from the view of the interests of society as a whole, Glaser and Strauss (1971) were more interested in the individual's perspective, and this approach is more relevant to our study. They identified a number of 'properties' of status passages, such as how 'desirable' the passage is to those concerned and how much 'control' the individual has over it. They questioned its 'centrality' and its 'clarity' to those involved and how far they could identify its phases and how long it is likely to last. These theoretical considerations carry practical implications for pupil transfer. Teachers could try to make the passage as attractive as possible, as they did in the Old Town scheme. Some argue for giving pupils more control over the passage, on the grounds that it will aid their negotiation of it (Hamblin 11978). Teachers could perhaps offer more signposts along the way to give the passage a clear schedule. Without such help there will be disarticulations – passages out of 'phase' and some who make only an uncomfortable accommodation to the new state.

Glaser and Strauss also draw attention to multiple status passages, and it is clear that pupil transfer at 12-plus consists not just of one status passage, but three. There is, firstly, the transfer within the formal culture, which is geared to teacher expectations and expressed through official policy; secondly, a transfer within informal culture, which is geared to pupil expectations and expressed in relationships among ones peers and among the pupils generally; thirdly, puberty. There is, at this stage, rapid physical, cognitive, emotional and sexual growth, embodied in the progression from child to adolescent. The actual status changes involve for the pupil a move from the top of one institution to the bottom of another (lower status), from primary to secondary pupil (higher status), from child to adolescent (higher status), and from *older* child to *younger* adolescent (lower status in the context of all teenage age-grades). It is in the interaction of these elements that this particular status passage has to be understood. One major aspect of this is how pupils prioritize the different passages. With some pupils, as we have seen, the passage into the informal hierarchy is more important than that into the school. Approaches that concentrate almost exclusively on the formal aspects such as the pupil's academic achievement miss a great deal, and may come to the wrong conclusions. We discuss the implications of this later.

We have been much concerned with the pupil's management of the passage. Myths, we argued, fulfil a major role in this, and it is likely that similar bodies of knowledge attend many other kinds of status passage. Myths were the key instrument of anticipatory socialization in the separation phase, and they continued to form a guide for action through transition and reincorporation. They signal that one has accomplished the passage, when pupils in their third term tell the myths to the next cohort. Their efficiency lies in their starkness, and in their ability to penetrate the subconscious and the emotions. These areas are usually left out of consideration, not least because of methodological problems in getting to grips with them. We have demonstrated their importance, and suggested one method of dealing with them.

Despite the preparation and general guide lines that myths afford, however, they leave a lot to be decided. As pupils encountered new problems and challenges, they seemed to engage in a trial-and-error search for new interpretations and definitions of the situation. We would support, therefore, those studies that have laid emphasis upon the individual's construction of meanings in response to situations as they occur (e.g. Davis 1963, Musgrove and Middleton 1981). Pupils employed psychological management, strategic invention and identity experimentation to feel their way through the passage. Solutions emerged gradually as a result of the ongoing adjustment process. This meant that pupils undergo considerable personal change during the transition, an aspect as yet little considered in the study of status passage.

Identity

We would wish to stress the degree of personal change in the status passage. There is not much theory to guide us here. Anthropological studies such as those of Van Gennep (1960) and Victor Turner (1969) were more interested in structural aspects. Glaser and Strauss (1971) considered the subjective properties, but did not venture into identity theory. In considering this status passage of pupil transfer at 11–13, it seemed essential to do so. This is because of the threat the move represents to the self. It occurs 'at a stage in life when the young teenager is concerned with . . . what sort of person one is to become, what sort of self is in the making' (Dewey 1922, p. 127; see also Rapoport and Rapoport 1975). As Erikson (1968) put it, 'Before the adolescent can successfully abandon the security of childhood dependence on others, he must have some idea of who he is, where he is going and what the possibilities are of getting there'.

Identity development does not begin, or end, of course, in adolescence. It is a continuous process throughout life. As soon as children gain a conception of the 'generalized other' (Mead 1934) and begin to see themselves as others see them, then a notion of identity, a sense of who one is, begins to be built up. It will involve roles, attributes of personality, appearance, values and beliefs, and it depends on how we see others seeing us, who *they* think we are.

The child first comes to a sense of the generalized other through play (Mead 1934). There is much role-experimentation in children's games, many of which are strongly featured in the primary or middle school playground. At this stage, this experimentation is transient, situational, and fun. With puberty, the question of identity becomes rather more serious as adolescents become more self-conscious and more conscious of themselves as unique individuals. Significantly, the experimentation changes from child's 'play' to more adolescent concerns regarding appearance and friendship patterns (Chapters 5, 7, 8 and 9). There is, also, a preoccupation with an *ens realissimus* (Berger *et al.* 1973), a central, unchanging component of self, which despite perhaps much variable behaviour represents 'the real me'. Thus, not only do they find themselves playing roles that shift from one situation, or one time, to another, and worry about 'which, if any, is the *real* me', they also self-consciously try out different roles in the hope of finding one that seems to fit (Conger 1977). They do not experiment alone. Parents and teachers often engage in great battles with children about whom they are to become.

There has been talk of 'identity crisis' or 'storm and stress' during adolescence, but, though some may go through such a dramatic experience, the evidence does not suggest it is an essential or widespread feature of this age range (Conger 1979). However, adolescence, and particularly the earlier stage of 11–13, does have its problems. It could hardly be otherwise, given the enormous changes that take place at this time – an acceleration of physical growth, intelligence and awareness, sexual maturation, emotional changes, distancing from family and growing influence of the peer group – all this, too, against a background of comparatively rapid social change, where norms and expectations are not as stable as they used to be. There may very well be therefore what we might term 'identity strain' or what Erikson (1968) calls 'identity confusion'.

The status passage of pupil transfer from primary or middle school to secondary occurs in the middle of these developments, and in the first instance would appear to heighten identity strain. Reputations, established over the years at middle school through hard work, prowess at games, or at fighting or whatever, now seem in jeopardy. How are pupils to cope with new forms of work, new challenges and forms of opposition? Will they be split up from their friends, who have hitherto sustained their sense of identity, and will they be put into separate classes with new people?

We found two major factors in pupil identities. One was basic attitudes to school, and one divide that was soon evident was a *conformist–deviant* one. The other was *gender*, promoting another divide, boys and girls, after initial interaction, soon separating along rigid lines. These were the two major elements noted in our study, but of course there may have been others we were unable to pick up for lack of comparative material. For example, we would expect social class and ethnicity to be big influences, and indeed we saw some indication of that in pupils' subjective conceptions of class. However, Old Town was too monolithic in those respects for thorough comparisons to be drawn. Further research could be designed to consider these aspects.

The way in which pupils treated and spoke of others leads us to suggest a 'polarities model' of identity construction. Pupils had their own conceptions of what constituted normal behaviour, belief and attitude, and projected their extremes along the two most important dimensions of attitude to school (ultra-conformist and ultra-deviant) and gender (ultra-masculinity or femininity, and the converse). These were personified in certain pupils, and the individual then located him or herself somewhere between these markers. Such a model may help to account for the highly stylized way in which adolescents seem to perceive others. There was evidence that pupils also employed teachers as 'markers' in these identification processes. The main criteria have been laid down by the peer culture, but teachers are judged by them. The teachers most attuned to them were the most popular and enjoyed most success. This illustrates a serious point about child socialization. It might be generally assumed that the 'significant others' exerting most influence on them are adults – parents and other relatives, and teachers. But it is clear from this study at least, that their own peer cultures may be a far more potent force, at least at this particularly important point in their career. The erstwhile 'significant others' are then interpreted through the peer culture. This yields a whole new range of pupil perspectives on teachers, deriving from the informal culture, to set beside those more formally related (such as 'good at control', 'explains well', 'has a laugh with you'). There are 'sex-pot' teachers, 'queer' teachers, teachers with 'big knockers', teachers who project the macho image or femininity, teachers who treat you 'more grown up' and others who treat you like 'little kids', teachers who are 'slow and old'. It seems clear that teachers act in a particular way as 'significant others' at this important stage of growth. The action is not direct and conscious on the teacher's part. Rather, pupils appear to see them as living examples of their own informal cultural properties, and to use them as sounding boards for their own development. A teacher's personal qualities, as well as teaching skill, is clearly of great importance. But we must recognize that negative role models play a part in helping pupils to locate themselves on any dimension.

Though the two divisions of academic orientation and gender were of crucial importance, they did on occasions cross-cut each other. Sometimes the masculine gender code put pressure on boys to try to perform well academically, but at others it required behaviour to show their tough and delinquent maleness. Girls felt more required by the feminine gender code to disguise their academic prowess. Both boys and girls solved these conflicts of interests and demands by employing what we term *'knife-edge strategies'*. These take the line of the thin divide between two opposing options, and may require vastly different forms of behaviour in different situations. Others have noticed similar strategies for the management of identity, and it appears to be a major way of handling conflicting pressures (Lambart 1976, Fuller 1980, Prendergast and Proust 1980, Turner 1983).

The study sheds light on the differences between primary and secondary socialization, and on the way individuals move between them. Primary socialization occurs early in life within the family and involves learning some basic strategical techniques – how to behave as boy or girl, how to act at table, speak to strangers, play games, relate to parents, brothers and sisters. For children, at this stage, before going to school, the family *is* the world, and what is mediated to them is the only reality that they know.

Secondary socialization, according to Berger and Luckmann (1967), involves 'the internalisation of institutional or institution-based "sub-worlds" . . . the acquisition of role-specific knowledge . . . role-specific vocabularies . . . and tacit understandings' (p. 158). The first lesson the child has to learn on going to school is how to become a pupil, in general terms, as distinct from 'a certain mother's child'. In the early years of infant school, the boundaries between school and home are softened to ease this transition. Eventually, however, other sub-roles come into play as the pupils become categorized into good or poor academically, well or badly behaved, proficient at certain subjects rather than others, and so on. There are fairly well-defined types, of which there are fairly clear expectations, and pupils, having signalled the appropriateness of their allocation to them, further learn to respond to these expectations.

As a method of handling a whole range of roles the child may also learn – though perhaps with varying degrees of success – to cultivate the art of 'role-distancing' (Goffman 1961). We have seen a number of examples of this during the first year of secondary school. That, perhaps, is not a bad recipe for education in modern industrial society, that is, learning to accommodate to a variety of roles in a flexible way, with maximum command, but personally adjustable commitment.

Cultures

The major thrust of the study has been to reveal how formal and informal cultures become interwoven, and how pupils chart their individual courses within and between them. The formal culture is introduced from above, as it were, by the teachers. They set the parameters within which it is formed, they set up the criteria by which it is defined, and initiate its inception. The informal culture is pressed up from below as it were, by one's peers and by more pervasive and widespread cultures expressed most notably in the media. These two cultures intermingled in many ways, sometimes harmoniously, sometimes conflictually. For example, the teachers took over some of the informal culture as they perceived it and blended it into their particular school ethos, one that we have depicted as 'middle-ground culture' (Measor and Woods 1984). Much of this came from the 'admass' world, to which both teachers and pupils had easy access. To much of this the pupils responded, playing their part in the construction of middle-ground culture.

At other times, however, the two cultures came into conflict. Sometimes the great informal pressures on pupils not only escaped teachers' perceptions, but were actually increased by them, albeit unknowingly. Such was the case with the operation of gender codes, particularly on girls. Girls' deviance went largely unperceived and unchallenged. Male teachers tended to reinforce a culture of femininity which celebrated incompetence. Sometimes pupils pressed the informal culture on teachers, as they did in making spaces and places for the play of their own concerns, and in attempted 'take-overs'. They exploited the uneven value of curriculum subjects to advance interests in opposition to the formal culture. Sometimes the informal was used in tacit alliance with the formal culture, though it might be interpreted differently by the teacher. This was the case with 'co-operative groups' – informal self-help groups that pupils formed themselves, often interpreted by teachers as counter-cultural agencies.

These are just some of the major ways the two cultures interacted, but they come into contact continuously in multifarious ways. Their further study is an urgent concern, not only for its own sake and further knowledge of cultures but because it is one of the chief social mechanisms through which learning either does or does not take place.

Apart from this distinction, there has been considerable debate in recent years about the form of pupil cultures, the nature of the peer group, indeed its relevance (Furlong 1976), the appropriateness of 'conformity' and 'deviance' as general modes of adaptation (Hammersley and Turner 1980), the impact of the institution on pupil cultures (Hargreaves 1967, Lacey 1970, Ball 1981), of social class (Willis 1977) and of gender (Sharpe 1976, Davies 1978, Deem 1978). Our study shows the power of the cultures of masculinity and femininity, but upholds the interactionist point about individual choice. Certain choices, however, are difficult to make, and pupils on occasions experience deep inner conflict. We felt this to be particularly true of girls who were ambitious academically.

The importance of friendship groups to pupils has been clearly demonstrated. Further, these groups do not simply have a redemptive function concerned with security in difficult situations. At this school, pupil associations soon moved to a new basis – of co-operative groups and of 'best friend' bonds. With regard to the latter, Lambart (1976) got close to their familial function. Our data, not all of which we can include in this study, suggest that this relationship was, for girls, almost a complete life-support system, and essential to their personal development. Boys seemed to have more generalized relationships within the culture of masculinity, with its emphasis on strength, toughness, and fighting ability.

The general applicability of conformity and deviance as modes of adaptation were confirmed, against doubts recently raised (Hammersley and Turner 1980). It was, in fact, how pupils themselves saw it, and was one of the main criteria in establishing their own identities and forming relationships with others. School processes and organization clarified this divide, rather than precipitated it.

We turn now to the implications of the study for educational policy and practice.

The informal passage

The informal passage is probably the more traumatic yet is least studied and understood, a fact reflected in its almost total negligence in Old Town's induction scheme.

Pupils seemed to cope better within the informal culture if they had a sympathetic brother or sister already at the school. They had the necessary inside knowledge, and perhaps were offered a degree of moral support. Some schools, on the same principle, encourage older pupils to take part in induction. For example, in one school, a sixth former is attached to each form on intake for a short period to help them through any initial problems. In another, the fifth formers put on a concert for the new intake, thus performing a similar function within the informal culture as the English staff did with their play within the formal culture. We were tempted to suggest that second year pupils, as the ones most recently initiated, might sponsor new recruits, by 'showing them the ropes' during the first few days. But we heard that one school does the opposite – keeps its second years away for the first one or two days – because most of the bullying and teasing comes from them! However, elsewhere *parents* have been invited to the secondary school during school time and escorted round by second year pupils, and this seems a useful compromise.

We have argued that identity concerns are prominent during the transition. There should be opportunities, therefore, for the safeguarding, recognition and promotion of individual identity. In this, friendship supports are vital, yet are severely threatened by the move. We were forced to conclude that 12-plus was not the best time to make such a change. At eleven, pupil friendships are still fragmentary, insubstantial and fleeting. At twelve, they are more stable and have a deeper emotional investment. This is probably connected with the biological and emotional changes connected with puberty that occur for many, particularly girls, during that year. When pupils transfer to a new school, many of these friendships will be disrupted. It makes their task of adapting to a vastly different situation that much harder. Eleven-plus, therefore, seems the better age for transfer, and this indeed was supported by parents, pupils, secondary school teachers and many of the middle school teachers. It was felt that pupils were 'held back a year' academically, socially and emotionally, because the middle schools lacked the resources to cope with the needs of the young adolescent. We should note here that the reasons for there being a break at all, and for its being at any particular age, are not all educational ones, and we have given a brief account in the Appendix of how current arrangements came into being.

Otherwise, teachers might consider the provision of private space and time both around and within lessons. In our study, pupils typically had to fight for this, and often arrived at cross-purposes with teachers. And not all teachers recognized the significance of the transfer to pupils in terms of heightened age-graded status. In one sense, the pupils are the babies in the new organization, but from a wider perspective they have left childhood behind and expect treatment and activities commensurate with their advanced status.

Such methods would help to give pupils more control of the passage as they go through it.

The formal passage

We have noted pupil fears of work difficulty, of new institutional size and organization, of bureaucracy, of teacher impersonality, of discipline – all in part but not completely assuaged by the induction scheme used by Old Town teachers. Some of these fears were resolved fairly easily, other less so. We noted, also, a certain amount of curriculum, teaching and task discontinuity.

There is clearly much that can be accomplished with minimal organizational change. For example, pupils could be initiated into specialist teaching and 'time-related' work in their final year of middle school, and there might be a measure of more generalist teaching and 'task-related' work in the first year of secondary school. The rules could be clarified. In Old Town, pupils could have been inducted more carefully into ways of handling homework. The punishment system was little understood, and it would have been a simple matter to advise what kinds of behaviour merited the cane, what constituted a 'detentionable offence' and what such a punishment entailed.

More continuity, however, can probably only be achieved by an interchange of personnel between middle and upper schools. In one area we know, teachers in the same subject field from the two schools meet to discuss curriculum and method, especially around the transition period. However, it may not be enough for them simply to talk. They may have to *work* in each other's schools to familiarize themselves with each other's tasks. This would carry another benefit, for pupils would have a chance to get to know some of the secondary teachers in advance, while on their own home, known territory.

Such an exchange of personnel makes sense from the point of view of the informal passage as well. We have drawn attention to the function of pupil transfer at this stage as rites of passage from childhood to adolescence. And as Blyth (1965, vol. 1, p. 144) notes, 'Rites of passage in preliterate societies are, after all, carried out before the faces of the elders of the tribe, rather than in a gap between two groups of elders facing in opposite directions.' This is an argument, of course, not only for teachers spreading themselves over the transition, but for their having better knowledge and greater awareness of processes within the informal culture.

Cross-fertilization of personnel alone, however, will not achieve maximum effect without joint planning. We agree with Power and Cotterell (1981, p. 36), who argue, 'If one takes the view that development is a continuous process which is optimised when there is a match between the learning experiences provided by the school and the knowledge, abilities and interests of the students, then it becomes clear that the school curriculum should be conceived and planned as a whole' (see also Neal 1975, Murdoch 1982). This might aid the resolution of some of the issues seen by pupils as problems.

However, other approaches are necessary to tackle pupils' 'informal' perceptions of the curriculum, which effectively reduce their learning experiences and, in some instances, their life-chances. We have described the pupils' evaluation of subjects in terms of their marketability, their use of certain areas for the play of the informal culture, and the influence of gender codes. As D. H. Hargreaves (1982) has argued, while schooling is ordered around the intellectual-cognitive domain of propositional knowledge, the aesthetic-artistic and the affective-emotional are relegated to an inferior position. In any consideration of how we might increase the currency of the expressive area, we must bear in mind its importance to the pupils' informal interests. This can meld with the formal if greater use is made of the pupils' own experiences and interests. As we have noted, in general, this was used to good effect in the Old Town ethos. But in the affective areas of the curriculum, arguably there is a case for making it the keystone of curriculum design. Vulliamy (1979), for example, argues that pop music is considered worthless and even delinquent beside the more serious pursuit of classical music. But if teachers were really interested in developing pupils' full musical appreciation in more than a purely cerebral way, they would try to get to grips with the affective-emotional content of pop.

Other problems are more intractable. We have seen how, for girls, their developing femininity works against their academic interests in some science subjects. Their non-competence is used as evidence that they are truly feminine, and those subject areas are then very useful to them within the informal culture, which here is at distinct odds with the formal. Diagnosis, however, is easier than cure, for the roots of these cultures lie deep within society. The least schools can do is to see that they do not aggravate divisions, reinforce inadequacies or endorse stereotypes. This in itself is not easy. Teachers themselves have been socialized into regarding cultural gender differences as natural, and the belief may form part of the bedrock of their whole approach to teaching. There is a task here, therefore, for teacher education.

It might, also, be acknowledged that there are no simple solutions. Making boys do needlework and girls metalwork, for example, appears to be counter-productive, judging from our case study. Separating boys and girls for science lessons removes some of the pressures on girls to under-perform, though there is little evidence as yet that it leads to greater achievement. There is scope here for new curriculum initiatives that render the form of science teaching more amenable to girls, and for a publicity drive to increase its marketability in the eyes of girls.

Old Town was a very successful school by usual state standards. They achieved good results, academically and socially. It was a happy school, with a strong sense of purpose, and it was oversubscribed with customers. All the more serious, therefore, are the implications for comprehensive education of some of our findings. There was no social mix, rather the differences appeared to be more vividly revealed by adjacency. We have seen, too, that the academically strong did not help the weak in mixed-ability situations, and that there were pressures on the aspiring conformist, whether boy or girl, actually to under-achieve. To these, streaming (or setting) came as a relief. Like most comprehensive schools, Old Town operated a selective system, which ministered to their formal requirements and also squared with the pupils' identity aspirations. These are powerful forces to set against the ideology of comprehensivization.

The need for discontinuities

Although the passage may certainly be eased in its structured aspects, we have already made the point in discussing primary and secondary socialization that it would be a mistake to aim for an entirely smooth, continuous transition. In other respects, too, the trauma associated with a sharp break is functional. As we have noted, in terms of personal and social development the passage is not a continuous one, but a 'going out' and a 'coming in' from one stage of life to another (Beattie 1959). Pain is a universal feature of puberty rites. As Lortie (1968) comments, 'Such ceremonies, in addition to dramatizing the child's movement to adulthood, test him ruthlessly for qualities prized in his society (p. 255)'. Our material certainly indicates a great deal of this 'ruthless testing'. It might be a mistake, therefore, *not* to have a transition point sometimes at this stage, and it might *not* be desirable to ease the passage too much and in all respects. Piggott (1977, p. 111), for one, argues on similar grounds that 'total continuity would do pupils a disservice'. Murdoch (1982, p. 225) also concludes that one might 're-consider attempts by teachers to blur the boundaries, because they may delay the maturation process.' One of her teachers commented that children who transfer at twelve are more immature than those who transfer at eleven. Blyth (1965, p. 138) also drew attention to the point. 'Just as pre-literate societies have their rites of passage from childhood to adolescence, so the transition from primary to secondary education fulfils a somewhat similar function in English society, marking the end of the Midlands' years'.

Our material shows that our pupils experienced mental and emotional pain when the requirements of the new stage were starkly presented. The price one has to pay for this may be a temporary fall-off in academic performance following transfer, but in terms of general socialization it may be for the best. For example, in relation to induction to work – another kind of status passage – Lortie pointed to the collective nature of the experience, which he terms 'shared ordeal', and notes that it:

> ... accompanies a shift to adult status, the development of self-esteem, tested commitment and inter-generational trust and the relevance of collegial ties in the work career. The absence of shared ordeal is associated in each instance, with an opposite outcome ...
>
> (Lortie 1968

There are some things, then, that pupils must learn for themselves. The root difficulty for teachers is that, while they might accept their roles as elders witnessing the pupils' ritual progress through the transition, some of that progress interferes with the continuities thought desirable in the formal passage – pupils' appropriation of the curriculum, pressures to under-achieve, their need to practise strategic deviance. Again, there are no easy solutions, but we thought that Old Town teachers were on the right track. Power and Cotterell (1981, p. 34) found that the successful schools in their sample 'seemed to have a sense of mission, an identity, and a wholeness which pervaded every aspect of their functioning. In such schools, induction programmes, pastoral care systems ... along with other features of school life, formed part of a hideen curriculum whereby the school conveyed the message that it cares about its students, their education and their well-being' (see also Hargreaves *et al.* 1975, Reynolds 1976, Rutter *et al.* 1979). At Old Town, teachers cultivated a 'middle ground', which, while insisting on control (specifying the boundaries), allowed a degree of latitude (for example in symbolic adjustments to the uniform), and attempted to convey the fun and excitement of learning and the rewards of hard work, in a friendly and caring atmosphere (see Measor and Woods 1984). It moved towards meeting pupils where it could do so profitably for both sides, but in other respects maintained a judicious distance. Much has to be left to the pupil's private, personal domain. But teachers should know about it, so that they can provide circumstances to aid it, or in those situations where conflict is inevitable or desirable, understand its cause. We concluded, therefore, that pupil transfer should be neither wholly 'continuous progress' nor wholly 'sharp break', but a bit of each, the former applying mainly to the formal passage, the latter to the informal, and that, where they merge and conflict, they are best tackled through a 'middle ground' ethos, which takes the needs of both cultures, and of teachers and pupils (which can vary in some important respects), into consideration.

⊃ *Appendix* ⊂

The origin of current transfer points

Fragmentation of the pupil career is dictated partly by administrative necessity, partly by the perceived demands of social justice, and partly by certain beliefs about the development of the adolescent.

The current transition points can be traced back to the beginning of the century. British education at the time was based on elementary education for the working classes (until 13 or 14 years of age) and secondary education for the better-off. Working-class children could only receive secondary education by winning scholarships, but many who did left grammar schools within a year of entering in order to begin work. Following the 1902 Education Act, regulations were introduced requiring secondary schools to provide four-year courses, beginning at the age of twelve (later reduced to ten). Some authorities also began imposing conditions upon entrants that they should give an undertaking to remain until their fifteenth birthday. The result was a steady trend towards 11–12 as the age of transfer. But there was still confusion in post-primary education, owing to the expansion of courses following the 1902 Act, and courses admitting at age 11 (grammar schools), 12 (central schools) and 13 (junior technical schools).

Added to a need for rationalization of these developments was the growing attack from Labour and Liberal politicians on the basic injustices of the system, which led R. H. Tawney to the conclusion that:

> The only policy which is at once educationally sound and suited to a democratic community is one under which primary education and secondary education are organized as two stages in a single and continuous process; secondary education being the education of the adolescent and primary education being education preparatory thereto. . . . (The Labour Party's) objective, therefore, is . . . that all normal children, irrespective of the income, class or occupation of their parents may be transferred at the age of eleven plus from the primary . . . school to one type of another of secondary school.
>
> (Tawney 1922, p. 7)

The prevailing psychology, also, was in favour of a division between 'childhood' and 'adolescence'. The views of Stanley Hall (1904) were very

172

influential. He saw the individual reliving the history of the species. 'Childhood' was equivalent to a primitive stage of existence, which stopped short of the higher forms of reason and morality and thus was the age of 'external and mechanical training', when teaching should take the form of 'drill, inculcation and regimentation' (typical of the elementary schools). But 'adolescence' was a new birth, for the higher and more completely human traits are now born (pp. xiii–xv). Consequently, new educational techniques were necessary, which made new appeals to 'freedom and interest'. What more natural and convenient than that these essentially different forms of education should take place in different schools and different parts of the system?

However, the main reasons were social and administrative. In considering the Hadow Report (Board of Education 1927), whose influence on educational stages still remains strong, Nisbet and Entwistle concluded that:

> a 'clean break' was necessary to eliminate the social division of education into parallel systems, one for the rich and the other for the poor. A fixed age of transfer was necessary in order to co-ordinate the various systems of post-primary education which had emerged at random throughout the country and 11-plus was the age produced by pressures to extend the secondary school course of elementary scholarship winners.
>
> (Nisbet and Entwistle 1966, p. 61)

Subsequently, the Hadow Committee (Board of Education 1927) recommended a 'clean break' in education across the system between the ages of eleven and twelve in a single, end-on system of primary and secondary schools. The choice of 11-plus as a natural dividing line received a further boost in the years following 1944 with the establishment of 'secondary education for all', though the development of tripartitism was in direct opposition to the principles enunciated by Tawney (1922). The Norwood Report (Board of Education 1943) had identified a difference in character between primary and secondary education, primary being for 'basic skills and aptitudes of mind' and 'general ability', secondary being for 'a special cast of mind to manifest itself'. The Norwood Committee, of course, argued for the general types of 'cast of mind', which could best be served, they thought, by a tripartite arrangement of grammar, technical and secondary modern schools. They did tone down the notion of a 'break' between primary and secondary, arguing more for a continuous process; but the 1944 Act none the less stamped a legal imprint on 'primary' pupils as those under twelve, thus confirming 11-plus in the post-war expansion as the one and only divide for the next twenty years.

The dominant consideration in British education at this time was the expansion of educational opportunity to all social classes. Though there was much debate about the nature of education and the relationship of primary to secondary, that division had been dictated by reasons other than purely educational ones connected with any individual's personal development (though that was part of the justification used). Nisbet and Entwistle (1966) have criticized the psychology of the Hadow Report. Research since then (e.g. Tanner 1961, 1962, Bloom 1964, Entwistle 1967) has pointed to continuous, uninterrupted growth in mental development between the ages of six and eighteen. In anthropology, Margaret Mead (1943) had already shown that the 'storm and stress' period, considered an essential element of adolescence, was not typical of the Samoan culture; she argued that it was a product of social conditions in certain societies. Other studies since have shown a wide range of individual rates in maturation, which undermines the argument for a 'natural' break. Moreover, successful systems are in operation in other countries, with a variety of breaks between the ages of ten and thirteen, or which run 'all-through systems' from six to 15 or 16 years of age.

In fact, our conceptions of phases of life are largely socially rather than biologically determined. Phillippe Aries (1965) has shown how recent our dominant conceptions of childhood and adolescence are, and how childhood was 'invented' in the seventeenth and eighteenth centuries as a means of separating the experience of the young from that of their elders. Similarly, Musgrove (1964) argues that 'adolescence' as a distinctive phase between childhood and adulthood is a myth, an invention of the last century and a half. Rousseau began the educational justification (continued later by Stanley Hall) with his notions of childhood as a distinctive phase (which could be abandoned to 'negative education'), and the 'second birth' that ushered in the flowering of adolescence. During the nineteenth century the concept of 'adolescence' was gradually defined. The rate of progress toward maturity had to be retarded as the demand for child and youthful labour declined. 'The adolescent was inappropriately located within the family: the characteristics which had been ascribed to him could more certainly be produced in the school' (Musgrove 1964, p. 54). So a boost was given to the education system, and a professional organization set about the legitimation of adolescence. These phases became institutionalized in the infant, junior and secondary divisions of school, and there was further legitimation from academic quarters, notably in the work of Piaget, who argued that the child developed through clearly identifiable stages.

Institutionalization of these phases consolidated them as 'natural' states. Blyth (1965) showed how teachers and administrators concentrated their interest on either primary or secondary education. Buildings, posts, finances, curricula, extra-curricular activities, etc., – all were viewed differently. Childhood and adolescence became integrated within themselves and differentiated from each. The primary stage, it could be argued, is concerned with primary socialization. It still has a 'family' ethos, and is most concerned with first principles. The secondary stage ushers in new fields of vision. The Newsom Report put it thus:

> The work in a secondary school becomes secondary in character whenever it is concerned, first, with self-conscious thought and judgement; secondly, with the

relation of school and the work done there to the world outside of which the pupils form part and of which they are increasingly aware, and thirdly, with the relation of what is done in school to the future of the pupils, that is, to the part they see themselves playing, or can be brought to see themselves playing in adult life.

(CACE 1967, pp. 112–13)

Again, it was largely the issue of social justice focusing on the inequities of selection at secondary level that eventually breached this system. Increasing interest in comprehensive education, the Leicestershire and West Riding experiments, Circular 10/65 (DES 1965), the Plowden Report (CACE 1967), the commitment to raising the school leaving age to 16 – all combined to destroy the sense of inevitability about 11-plus as the age of transfer.

Leicestershire tried a two-tier secondary system of 11–15 high schools and 14–18 grammar schools, with voluntary transfer. The West Riding employed a middle-school of 9–13. The Plowden Committee came down in favour of twelve as the appropriate age of transfer, and recommended a restructured national system which included middle schools, preferably for the age-range 8–12. The Education Act of 1968 legalized conversions, and, gradually, authorities began to reorganize. They could not, of course, begin from scratch, but had to make use of existing buildings, and this, inevitably, had its own influence on developments. However, by the terms of the 1964 Act, though middle schools were authorized, they still had to be 'deemed' either 'primary' or 'secondary' by the Secretary of State.

If the evils of selection, according to this account, were the driving force behind this trend, coupled with economic and administrative considerations, there was an equally strong emphasis on child development, which countered the 'clean break' psychology of the Hadow Committee. Nisbet and Entwistle (1966, 1969) concluded tht 'childhood and adolescence merge without any immediate or obvious changes in behaviour' (1966, p. 19) and that the after-effects of transfer 'seem to leave their mark on children's academic performance throughout the first year at secondary school' (1969). They recommended that the years 9–13 should be a period of gradual change in style of teaching and method of reorganization.

It has been variously argued that there is stability in physical development between the ages of eight and thirteen, that this represents the stage of concrete operations identified by Piaget, and that there is distinctive social and emotional development during these years, which outgrows the primary atmosphere but for which the teenage culture of the secondary school is not suitable. However, as Blyth (1980, p. 25) concludes: 'There is indeed a lack of firm evidence, and even a lack of the means of establishing firm evidence, about the educational advantages of middle schools, or for that matter of any alternative age-pattern'. As with the Hadow Committee, one gains a sense of the psychology being made to fit the practical pattern that had emerged. It does contain a fair degree of elasticity. Piaget, for example, has placed the 'nominal' age of 'concrete operations' at 7–11, followed by 'formal operations' at 11–15, thus apparently supporting the 11-plus divide.

However, as Nisbet and Entwistle (1966) argue, we do not know how representative Piaget's samples were. And while his characterization of the sequence of phases may be sound, judging from other research, the age-stages remain problematic. Piaget can thus be quoted to support almost any system, as long as it is sequential – one that has a 'clean break' at 11-plus, one that has middle schools for the phase of 'concrete operations', and one that has a mixture of schools with different starting and leaving dates that might cater for individuals who develop at different rates. As the system now stands, there are transfer ages of 11, 12 and 13, depending on area and type of system in use.

References

ARGYLE, M. (1969). *Social Interaction*. London, Methuen.

ARIES, P. (1965). *Centuries of Childhood: a social history of family life*. New York, Vintage Books.

BALL, S. (1980). Initial encounters in the classroom and the process of establishment, in WOODS, P. (ed.). *Pupil Strategies*. London, Croom Helm.

BALL, S. (1981). *Beachside Comprehensive*. Cambridge, Cambridge University Press.

BARTHES, R. (1973). *Mythologies*. London, Paladin.

BEATTIE, J.H.M. (1959). *Other Cultures: aims, methods and achievements in social anthropology*. London, Cohen and West.

BECK, J. (1972). *Transition and Continuity: a study of an educational status passage*. Unpublished MA thesis. London, University of London Institute of Education.

BECKER, H.S. *et al.* (1961). *Boys in White*. Chicago, University of Chicago Press.

BEYNON, J. (1984). 'Sussing-out' teachers: pupils as data gatherers, in HAMMERSLEY, M. and WOODS, P. (eds). *Life in School: the sociology of pupil culture*. Milton Keynes, Open University Press.

BERGER, P.L., BERGER, B., and KELLNER, H. (1973). *The Homeless Mind*. Harmondsworth, Penguin.

BERGER, P.L. and LUCKMANN, T. (1967). *The Social Construction of Reality: a treatise in the sociology of knowledge*. Harmondsworth, Penguin.

BIRD, C., CHESSUM, R., FURLONG, J. and JOHNSON, D. (1981). *Disaffected Pupils*. London, Brunel University, Educational Studies Unit.

BLOOM, C.J. (1964). *Stability and Change in Human Characteristics*. New York, Wiley.

BLYTH, W.A.L. (1965). *English Primary Education: a sociological description*. London, Routledge.

BLYTH, W.A.L. (1980). Middle schools and the historical perspective, in Hargreaves A. and Tickle A. (eds). *Middle Schools: origins, ideology and practice*. London, Harper and Row.

BOARD OF EDUCATION (1927). *The Education of the Adolescent*. Report of the Consultative Committee. London, HMSO, (The Hadow Report.)

BOARD OF EDUCATION (1943). *Curriculum and Examinations in Secondary Schools*. Report of the Committee of the Secondary School Examination Council. London, HMSO. (The Norwood Report.)

BURGESS, R.G. (1984). *In the Field: an introduction to field research*. London, Allen and Unwin.

BRYAN, K. (1980) Pupil perceptions of transfer between middle and high schools, in HARGREAVES, A. and TICKLE, L. (eds). *Middle Schools: Origins, Ideology and Practice*. London, Harper and Row.

BURNS, A.B. (1977). The self-concept and its relevance to academic achievement, in CHILD, D. (ed.). *Readings in Psychology for the Teacher*. London, Holt, Rinehart and Winston.

BYRNE, E.M. (1978). *Women and Education*. London, Tavistock.

CENTRAL ADVISORY COUNCIL FOR EDUCATION (1963). *Half Our Future*. London, HMSO. (The Newsom Report.)

CENTRAL ADVISORY COUNCIL FOR EDUCATION (ENGLAND) (1967). *Children and their Primary Schools*. London, HMSO. (The Plowden Report.)

CONGER, J.J. (1977). *Adolescence and Youth: psychological develkopment in a changing world*. New York, Harper and Row.

CONGER, J.J. (1979). *Adolescence: generation under pressure*. New York, Harper and Row.

COOLEY, C.H. (1902). *Human Nature and the Social Order*. New York, Charles Scribner.

DAVIES, B. (1982). *Life in the Classroom and Playground: the accounts of primary school children*. London, Routledge and Kegan Paul.

DAVIES, L. (1978). The view from the girls. *Educational Review*, 30 (2).

DAVIS, F. (1963). *Passage through Crisis*. Indianopolis, Bobbs-Merrill.

DEEM, R. (1978). *Women and Schooling*. London, Routledge and Kegan Paul.

DELAMONT, S. (1976). *Interaction in the Classroom*. London, Methuen.

DENSCOMBE, M. (1980a). 'Keeping 'em quiet': the significance of noise for the practical activity of teaching, in WOODS, P. (ed.). *Teacher Strategies*. London, Croom Helm.

DENSCOMBE, M. (1980b). Pupil strategies and the open classroom, in WOODS, P. (ed.). *Pupil Strategies*. London, Croom Helm.

DEPARTMENT OF EDUCATION AND SCIENCE (1965). *The Organisation of Secondary Education*. Circular 10/65. London, HMSO.

DEWEY, J. (1922). *Human Nature and Conduct*. New York, Henry Holt.

DITTON, J. (1977). *Part-time Crime: an ethnography of fiddling and pilferage*. London, Macmillan.

DOUGLAS, M. (1968). Meaning of myth, in LEACH, E. *The Structural Study of Myth and Totemism*. ASA Monograph No. 5. London, Tavistock Publications.

EBBUTT, D. (1981). Girls' Science: boys' science revisited, in KELLY A. (ed.). *The Missing Half*. Manchester, Manchester University Press.

ELIADE, M. (1959). *The Sacred and the Profane*. New York, Harcourt Brace.

ENTWISTLE, N.J. (1967). The transition to secondary education. Unpublished PhD thesis, University of Aberdeen.

ERIKSON, E.H. (1968). *Identity: youth and crisis*. New York, Norton.

FULLER, M. (1980). Black girls in a London comprehensive school., in DEEM, R. (ed.). *Schooling for Women's Work*. London, Routledge and Kegan Paul.

FURLONG, J. (1976). Interaction sets in the classroom, in HAMMERSLEY, M. and WOODS, P. (eds). *The Process of Schooling*. London, Routledge and Kegan Paul.

FURLONG, J. (1977). Anancy goes to school: a case study of pupils' knowledge of their teachers, in WOODS, P. and HAMMERSLEY, M. (eds). *School Experience*. London, Croom Helm.

GALTON, M. and WILLCOCKS, J. (eds) (1982). *Moving from the Primary Classroom*. London, Routledge and Kegan Paul.

GANNAWAY, H. (1976). Making sense of school, in STUBBS, M. and DELAMONT, S. (eds). *Explorations in Classroom Observation*. London, Wiley.

GLASER, B. and STRAUSS, A. (1968). *Time for Dying*. Chicago, Aldine.

GOFFMAN, E. (1959). *The Presentation of Self in Everyday Life*. Garden City, Doubleday.

GOFFMAN, E. (1961). *Asylums*. Garden City, Doubleday; also in Harmondsworth, Penguin, 1968.

HALL, G.S. (1904). *Adolescence – its psychology*. New York, Appleton.

HALLOWELL, A.J. (1937). Temporal orientation in western civilization and in a pre-literate society. *American Anthropology*, 39.

HAMBLIN, D.H. (1978). *The Teacher and Pastoral Care*. Oxford, Blackwell.

HAMMERSLEY, M. and TURNER, G. (1980). Conformist Pupils? in WOODS, P. (ed.). *Pupil Strategies*. London, Croom Helm.

HAMMERSLEY, M. and WOODS, P. (eds) (1976).*The Process of Schooling*. London, Routledge and Kegan Paul.

HARGREAVES, A. (1979). Strategies, decisions and control: interaction in a middle school classroom, in EGGLESTON, J. (ed.). *Teacher Decision-Making in the Classroom*. London, Routledge and Kegan Paul.

HARGREAVES, D.H. (1967). *Social Relations in a Secondary School*. London, Routledge and Kegan Paul.

HARGREAVES, D.H. (1982). *The Challenge for the Comprehensive School*. London, Routledge and Kegan Paul.

HARGREAVES, D.H., HESTER, S.K. and MELLOR, F.J. (1975). *Deviance in Classrooms*. London, Routledge and Kegan Paul.

HART, N. (1976). *When Marriage Ends: a study in status passage*. London, Tavistock Publications.

JONES, R. (1980). Fostering femininity in middle school girls. Paper delivered to the Middle Schools Research Group Conference, Maryland College, Woburn.

KELLY, A. (ed.) (1981). *Missing Half: Girls and Science Education*. Manchester, Manchester University Press.

KLAPP, O.E. (1949). The fool as a social type. *American Journal of Sociology*, LV, pp. 157–62.

LACEY, C. (1970). *Hightown Grammar*. Manchester, Manchester University Press.

LAMBART, A.M. (1976). The sisterhood, in HAMMERSLEY, M. and WOODS, P. (eds). *The Process of Schooling*. London, Routledge and Kegan Paul.

LEACH, E. (1968). *The Structural Study of Myth and Totemism*. ASA Monograph No. 5. London, Tavistock.

LÉVI-STRAUSS, C. (1955). *Tristes Tropiques*. Paris, Plon.

LEWIS, G. (1980). *Day of Shining Red*. Cambridge, Cambridge University Press.

LLEWELLYN, M. (1980). Studying girls at school: the implications of confusion, in DEEM, R. (ed.). *Schooling for Women's Work*. London, Routledge and Kegan Paul.

LORTIE, D. (1968). Shared ordeal and induction to work, in BECKER, H.S. *et al.* (eds). *Institution and the Person*. Chicago, Aldine.

McROBBIE, A. and GARBER, J. (1976). Girls and subcultures, in HALL, S. and JEFFERSON, T. (eds). *Resistance through Rituals*. London, Hutchinson.

MALINOWSKI, B. (1926). *Myth in Primitive Psychology*. London, Routledge and Kegan Paul.

MARTIN, W.B.W. (1976). *The Negotiated Order of the School*. Toronto, MacMillan.

MEAD, G.H. (1934). *Mind, Self and Society*. Chicago, University of Chicago (edited by C.W. Morris).

MEAD, M. (1943). *Coming of Age in Samoa*. Harmondsworth, Penguin.

MEASOR, L. (1983). Gender and curriculum choice: a case study, in HAMMERSLEY, M. and HARGREAVES, A. (eds). *Curriculum Practice: some sociological case studies*. Lewes, The Falmer Press.

MEASOR, L. and WOODS, P. (1984). Cultivating the middle ground: teachers and school ethos. *Research in Education*.

MERTON, J. (1975). Transfer from primary to secondary education: problems of adjustment. Unpublished Dip.Ed. dissertation. Birmingham, University of Birmingham, School of Education.

MEYENN, R. (1980). School girls' peer groups, in WOODS, P. (ed.). *Pupil Strategies*. London, Croom Helm.

MORGAN, J., O'NEILL, C. and HARRÉ, R. (1979). *Nicknames: their origins and social consequences*. London, Routledge and Kegan Paul.

MURDOCH, A. (1982). Forty-two children and the transfer to secondary education. PhD thesis. Norwich, University of East Anglia.

MURDOCH, W.F. (1966). The effect of transfer on the level of children's adjustment to school. Unpublished MEd thesis. Aberdeen, University of Aberdeen.

MUSGROVE, F. (1964). *Youth and The Social Order*. London, Routledge and Kegan Paul.

MUSGROVE, F. and MIDDLETON, R. (1981). Rites of passage and the meaning of age in three contrasted social groups. *British Journal of Sociology*, 32 (1), March 1981.

NASH, R. (1976). Pupils' expectations of their teachers, in STUBBS, M. and DELAMONT, S. (eds). *Explorations in Classroom Observation*. London, Wiley.

NEAL, P.D. (1975). *Continuity in Education, EDC Project Five*. Birmingham, City of Birmingham Education Department.

NISBET, J.D. and ENTWISTLE, N.J. (1966). *The Age of Transfer to Secondary Education*. London, University of London Press.

NISBET, J.D. and ENTWISTLE, N.J. (1969). *The Transition to Secondary Education*. London, University of London Press.

NISBET, J.D. and ENTWISTLE, N.J. (1970). Transfer from primary to secondary education, in BUTCHER, H.J. and PONT, H.B. (eds). *Educational Research in Britain 2*. London, University of London Press.

OAKLEY, A. (1980). *Women Confined: towards a sociology of childbirth*. Oxford, Martin Robertson.

PIGGOTT, C.A. (1977). *Transfer from Primary to Secondary Education*. Unpublished MA dissertation. Southampton, University of Southampton.

POWER, C. and COTTERELL, J. (1981). *Changes in Students in the Transition from Primary to Secondary School*. ERDC Report No. 27. Canberra, Australian Government Publishing Service.

PRENDERGAST, S. and PROUT, A. (1980). What will I do ? Teenage girls and the construction of motherhood. *Sociological Review*, 28 (3).

RAPOPORT, R. and RAPOPORT, R.N. (1975). *Leisure and the Family Life Cycle*. London, Routledge and Kegan Paul.

REYNOLDS, D. (1976). When teachers and pupils refuse a truce, in MUNGHAM, G. and PEARSON, G. (eds). *Working Class Youth Culture*. London, Routledge and Kegan Paul.

ROSSER, E. and HARRÉ, R. (1976). The meaning of disorder, in HAMMERSLEY, M. and WOODS, P. (eds). *The Process of Schooling*. London, Routledge and Kegan Paul.

RUTTER, M., MAUGHAM, B., MORTIMORE, P. and OUSTON, J. (1979). *Fifteen Thousand Hours*. London, Open Books.

SCHOFIELD, M. (1965). *The Sexual Behaviour of Young People*. London, Longmans.

SCHUTZ, A. (1962). *Collected Papers*. The Hague, Nijhoff.

SHARPE, S. (1976). *Just Like a Girl*. Harmondsworth, Penguin.

SHAW, J. (1980). Education and the individual: schooling for girls, or Mixed schooling – a mixed blessing? in DEEM, R. (ed.). *Schooling for Wlmen's Work*. London, Routledge and Kegan Paul.

SOREL, G. (1950). *Reflections on Violence*. Glencoe, Illinois, The Free Press.

SOROKIN, P.A. and MERTON, R.K. (1937). Social time: a methodology and functional analysis. *American Journal of Sociology*, XLII (5).

SPELMAN, B.J. (1979). *Pupil Adaptation to Secondary School*. Belfast, Northern Ireland Council for Educational Research.

SPENDER, D. and SARAH, E. (eds) (1980). *Learning to Lose: sexism and education*. London, The Women's Press.

STEBBINS, R. (1970). The meaning of disorderly behaviour: teacher definitions of a classroom situation. *Sociology of Education*, 44, pp. 217–36.

STEBBINS, R. (1975). *Teachers and Meaning: definitions of classroom situations*. Leiden, E.J. Brill.

STILLMAN, A. and MAYCHELL, K. (1982). *Transfer Procedures at 9 and 13*. Slough, National Foundation for Educational Research.

STONE, G.P. (1962). Appearance and the self, in ROSE, A.M. (ed.). *Human Behaviour and Social Processes*. London, Routledge and Kegan Paul.

STRAUSS, A. *et al.* (1964). *Psychiatric Ideologies and Institutions*. London, Collier–Macmillan.

SYKES, A.T.M. (1965). Myth and attitude change. *Human Relations*, 18 (4).

TANNER, J.M. (1961). *Education and Physical Growth*. London, University of London Press.

TANNER, J.M. (1962). *Growth of Adolescence*. London, Blackwell.

TAWNEY, R.H. (1922). *Secondary Education for All: a policy for Labour*. London, Allen and Unwin.

TURNER, G. (1983). *The Social World of the Comprehensive School*. London, Croom Helm.

TURNER, V.W. (1969). *The Ritual Process*. London, Routledge and Kegan Paul.

VAN GENNEP, A. (1960). *The Rites of Passage*. London, Routledge and Kegan Paul.

VULLIAMY, G. (1979). Culture clash and school music: a sociological analysis, in BARTON, L. and MEIGHAN, R. (eds). *Sociological Interpretations of Schooling and Classrooms*. Driffield, Nafferton Books.

WILLIS, P. (1977). *Learning to Labour*. Farnborough, Saxon House.

WOODS, P. (1978). Negotiating the demands of schoolwork. *Journal of Curriculum Studies*, 10 (4), pp. 309–27.

WOODS, P. (1979). *The Divided School*. London, Routledge and Kegan Paul.

WOODS, P. (1980). *Pupil Strategies*. London, Croom Helm.

YALMAN, N. (1968). Observations on *Le Cru et le Cuit*, in LEACH, E. *The Structural Study of Myth and Totemism*. ASA Monographs No. 5. London, Tavistock Publications.

Index

186